MOTIVATION

MOTIVATION

UNDERSTANDING AND INFLUENCING HUMAN BEHAVIOR

Walter B. Kolesnik
UNIVERSITY OF DETROIT

ALLYN AND BACON, INC.
Boston   London   Sydney   Toronto

Library of Congress Cataloging in Publication Data

Kolesnik, Walter Bernard, 1923–
    Motivation.

    Bibliography: p.
    Includes index.
    1. Motivation in education.   2. Classroom management.   I. Title.
LB0165.K58   370.15'4   77-13510
ISBN 0-205-05973-2

To Kathryn and Martha Kolesnik
The Hanleys and the Stallards

CONTENTS

Preface

The purpose of this book is to help the reader to understand and influence human behavior, particularly in the area of education. The book therefore addresses itself to two main questions:

1. Why do people behave as they do?
2. How can teachers effectively motivate students to study, learn, develop their potentialities, observe necessary classroom regulations, and otherwise do what they should like them to do?

This book does not, of course, attempt to provide all of the possible answers to these questions. But it does, I believe, clearly and concisely survey many of them.

The short introductory chapter includes a brief rationale for the book and a preview of the nine longer chapters that follow.

Chapters 2 through 6 include insights from psychoanalysis, Individual psychology, behaviorism, cognitive, and humanistic psychology, respectively. They bring out some general educational implications of each of those positions, but relate primarily to the first of our two questions.

The last four chapters pertain more directly to the second question. Chapters 7 and 8 deal, respectively, with intrinsic and extrinsic motivational procedures in classroom situations. Chapter 9 includes several specific recommendations for handling discipline problems, whereas chapter 10 summarizes a number of suggestions for motivating students toward scholastic achievement. Organized around clearly stated directives for the most part, the last two chapters offer readers something less than precise cookbook formulas, but are intended to leave them with something more than vague general principles.

Although this book was written primarily for prospective and beginning teachers, it is intended also for those who will participate in the education-motivation process in other capacities— as parents, for example—and as a review for advanced students in psychology or education. Introductory in style and not very technical in content, the book does not presume any previous course work in either of those disciplines.

For the constructive criticism and helpful suggestions they offered for improving the manuscript, I should like to thank Don Treffinger, University of Kansas; Myron Dembo, University of Southern California; Richard Schmid, Arizona State University; and Jim Oleman, New York University.

W. B. K.

CHAPTER ONE

An Introduction to Motivation

Most of us study psychology for one or another or both of two reasons. One is that we want to *understand* human behavior. The other is that we want to *influence* (or change or improve) it. The first reason centers on the question of *Why?* Why do we think, feel, or act as we do? The second is more a question of *How?* How can we use psychology in our everyday lives? The first question is largely theoretical. The second is considerably more practical. But both center on the problem of motivation: What motivates people to behave as they do? How can we motivate others to do what we should like them to do?

MOTIVATION AND EDUCATION

Motivation is not only one of the central problems of psychology but one of education as well. Among the kinds of questions most frequently asked by beginning teachers and seasoned veterans are

1

How can I get my students to pay attention?
How can I get them to do their assignments?
How can I get them to behave themselves?
How can I get them to learn?
How can I get them to at least try?

In each of these questions, by the word *get* I presume that they mean *motivate*.

With respect to scholastic achievement, two of the main requisites are ability and motivation. The vast majority of students undoubtedly have the ability to learn the subject matter, skills, and behavior patterns that they are expected to learn. However, they do not always have the desire, the inclination, the drive, or the will to use their abilities in the way that their teachers and parents would like.

When students are highly motivated to learn, when they want to learn and are willing to try to learn, they almost surely will learn even if the instructional materials and methods employed by their teachers leave something to be desired. Moreover, when students are motivated toward scholastic achievement, the problems of classroom management and dealing with student misbehavior ordinarily do not arise. The first piece of advice usually given to teachers for preventing classroom misbehavior is to keep their students busily engaged in some interesting, challenging, or rewarding task. But, like a lot of other advice given to teachers, this is easier said than done.

Not only teachers, but such people as advertisers, salespersons, politicians, social workers, lawyers, journalists, law enforcement officers, members of the clergy and health care professions, and parents are necessarily involved in the motivation process. The very nature of their jobs requires them to understand and try to affect the thoughts, feelings, desires, and overt acts of others. Although much of the material in this book is directly addressed to teachers, let us recognize that people in many other professions are also engaged in the work of education. Most of what will be said to or about teachers applies to these others as well.

Theories of Motivation

Teachers, parents, and these other motivating agents ordinarily are not as concerned with elaborate theories of motivation as

they are with practical techniques. But, to carry out their responsibilities effectively, they do need some insight into the *why*
of human behavior. They need some theory—or at least some principles or assumptions—on which to base their practices. To motivate your students to study, to complete their assignments, or
to be quiet while you are talking, it might not be absolutely
necessary for you to draw on any particular formal theory of
motivation. However, your efforts are likely to be far more productive if you understand why it is that some students do these
things and why others don't.

When we turn to psychology for elucidation about what
makes people tick, we find that reputable psychologists are by
no means in complete agreement with one another. As K. B.
Madsen (1974), McClelland and Steele (1973), Teevan and Birney
(1964), Bernard Weiner (1974), and others suggest, there are
dozens of theories about what motivation is and how it energizes
or directs human behavior. (Full references to the pertinent
writings of these and other individuals mentioned in this book
are given in the general bibliography that follows the last chapter.)
Some of these theories attempt to explain our behavior in terms
of innate drives, urges, instincts, impulses, tensions, needs, or
other activating forces over which we have little or no control.
Others try to explain our behavior in terms of our freely chosen
goals, purposes, plans, values, beliefs, or aspirations. Our concepts
of motivation are likely to be inextricably tied to our assumptions
about human nature. We act as we do—or we are motivated to
act as we do—because of what we are. But what are we? Here
again, we have a variety of theories from which to choose (W.
Russell 1970; Sahakian 1974).

In the pages that follow, we will not, of course, discuss all of
the theories of human nature, behavior, and motivation that have
been proposed. Rather, we will look closely at Freudian, Adlerian,
behavioral, cognitive, and humanistic theories. The model in
Figure 1 includes elements from all five. This model can serve as
an overview to help you to organize and interrelate some of the
concepts, principles, and recommendations that you will encounter in the chapters ahead. It can also be adapted to help you
to plan and implement a classroom motivation program based on
your own eclectic theory of motivation. For example, in a particular situation you might capitalize on your understanding of

TRY TO UNDERSTAND AND CAPITALIZE ON YOUR STUDENTS'		
needs	drives	potentialities
interests	urges	anxieties
goals	values	beliefs
aspirations	attitudes	perceptions
unconscious		developmental
motives		characteristics
	etc.	

AND USE A VARIETY OF STRATEGIES AS		
modeling	grades	competition
positive reinforcement	tests	cooperation
negative reinforcement	programming	punishment
performance objectives	contracts	verbal approval
curiosity/stimulation	assignments	verbal disapproval
contingency management	games	questions
discovery methods	simulations	explanations
	etc.	

THAT WILL ENABLE YOUR STUDENTS TO

experience a feeling of success
receive tangible or symbolic rewards
be granted certain privileges
acquire or maintain a feeling of personal worth
develop a more favorable self-concept

win your praise	overcome their fears
earn parental approval	satisfy their needs
gain peer-group recognition	reduce their drives
feel good about themselves	resolve their conflicts
enjoy themselves	grow in self-confidence

etc.

AND HELP TO BRING ABOUT

orderly classroom behavior
and
scholastic achievement

FIGURE 1. A Model for Classroom Motivation. This model can be used to help you to organize some of the concepts that are discussed in later chapters and to guide you in planning your own motivation program.

students' needs and interests by using discovery methc positive reinforcement that will enable your students to rience a feeling of success that, in turn, will contribute tc subsequent scholastic achievement.

Techniques of Motivation

Whatever else it might be, motivation is not a prepackaged bag of tricks that can be handed down from one generation of teachers to the next. There are no formulas "guaranteed to work or double your money back" for getting students to do this, that, or the other thing. In later chapers, we discuss a number of strategies that *some* teachers have found to be effective in *some* situations. But the effectiveness of a particular kind of strategy depends on at least three variables: the teacher, the student, and the material to be learned.

A procedure that works beautifully for one teacher might not work at all for another. For example, verbal expressions of approval, encouragement, or disapproval from Teacher A do not necessarily have the same meaning or the same effect that they do when they come from Teacher B. A technique that is highly effective with one student or group of students might not be nearly as productive with another individual or class. Even with the same teacher and the same students, a strategy that produces the desired results in, say, an English class could turn out to be disastrous in a science, a mathematics, or a gym class.

Because of these three variables, you will have to experiment with a variety of motivational devices to find out for yourself which work best for you in your particular teaching situation.

The Individual Student

While all of the above-mentioned variables are significant, the most critical is the individual student. Perhaps the most important single principle in the entire field of psychology is that no two human beings are exactly alike. Besides differing from one another physically, socially, emotionally, and intellectually, students at every age and grade level differ in their interests and attitudes, their values and their goals, their special talents and their particular needs. They differ in their inherited potentialities and in the kinds of environments in which they have been raised. They differ with respect to their racial, ethnic, cultural, socioeconomic, and religious backgrounds and in the varieties of previous experiences that they have accumulated in their homes, with their families, in their neighborhoods, etc.

In short, within a particular classroom, students are almost certain to differ not only in their abilities to learn and in what they have already learned, but also in what they want to learn and, perhaps, even in what they need to learn. Thus, your students are likely to differ, even widely, in the kinds of motivational stimuli to which they respond and the kinds of responses that they make to the particular techniques you might choose to employ.

From what has just been said, it would seem to follow that, before we concern ourselves too much with methods and techniques of motivation, we should try to understand the existing motives of our individual students. The first part of this book is intended primarily to help to bring about such an understanding.

Extrinsic and Intrinsic Motivation

For purposes of understanding as well as changing or influencing human behavior, an important distinction is commonly made between extrinsic and intrinsic motivation.

Extrinsic motives are so called because they arise from a source outside the individual. We are said to be motivated extrinsically when we do something because someone else wants us to do it, when someone somehow will reward us for doing it, or when we simply want to please or impress someone else. The classic example of extrinsic motivation in a classroom setting is the practice of working for grades.

Intrinsic motives are those that arise from within the individual. We are motivated intrinsically when we do something because we want to do it. We enjoy the activity as an end in itself or we are sufficiently interested in doing it so that external inducements are unnecessary. An example of an intrinsically motivated student is one who reads novels simply because he likes to read novels or studies mathematics because he readily perceives that it is somehow to his advantage to do so.

Chapters 7 and 8 are specifically organized around intrinsic and extrinsic motivation, respectively. However, these two concepts appear and reappear as a theme in the other chapters as well. The distinction between them is worth keeping in mind for two reasons that correspond to the two questions posed at the beginning of this chapter.

First, the various theories of motivation that we shall discuss tend to rely on one or the other or a combination of the two in attempting to explain the *why* of human behavior. Both intrinsic and extrinsic motivation are concepts indispensable to a full *understanding* of why we do the things we do.

Second, from the consideration of *how to influence* human behavior, we should recognize that neither an intrinsic nor an extrinsic strategy is better than the other in general, but that either has its uses as well as its limitations. Although intrinsic methods might work well with some students, extrinsic techniques might be more productive with others. Moreover, intrinsic and extrinsic strategies might differ widely in their effects. For example, while extrinsic motivation might seem to be more useful in bringing about immediate observable results, the long-range benefits of intrinsic strategies might be far more desirable.

PREVIEW OF CHAPTERS AHEAD

In Chapter 2, we shall examine the complex, revolutionary, and highly controversial theories of Sigmund Freud. We begin with Freud's views because of their historic importance, their impact on the development of subsequent psychological systems, and their bearing on some of the concepts, principles, and recommendations brought out in later chapters. According to Freud, as we shall see, we are often totally unaware of the real motives underlying many of the things that we do because so much of our behavior is determined by repressed unconscious drives. Freud believed that these unconscious motives are essentially outgrowths of impulses toward sexual gratification and aggression which are instinctive and part of our nature as human beings.

Chapter 3 reflects the theory of Alfred Adler that motivation can be understood best in terms of our basic feelings of inferiority and our attempts to overcome them. Adler stresses our striving for individual perfection, power, or dominance along with our natural inclination toward social awareness or concern for the welfare of others. Adler helps to bridge a gap between psychoanalysis and humanism and offers what an apparently growing number of psychologists accept as a down-to-earth explanation of human behavior that squares with their own observations and common sense.

Chapter 4 deals with the theories of behavioral psychologists, such as B. F. Skinner, who have little or no use for the very concept of motives but instead explain human behavior in terms of its consequences or payoff. In terms of behavioral psychology, motivation is essentially a matter of operant conditioning. We behave as we do because we are somehow reinforced for doing so. In addition to a discussion of various forms of reinforcement and punishment, Chapter 4 also includes an explanation of frustration, anxiety, conflict, and aggression from a behavioral point of view.

Chapter 5 is based on ideas about motivation that are based on or derived from cognitive psychology. Cognitive psychology is so called because it is concerned particularly with our cognitive processes: knowing, thinking, believing, etc. To the cognitive psychologist, we behave as we do because of what we know, think, feel, or believe about the world around us and about ourselves in relation to the world as we perceive it.

Chapter 6 focuses on humanistic theories of motivation in general and those of Abraham Maslow in particular. There we will see that, according to humanistic psychology, most human behavior is an attempt to satisfy such needs as those for self-preservation, security, attention, belonging, love, self-esteem, and, above all, self-actualization or self-fulfillment.

Chapter 7 has to do with intrinsic motivation, which is especially recommended by humanistic, cognitive, and Adlerian psychology and is compatible with the views of Freud. Intrinsic motivation, as we shall see, is closely related to the concept of interest. Much of that chapter, therefore, deals with the nature and development of students' interests and classroom strategies for making schoolwork interesting. A number of suggestions with respect to creativity, curiosity arousal, and attention also are included.

Chapter 8 shifts our attention to extrinsic motivation, the type that is more closely associated with behavioral psychology. Extrinsic motivation implies the use of incentives, which come from outside the individual, rather than interests, which come from within. In that chapter, we look at the use of teacher feedback or the expression of approval and disapproval as a motivational device; some problems pertaining to the use (and misuse) of grades as incentives; the behavior modification or contingency management approach to motivation; and some advantages and disadvantages of competition.

Chapter 9 zeroes in on the problem of classroom management and coping with student misbehavior. It includes a discussion of some of the main reasons for misbehavior, but it is devoted mainly to specific recommendations for preventing misbehavior in the classroom and for correcting it when it occurs.

Chapter 10 is a short summary of practical suggestions for motivating students toward scholastic achievement. While Chapter 9 is primarily concerned with order and discipline in the classroom, the main thrust of Chapter 10 is toward learning. Thus, we conclude with a concise chapter that pulls together a number of recommendations made in earlier chapters and adds some new ones that I hope you will be able to adopt for yourself and put to good use in your particular teaching situation.

Preview Questions

Preceding each of Chapters 2 through 10, you will find a list of Preview Questions. These are intended to help you to organize, summarize, and reflect on some of the main ideas in that chapter. The questions can be used for purposes of *pre*view or *re*view or both. As previews, they indicate the kinds of things you should be looking for as you read the chapter. After you have finished reading the chapter, you might try to answer them as a means of review.

Recommended Readings

Since this book is essentially a survey rather than an in-depth analysis of motivational theories and practices, there are many concepts, principles, research findings, etc., that we shall only touch upon in the pages ahead. For this reason, each chapter includes a list of twelve Recommended Readings for further information about some of the major points dealt with in that chapter. In addition, the Bibliography at the end of the book includes references to the writings of each of the individuals who are mentioned in the text.

CHAPTER 2: PREVIEW QUESTIONS

(After you have finished reading Chapter 2, you should be able to answer the following.)

1. Explain what Freud considered to be the primary source of all motivation. In what respects can Freud's theories of human nature, behavior, and motivation be considered revolutionary?
2. What is the id? What does it do? Does your id differ from mine? If so, why? If not, why not?
3. What is the ego? What is its function? Where does it get its energy? Are all egos alike or is each one unique? Why?
4. What is a superego? What is the difference or relationship between one's superego, conscience, and ego ideal? On what does the development of one's superego depend?
5. How is repression related to motivation? What are some kinds of ideas, experiences, or urges that are commonly repressed? What are some effects of repression?
6. According to psychoanalysis, how or why do conflicts arise? What are some basic kinds of conflicts? How or why do people differ in their responses to conflict?
7. Explain the five stages of psychosexual development according to Freud. What are some distinguishing characteristics of each? What effects might sexual experiences in early childhood

have on an individual's subsequent personality development?

8. What, according to Erikson, is the central crisis of each of the eight stages of human development? What difference does it make whether or not these crises are resolved at the appropriate time of life?

9. What is the difference or the relationship between sublimation and displacement? How and why are these mechanisms used? Give a few examples of each.

10. What is identification? Projection? Reaction formation? What are some other commonly used psychological mechanisms? Give a couple of examples of each.

11. What light does Freudian psychology shed on the motives of people who tell dirty jokes? Go to church regularly? Have nightmares? Make certain mistakes repeatedly? Are neat and orderly? Help other people? Hurt other people?

12. Summarize what you consider to be the most significant educational implications of Freudian psychology.

13. What is the Pleasure Principle? The Reality Principle? How can these be related to curriculum planning?

14. How can psychoanalysis be interpreted to support either permissiveness or firm discipline in education, or both?

15. What is your overall opinion of, or general feeling about, Freudian psychology? What features of psychoanalysis, if any, are you inclined to accept? Which, if any, are you inclined to reject? Give the reasons for your position.

CHAPTER TWO

Unconscious Motivation

Sigmund Freud (1856–1939) opened up a whole new world for psychology: the world of the unconscious. His radical theories of human nature and his explanations of the dynamics of the human personality revolutionized people's thinking about themselves with an impact comparable in intensity to the views of Charles Darwin on the origin and evolution of human life. For centuries, it had been generally assumed that human beings were rational animals, members of a unique species with intellects and free will as their distinguishing characteristics. People were presumed to know what they were doing and why they were doing it. It was generally believed that we act as we do because we consciously, deliberately choose to act in that particular way.

Freud, however, maintained that much human behavior is literally irrational. He claimed that some of the most common and important behavior not only of emotionally disturbed or neurotic individuals but of ordinary, normal people as well is not freely chosen but determined by repressed, unconscious drives. He believed that a person's motives for acting, as well as the real meaning of those acts, are often unknown, even to the individual himself. In short, he advanced the proposition that there is a lot more to human behavior than meets the eye, that observable behavior is like the proverbial tip of the iceberg, and that an understanding of that behavior requires an in-depth analysis of that which lies below the superficial threshold of consciousness. This in-depth analysis is referred to as psychoanalysis.

The term *psychoanalysis* is used to denote (1) the methods devised by Freud and extended by some of his followers for treating emotionally disturbed people and (2) his theory of personality and human behavior on which those methods are based. The discussion that follows is limited to a brief overview of the latter, with emphasis on those aspects of psychoanalysis that pertain most directly to motivation.

THE HUMAN PERSONALITY

Basic to Freud's theory of motivation is his concept of psychic energy. Just as mechanical, chemical, electrical, and other forms of energy perform certain kinds of work and activate the physical universe, so does psychic energy perform psychological works and activate the human organism. Among these psychological workings are such activities as thinking, desiring, remembering, and perceiving.

Every person, Freud maintained, is endowed by nature with a fixed amount of psychic energy. This amount remains constant throughout the life of the individual. It can be neither increased nor decreased. It can, however, be transformed. Transformations from one form of psychic energy to another are taking place constantly. So are transformations from psychic to physical energy (we want something and then we do something) and from physical to psychic (we do something and then we feel or remember something).

Freud explains the mature human personality as consisting of three levels or energy systems: the id, the ego, and the superego. These are not literal parts of the personality. They are, rather, names that he gave to three different psychic processes or ways in which the personality functions. The most fundamental of these, the first to emerge, and the one from which the energy of the ego and superego is derived, is the id (Freud 1938, 1969).

The Id

The id is what every person basically and originally *is*. It is the very core of human nature and the primary source of all motivation. The id consists of unlearned drives or instinctive tendencies toward the bare necessities of life, such as food, drink, and the avoidance of pain. It is also directed toward sexual gratification. The only function of the id is to fulfill what Freud calls the *Pleasure Principle.* The Pleasure Principle, which is the basic principle of life, refers to a person's inborn drives toward reducing or, if possible, eliminating tensions. Tensions are feelings of pain or discomfort that result, for example, from hunger or coldness. Relief from tension is experienced as pleasure or satisfaction.

A human being does not acquire an id. The id is innate. For the newborn infant, before it has had any experience with the external world, the id is the *only* reality. The id cannot think, reason, plan, or deliberate but is irrational and really quite stupid. The id wants to reduce the discomfort of hunger, for example, but it cannot distinguish between edible and nonedible objects. The id cannot distinguish even between an object (such as food) and the memory or an image of the object.

The id has no contact whatsoever with the environment; it is completely out of touch with reality. It recognizes nothing outside itself. All it does is seek and demand immediate satisfaction. Unable to tolerate tensions, it wants gratification here and now. The id is not only impulsive; it is also amoral. It will do anything possible to obtain satisfaction, and to hell with the consequences. Actually, it does not (because it cannot) even think of consequences. It has no foresight and no concern at all for the welfare of others or with any principles of morality.

Ids, being in effect raw human nature, are all alike. Because the id is isolated from reality, it cannot be changed. However, it can be regulated by the ego. Egos and superegos, as we shall see, are all different, resulting from environmental stimulation and experience, including education. But the id—the foundation upon which one's later personality is built, and the ultimate source of all motivation—remains constant throughout the life of an individual (Freud 1960).

Sex and Aggression

The psychic energy of the id is divided between the life instinct and the death instinct. The life instinct, or the eros, is the tendency toward physical survival and reproduction of the human species. The energy of the life instinct is called the *libido*. Most significant of the life instincts is sex. Sex plays such an important role in Freudian psychology because Freud believed that it is the frustration of that drive more than any other that contributes to personality maladjustment and neuroses. Moreover, he believed that the largest part of an individual's energies is devoted to reducing sexual tensions and obtaining the corresponding sexual pleasure (Freud 1938).

Freud's concept of sex is considerably broader than the common understanding of that term. It includes but is not limited to genital stimulation. It underlies practically all forms of what we might call love, including brotherly love, Platonic love, the mutual love of parents and children. Thus, the eros is not only the ultimate source of one's desire for sexual satisfaction in the biological sense. Modified by the ego, it is also the source of all of our constructive, altruistic activities. We shall return to this subject shortly, but first let us attend to the second kind of instinct, the so-called death wish (Freud 1959).

The death instinct, or the *thanatos*, is an unconscious desire to die, to end it all, to return to an organic state, to destroy ourselves and others. Freud did not develop the concept of the thanatos until rather late in his career. He does not have as much to say on this subject as on the eros. However, he suggests that the death wish is apparent in the behavior of daredevils, reckless drivers, and others who are careless about their health and safety, as well as in the behavior of those who commit or attempt suicide. Just as he believed that the eros is the ultimate source of our good (or constructive or loving) behavior, he suggests that the thanatos, along with frustrations of sex impulses, is the source of hostile, destructive, and sometimes brutally violent behavior.

Human Nature

Freud's picture of human nature is quite pessimistic and not particularly pretty. The id, as we have seen, is stupid, selfish, demanding, and amoral. It includes a strong predisposition toward lust as well as a tendency toward aggression (Freud 1961). Those who maintain that there will always be wars and crime and cruelty because of human nature can find support for their position in Freudian psychology. So can those who attribute sexual perversions and depravity to irresistible drives over which the individual has no control and for which he cannot therefore be held entirely responsible. But still, as critical and unchangeable as the id is, it is only one of the three psychic forces operative within us and determining our behavior.

The Ego

The ego is the rational dimension of the human personality, the only dimension of which we are consciously aware. The ego corresponds to what we ordinarily mean by I or me or self. Its main function is to take reality into account and regulate the impulsive tendencies arising from the id. It is the ego that thinks, judges, foresees consequences, makes decisions, solves problems, and postpones gratification of our sexual or aggressive urges until suitable means of satisfying them can be found. The ego, then, is the sole determinant of our voluntary behavior.

The id can wish and generate images pertaining to wish fulfillment, but a person cannot survive on wishes and images alone. The infant who is hungry cannot eat or try to eat just anything. Nor can an older child or an adult immediately satisfy every sexual or aggressive urge that he experiences without taking the rights and welfare of others into account. Survival demands that the individual learn to wait, to tolerate tensions until they can be discharged in a civilized manner, and to distinguish between appropriate and inappropriate, harmful and helpful activities. The Pleasure Principle, in short, must be temporarily suspended in the interest of reality. Because it is so directly involved with the objective, physical environment, the ego is said to be governed by the *Reality Principle*.

The ego of the well-adjusted person has been likened to an executive, controlling the id on the one hand and the superego on the other, all the while keeping in touch with the external world to promote the best interests of the person (or the personality) as a whole. The ego begins to develop slowly and gradually very early in the life of an individual as some psychic energy is displaced or diverted from the id. Thus, the stronger one's ego becomes, the less energy remains for the id (Freud, 1960, 1966).

The Superego

Just as the ego grows out of the id, so does the third branch of the human personality, the superego, grow out of the ego. The superego has been referred to as the moral or judicial branch. It perceives things not as they are but as they should be. Representing the ideal rather than the real, it strives for a kind of perfection rather than simple pleasure or the reduction of tensions. Its main function is to restrict or inhibit the impulses arising from the id that are repugnant or potentially harmful to the individual or to society or both. Thus, the superego can be thought of as a moral censor or as the person's social sense (Freud 1938).

The superego begins to develop by about the age of four or five, as the child begins to assimilate the parents' standards of what is good and what is bad. It has two subsystems: the *ego ideal* and the *conscience*. The ego ideal refers to those internalized values or standards of behavior that are considered good; the conscience to those that are bad. Both are derived by a process known as *introjection*, which is an uncritical, irrational acceptance and assimilation of the standards of others.

In childhood, the values of one's parents and the examples they set are likely to be most crucial in the formation of one's superego. If, for example, parents regularly practice honesty or cleanliness, these become part of the ego ideal. The child does not analyze the concept of honesty logically. He does not weigh the pros and cons of cleanliness. He simply accepts these as virtuous or desirable and incorporates them into his emerging value system. Similarly, if his parents scold or otherwise punish him for, say, using certain words or touching certain parts of his body, he comes to assimilate these into his conscience as bad or sinful activities. Later in life, as the child's social horizons are broadened and other moral points of view are encountered, his ego compares and judges them and decides on what it considers appropriate in a given situation.

The superego is partly, though not entirely, an unconscious process. Like the id, the superego is unable to distinguish between inner, subjective experience and the objective world of external reality. It rewards the ego, usually with a feeling of satisfaction, not only for good acts but also for good thoughts and feelings and wishes. Similarly, it punishes the ego, usually with a feeling of guilt or shame, for bad thoughts, feelings, and desires as well as for bad overt behavior.

The Unconscious

Early in his career, Freud made a distinction among three regions of the human mind: the conscious, the preconscious, and the unconscious. These, of course, are not literally places or areas within the human organism. They represent, rather, levels of awareness or contents of the mind.

Consciousness refers to any and all thoughts, ideas, experiences, etc., of which the individual is currently aware. Whatever it is that we focus our attention on at a given moment is said to be in the forefront of consciousness.

The preconscious refers to ideas of which we are not currently aware, or on which our attention is not currently focused, but which can be voluntarily and rather easily brought to consciousness. For example, much of the material that you learned in high school and many of your past experiences are at this level. Perhaps you have not thought about these things for years, but you could recall them if you wanted to. Sometimes they are recalled spontaneously, often because of an association with some present experience.

The unconscious refers to thoughts, experiences, etc., that cannot be brought to consciousness voluntarily. They are not literally buried below the threshold of consciousness. However, because of strong inhibiting or repressive factors, they are not amenable to ordinary means of recall. We are presently unaware not only of our unconscious thoughts but we are unaware also of ever having entertained them. It is usually only through psychoanalysis that ideas and urges from the unconscious can be brought to consciousness and there dealt with rationally.

The id, as we have seen, is totally and completely unconscious. This is why it is sometimes referred to as the hidden part of the personality. The superego is partly conscious, partly preconscious, and partly unconscious. Our so-called primary motives arise from the id; our secondary motives are products of the superego. Secondary motives are not innate but learned. They are social rather than biological in nature and include goals such as recognition, attention, and acceptance. It is the unconscious aspect of the superego that is likely to be most critical in bringing about conflicts and anxieties. The ego is mainly a conscious process, but it also includes unconscious as well as preconscious ideas (Freud 1938, 1969). Id/ego/superego and conscious/preconscious/unconscious relationships are shown in Figure 2.

Conflicts

As Figure 3 shows, the ego is often in conflict with the id, the superego, and the demands of reality. These conflicts give rise to a variety of psychological disturbances, including several forms of neuroses, such as phobias, obsessions, compulsions, depression, and anxiety reactions. But much of the everyday behavior of normal people can also be understood as a means of trying to resolve these conflicts. The ego, as has been suggested, acts as a kind of buffer or mediator between the id on the one hand and the superego on the other. When, for example, impulsive sexual desires arise from the id demanding immediate gratification, the

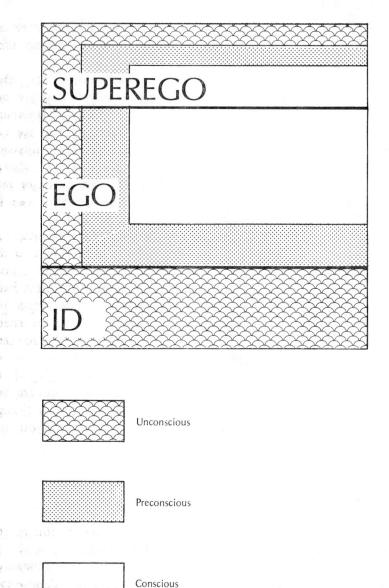

FIGURE 2. Freudian Levels of Personality and Consciousness. While the id operates completely at the unconscious level, the ego and super-ego are partly conscious, partly preconscious, and partly unconscious processes.

superego counters with moral or social restraints or prohibitions.

The id, in effect, says, "I want it now."

The superego says, "You can't. It's a sin." Or: "It's against the best interests of society." Or: "Your parents wouldn't approve."

The ego's function is to consider reality, weigh the pros and cons, consider the consequences, and make a decision. Sometimes, the ego decides to go along with the id and let it have its way. Sometimes, it supports the superego. Most commonly, in a well-adjusted person, it tries to work out a compromise, perhaps by devising some substitute activity where the demands of the id can be fairly well satisfied but in a manner that is acceptable to the superego. Strictly speaking, the id and the superego do not enter directly into conflict with one another. Rather, the ego conflicts with either the id or the superego.

When these conflicts can be rather easily resolved, as is usually the case, the individual is said to be well adjusted. The normal, healthy, well-adjusted person has achieved harmony among the three processes, with the ego in control of the other two. Such a person is said to have ego strength, the ego having the lion's share, as it were, of the individual's psychic energy. When the id is in control, the individual is amoral, impulsive, and possibly psychopathic. Such a person has little or no regard for others, little or

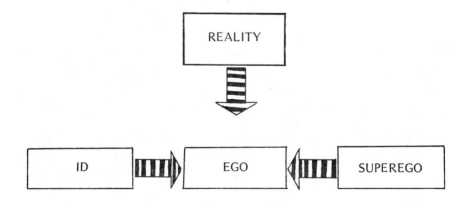

FIGURE 3.   Freudian Conflicts. Typical conflicts occur among the ego and the id, the superego, and the demands of reality.

no sense of right and wrong, and few if any guilt feelings or feelings of remorse. When, on the other hand, the superego is dominant, the individual is likely to be rigidly moralistic, perhaps with a holier-than-thou attitude. Such a person has an irrational, inflexible set of moral standards to which he adheres scrupulously, and he may experience severe guilt feelings and maybe feelings of depravity if he does not.

PSYCHOSEXUAL DEVELOPMENT

One of Freud's most revolutionary and controversial theories has to do with the sex life of very young children and its effects on their later personality development and motivation. Contrary to the earlier belief that sex drives begin to emerge at puberty, Freud maintained that they have their origins in early infancy. He identified five stages in the psychosexual development of human beings: the oral, anal, phallic, latency, and genital stages (Freud 1938, 1966).

Oral Stage

The oral stage lasts for about the first year and a half of life. This stage is so called because tensions during that period are localized in and around the mouth, and erogenous pleasure is derived from the stimulation of that part of the body. At later stages of development, the anal region and finally the genitals become the primary erogenous zones.

Freud maintained that during the oral stage the infant not only satisfies its need for food by eating but also derives sexual pleasure from the acts of sucking, chewing, swallowing, etc. During this stage, the infant learns to associate the feeding process with its mother and with her attitudes and feelings while she nurses or feeds it. One of the cornerstones of Freudian psychology is that the feelings and modes of adjustment acquired during the first few years determine to a great extent one's personality characteristics in later life. Psychoanalysts speculate that, other things being equal, an infant who is fed regularly and sufficiently is therefore likely to develop a sense of trust and a feeling of security that will remain with it throughout life. On the other hand, the infant who is frequently frustrated in this respect or is made to feel uncertain of its food supply is likely to develop a basic feeling of insecurity or mistrust that will characterize its subsequent personality.

Another possibility is that excessive frustration of the need for nourishment and the accompanying oral pleasure might cause the individual to become fixated at this stage of development. The behavior of an adult who engages in excessive eating, drinking, smoking, or even talking can be attributed to this type of fixation. Activities such as thumb-sucking, humming, and whistling, as well as the more obvious act of kissing, are among the everyday behaviors that can be regarded as attempts at oral gratification.

Anal Stage

During the second stage of psychosexual development, from about ages two to three, the locus of tension and satisfaction shifts from the oral region of the body to that around the anus. Now, the individual receives erotic pleasure not only from the stroking or patting of the buttocks but also from the elimination and retention of solid bodily wastes. This anal erotic phase of Freud's theory often is ridiculed. However, many of his followers still maintain that the kind of toilet training that a child receives at this stage, especially with respect to defecation, is likely to leave its mark on later personality development.

The expulsion of feces is often a pleasurable, tension-reducing activity and, under certain conditions, the retention of the feces can be just as pleasurable. No one, two-year-old children included, likes to have someone else interfere with and try to regulate his (or her) pleasures. But such interference and regulation is usually at the very heart of the act of toilet training that is ordinarily a child's first major encounter with discipline imposed by an external authority. The methods that parents employ in toilet training and the attitudes that they display with respect to defecation, feces, cleanliness, schedules, routines, etc., have been postulated as contributing factors to generosity, stinginess, rigidity, compulsive neatness, disorderliness, and a host of other personality traits. For example, it is claimed that one who has been highly praised for defecating is likely to develop a so-called anal-expulsive character. Such a person is inclined to be generous to a fault, regarding material possessions ("filthy lucre") as something to get rid of. On the other hand, one who has been overly rewarded for *not* defecating is more likely to become anal-retentive. Such a person is inclined to savor possessions, keeping them to himself, value cleanliness and order, and perhaps indulge in extreme selfishness.

Phallic Stage: Male

The phallic stage of psychosexual development extends from about ages three to six. During these years, Freud maintained, children become increasingly aware of their genitals and the pleasure to be derived from stroking and manipulating them. They also begin to engage in sexual fantasies involving their own genitals and their opposite-sex parents. Because of the anatomical or biological differences between the reproductive organs of girls and boys, corresponding psychological differences between males and females begin to appear at this time. These biological differences underlie the Freudian principle that "anatomy is destiny" (Gilman 1971).

During the phallic stage, the boy experiences the Oedipus complex, named after the character in Greeek mythology who unknowingly killed his father and married his mother. Freud believed that it is quite normal for a boy of this age to long for intimate relations with his mother and to perceive his father as a rival. The boy fears that, if his incestuous desires persist, his father will punish him by removing the offending sex organ. Thus, he develops the so-called *castration anxiety*. Largely, though not entirely, as a consequence of this anxiety, the boy represses his sexual desire **for** his mother as well as his hostility toward his father.

Through the efforts of the ego and the emerging superego, the boy fairly well resolves or outgrows the Oedipus complex by about the age of five. When he does so, he begins to identify more strongly with either his mother or his father or both. The boy's particular relationships with his respective parents as well as his other contacts with reality are among the major factors that determine his subsequent character, personality, attitudes toward the opposite sex, and feelings about himself. Much of the adult male's everyday behavior, moreoever, can be explained psycho-analytically in terms of his individual satisfactions and frustrations during the phallic stage of his development and by vestiges of the Oedipus complex that remain buried in his unconscious (A. Freud 1935).

Phallic Stage: Female

The feminine counterpart of the castration anxiety is what Freud calls penis envy. Upon observing that she does not possess the external male genitals, the little girl feels that she has already been castrated and blames her mother for this deficiency. Her love for her mother thereby becomes weakened and her love for her father begins to grow. Whereas castration anxiety is the main reason for the termination of the Oedipus complex in males, penis envy is the main reason for the onset of a similar complex in females. Thus, the girl loves her father, announces that when she grows up she is going to marry daddy, and perceives her mother as a rival.

As is the case with boys, the Oedipus complex in girls is ordinarily fairly well resolved by about the age of five or six. But, Freud maintained, the female version is more likely to persist. The manner in which this complex is resolved and the consequent feelings, behavior, and personality characteristics that result are affected, as is the case with boys, by biologically determined sex tendencies. Freud maintained that males and females alike are bisexual in that they inherit the predispositions of the opposite sex as well as their own. The relative strength of each of these tendencies within an individual goes a long way toward determining his or her subsequent masculinity or femininity, attitudes toward the opposite sex, and other individual personality variables.

Latency Period

Between the age of about five or six (when the Oedipus complex has been resolved) and puberty (when drastic physiological changes in the reproductive system take place), boys and girls go through the latency period. During these years, the sexual impulses remain dormant, and relatively unimportant as motivational factors. During these years, boys and girls alike appear to have little or no interest in sex as such. When they attend to members of the opposite sex at all, it is likely to be with disdain. Throughout the latency period, the ego and superego are developing and the child accumulates experiences, values, and interests that will contribute toward determining not only his reactions to the crises of adolescence but also the basic personality and motivational structure that will remain with him for life.

Genital Stage

The final stage of psychosexual development begins at puberty, with the reawakening of the sex impulses, and continues throughout adulthood. During the earlier, pregenital stages, the sexual instincts are directed inward, as the child's own body is the primary source of his erotic satisfaction. He is attracted toward his parents—particularly toward his mother because she is one of the first sources of pleasure—and the hugs, kisses, strokes, and caresses of both parents are sensually satisfying. In the genital stage, however, the sexual impulses are directed outward toward reproduction. Earlier modes of satisfaction, including masturbation, are no longer completely satisfying. Now the individual is attracted toward a person of the opposite sex with copulation as the objective. It is, of course, during this stage that the person either marries and perhaps begins to raise a family or experiments with what have come to be called alternative life-styles. In any case, many of the individual's day-to-day problems, activities, and motives remain primarily sexual in nature, or are at least derived from the sex impulses arising from the id.

Erikson's Model of Psychosocial Development

Freud's theory of psycho*sexual* development is significant not only in its own right, but also because it has served as a basis for the model of psycho*social* development formulated by the prominent contemporary psychoanalyst, Erik Erikson. Like a number of other neo-Freudians, including Alfred Adler, Erikson places less emphasis than Freud on the sexual and more on the social aspects of development. According to Erikson's model, between birth and death a person ordinarily passes through the eight stages of development that are outlined in Figure 4. Each of these stages is characterized by a dominant problem to be solved, need to be filled, or crisis to be overcome. During each stage, the individual must come to grips with the central crisis of that stage before he can move on to and cope with the crisis that is characteristic of the next (Erikson 1968).

In the first stage, *infancy*, which Erikson regards as the first year and a half of life, the individual has the best opportunity to develop a basic feeling of trust. If the infant receives enough tender loving care during this period, learning that it can count on its parents for food and comfort, and if other similar conditions are met, it is likely to develop the sense of trust that Erikson regards as the foundation of a healthy adult personality. If, on the other hand, the infant is raised in an unpredictable environment and is neglected by its parents, it is more likely to develop a distrust of other people that might remain with it for the rest of its life. If the infant does not develop a sense of trust in the first stage, it will not be impossible—but rather difficult—to acquire later in life.

In the second stage, *early childhood,* which extends from about age one-and-a-half to three, the child begins to assert his individuality, to test himself as a unique, independent person, and to find out what he can and cannot do by and for himself. During this phase, he has the potential to develop a sense of personal autonomy as opposed to feelings of shame and doubt about his adequacy. His future personality development, according to Erikson, depends in no small measure on the support and encouragement that he receives during these years and on how successful or unsuccessful he is in establishing his role within the family structure.

	1	2	3	4	5	6	7	
Maturity or Old Age								Integrity vs. Despair
Adulthood							Generativity vs. Stagnation	
Young Adulthood						Intimacy vs. Isolation		
Puberty and Adolescence					Identity vs. Role Confusion			
School Age (Latency Period)				Industry vs. Inferiority				
Childhood (Locomotor - Genital Stage)			Initiative vs. Guilt					
Early Childhood (Muscular - Anal Stage)		Autonomy vs. Shame, Doubt						
Infancy (Oral - Sensory Stage)	Trust vs. Mistrust							

FIGURE 4. Erikson's Model of Personality Development: Eight Psycological Stages and Their Accompanying Crises.

In the third stage (childhood, sometimes called the *play age*, ages three to seven), the child's social horizons are broadened and he has a chance to become more assertive in situations outside the home. If he is successful in channelling his social tendencies toward socially acceptable behavior, he will develop what Erikson calls a sense of initiative. Otherwise, he is likely to develop a basic feeling of guilt about the impropriety of his social behavior. This guilt feeling might remain with the individual for a long time and affect his future social relationships.

In the fourth stage, the *school age*, ages seven to twelve, the crisis involves a sense of industry versus one of inferiority. By industry Erikson means what we refer to in later chapters as a feeling of competence or achievement. Inferiority, to Erikson, implies not only a feeling of failure and frustration, but also the acquisition of poor work and study habits. The direction in which the person develops at this stage is, of course, dependent largely upon the quality of his schoolwork plus the support and assistance that he receives from his teachers.

In the fifth stage, *adolescence*, ages twelve to eighteen, the individual experiences what is perhaps the best known of the crises Erikson has discussed: the identity crisis. According to Erikson, this crisis must be resolved before the individual can function fully as a young adult and move on to meet the problems and demands of that stage. Consequently, much adolescent behavior is motivated by a need to find oneself and involves a certain amount of experimentation with diverse kinds of possible roles or identities. Ordinarily, the person who has previously developed a sense of trust, autonomy, initiative, and industry will have no great difficulty at this stage. But, a less fortunate individual might develop a sense of role diffusion (or confusion) that also might remain with him for years to come.

In the sixth stage, *young adulthood*, from approximately eighteen until the mid-thirties, the developmental crisis centers on a sense of intimacy with other people as opposed to a sense of isolation. At this stage, one of the major problems involves the sharing or fusing of one's identity with that of another person.

In the seventh stage, *adulthood*, the crisis involves a possible conflict between generativity and self-absorption or stagnation. Generativity implies helping the next generation. It also implies a feeling of productivity, creativity, usefulness, and concern for others as opposed to preoccupation with one's own problems and a feeling that one is no longer going anywhere. This stage is considered to extend from about the mid-thirties to the mid-sixties or until the person retires.

In the final stage, *late adulthood*, the individual develops a sense of integrity or one of despair, depending upon how successful or unsuccessful he has been in finding meaning in his life and accepting the inevitability of death. Integrity, as the term is presently used, involves a feeling of wisdom, personal satisfaction, and inner peace. As Erikson sees it, these qualities depend largely on the successful resolution of the seven earlier crises.

Unlike Freud, whose dismal view of human nature seems so pessimistic, Erikson is highly optimistic about the individual's potential to resolve each of these crises and to develop in a healthy direction. In this respect, his views are generally compatible with some of the principles of humanistic psychology that we discuss in Chapter 6.

DEFENSE MECHANISMS

Thus far, we have noted that, according to Freudian psychology, much human behavior is motivated unconsciously. These motives are primarily sexual in nature but include a strong element of hostility as well. As we have seen, one of the major functions of the ego is to protect the individual against threats and dangers and to reduce or eliminate anxieties. One way in which the ego fulfills this function is through the use of rational, problem-solving processes. Taking reality into account, the ego studies the situation and makes an intellectual judgment as to what should be done. Another way in which the ego fulfills this purpose is through the use of one or another of the so-called defense mechanisms (A. Freud 1968). Also referred to as escape or ego-protective mechanisms, defense mechanisms are irrational means of dealing with anxiety. They are said to be irrational because they cause one to distort, or deny, or attempt to escape from reality. One of the most important of these reactions is repression.

Repression

When harmful or repulsive urges, ideas, or memories arise from the id and are opposed by the superego, they are forced out of consciousness by the ego. They are, in a word, repressed. Repression is an unconscious process that is basic to the entire system of psychoanalysis. Essentially a response to an inner conflict, repression is one of the principal ways in which the ego defends itself against the unreasonable and often immoral or antisocial demands of the id. Repression reduces anxiety, in effect, by denying the very existence of an internal or external threat. But it does not eliminate the urge itself. It simply forces it into the unconscious, where it remains submerged, concealed, and apparently forgotten. However, the urge remains potentially operative, seeking its release or expression, often in some disguised form. Although any anxiety-producing or potentially dangerous desire or experience or fantasy is subject to repression, the urges that are most significant in this respect are those growing out of the eros or the thanatos.

Effects of Repression

Sometimes repressed desires are released from the unconscious in dreams. Dreams, according to Freud, are always means of wish fulfillment (Freud 1955). Some dreams bring about sexual pleasure in a rather obvious manner. Others have sexual implications, but they involve such complex symbolism that the individual does not recognize them for what they are. Even nightmares can be interpreted as a means of wish fulfillment growing out of the individual's unconscious desire for punishment as a means of ridding himself of guilt feelings.

    Jokes are another outlet for repressed urges (Freud 1938, 1960). For example, jokes involving sex or matters pertaining to the toilet give an individual a chance to receive, in a manner acceptable to the superego, a kind of vicarious satisfaction that he might otherwise be unable to obtain. Similarly, jokes in which certain classes of people, such as members of another ethnic or occupational group, are ridiculed provide a socially acceptable means of releasing pentup hostilities toward these people.

Some of the little mistakes that we make in everyday life, the slips of the tongue or of the pen, are still another way in which repressed ideas are released. These are forms of parapraxia, better known as Freudian slips (Freud 1965). For example, a typing error in which we accidentally refer to a *friend* as a *fiend* might be interpreted by a Freudian as revealing our true feelings toward that person. More than one critic of psychoanalysis has unintentionally referred to its founder as Sigmund Fraud. Similarly, memory lapses, such as forgetting an appointment that we really want to forget, even accidents involving injury to oneself or to the property or welfare of others, can be attributed to unconscious motivation.

Sometimes the repressed desire overwhelms the resistance all at once so that the result is an intense emotional outburst. This is what happens when, for example, an ordinarily quiet, well-behaved person cuts loose and releases his bottled-up sex or aggression drives in a kind of rampage. Sometimes, these repressed urges are not released at all, thus causing the individual to go through life unhappy, and perhaps at least mildly neurotic, without having the slightest idea why. Psychoanalysis as a system of therapy is the process by which these repressed urges are brought to consciousness and dealt with accordingly.

In and of itself, repression is not bad. It helps a person adjust to prevailing social, cultural, and moral standards and expectations, and serves as a control over one's thoughts, speech, and overt behavior. It protects the ego against repugnant feelings and desires. But repressed emotions, as we have noted, do not remain repressed forever. They need some outlet. If they are not given release in a morally acceptable, socially approved manner, they might erupt in some form of unsocial or immoral behavior. The mechanism of displacement is one way in which this release is obtained.

Displacement

Displacement is the channelling of psychic energy away from one object toward another. The urge remains the same but the means of expressing it is changed. By means of this mechanism, a person is able to release an impulse or a repressed emotion in some disguised form so as not to arouse feelings of guilt and to avoid being punished by either his superego or society. The most common form of this mechanism is displaced hostility whereby the individual substitutes one person (or group or object) for another as the target of his hatred.

A young boy, for example, might wish to inflict physical harm on the newly arrived baby sister of whom he is intensely jealous. But hitting the baby sister is a No-No. Fortunately, for the baby, the older sibling rival therefore directs his energies into some constructive or harmless kind of activity that enables him to rid himself of aggressive feelings. Calling her names, spanking a doll, kicking a football, or pounding a piece of modeling clay might provide this outlet.

At a later stage of development, the boy might take out his repressed hostility toward his father on some other person. Thus, a teacher, a policeman, some other authority figure, or an innocent bystander becomes the object of his verbal abuse or even actual physical attack. The father, in turn, might displace his hostilities by slamming doors, kicking his automobile tires, or mistreating his wife instead of his boss or someone else whom he'd *really* like to injure.

The behavior of the bully, the vandal, the gossip, and the rumormonger, among others, is commonly explained in terms of this mechanism. So is that of the avid sports fan who releases his or her aggressive tendencies by yelling, "Kill the umpire!" (the authority figure); "Murder the bum!" (the symbol of the boss?); or "Hit 'em again, harder, harder!" In fact, any form of competitive activity in which one person tries to beat another—in sports, in the business world, or in the classroom—can be interpreted as a case of displaced hostility.

Sublimation

Sublimation is a particular form of displacement. While the term *displacement* is commonly used with respect to aggressive drives and is often basically destructive, sublimation is more commonly associated with the sex drive and usually implies a substitute activity that is constructive in nature. Through this mechanism, the individual directs his energy away from primitive unsocial or immoral activities toward those which are socially useful or at least acceptable.

An adolescent, for example, who is prevented by his ego and his superego from satisfying his sex needs directly might satisfy them indirectly by being especially nice to girls, writing love poems, or expressing his love by doing good deeds of one kind or another. Teachers, social workers, nurses, clergymen, and others who devote themselves professionally to helping others are considered to be sublimating. So is the student who works hard in school to please his parents or perhaps his teachers. Sublimation also explains the behavior of a person who, for example, "loves" his new car, pats it affectionately, thinks of it as sexy, and refers to it as a beauty. The artist who, instead of using his sex impulses to create a new human life, creates instead a picture or a musical composition is also thought to be sublimating. In short, all forms of creative activity as well as nurturing, altruistic behavior and all forms of love can be explained psychoanalytically as essentially the sublimation of sex impulses.

Reaction Formation

Reaction formation is the directing of one's psychic energies away from a desired object to its exact opposite. This mechanism manifests itself in behavior that is diametrically opposite to that which a person wants but fears to express. The individual leans over backward to appear the opposite of what he is or feels. Hostility, for example, might take the form of overprotection or overconcern for the welfare of others, whereas fondness or attraction might be expressed through mistreatment. Rather than admit that she likes a certain boy, for example, a ten-year-old girl might torment him with insulting remarks. Similarly, overindulgent parents might really, albeit unconsciously, reject their children and be attempting to alleviate their consequent feelings of guilt by showering them with gifts and special privileges. Whistling in the dark to cover up one's fears, making light of serious matters to conceal one's anxieties, conforming excessively to external standards of moral behavior, and trying too hard to act in a stereotyped masculine/feminine manner might also be examples of this ego-protective device.

Identification

Identification is the process by which an individual incorporates into his own personality certain admired qualities of another person. It is largely through identification that one's ego and superego are formed. By identifying with and imitating first his parents and then others, the individual assimilates their values and behavior patterns and eventually comes to think, feel, believe, and act much as they do. Identification, however, is not the same as imitation. While imitation is likely to be a conscious attempt to copy someone else's behavior, identification is the unconscious assimilation or introjection of certain aspects of the other person's very personality.

As an ego-protective measure, identification is used to alleviate anxieties about one's own shortcomings by attributing to oneself the strengths or virtues of others. A frustrated person, for example, is likely to identify with someone who is successful in order to experience some of that reflected success himself. It is for this reason that we often identify with public figures or fictional characters in books or movies. Identification also serves to strengthen one's feeling of security by giving one a feeling of belonging to some group or organization. It is interesting to note that we sometimes identify with others not because we want to be like them but because they are somehow like us. This form of identification is referred to as narcissistic because, like the young man in Greek mythology, we are attracted by the image of ourselves as it is reflected in others.

Projection

Projection is, in effect, the opposite of identification. By projecting, the individual alleviates his feelings of guilt or anxiety by unconsciously attributing to others his own faults, weaknesses, or forbidden impulses. For example, a person whose sex drives are unsatisfied might accuse someone else of being oversexed. Projection also involves blaming some other person or some external condition for one's own shortcomings. Thus, a student who does not do particularly well in mathematics explains away failure by alleging that the teacher really does not know much about mathematics or that, if he does, he doesn't know how to teach it. Blaming society, or the system, or unsettled world conditions, or the government, or one's family for one's failures are other common cases of projection.

By means of this mechanism, a person transforms neurotic or moral anxiety into objective reality. With respect to neurotic anxiety (fear of the id), the feeling of "I want to hurt him" is transformed to one of "He wants to hurt me." With respect to moral anxiety (fear of the superego), the feeling of "I am guilty" is changed to "Someone else is guilty of causing my frustration and anxiety."

Rationalization

Projection is closely related to the mechanism of rationalization. Rationalization is the use of plausible but untrue reasons to justify doing something, or wishing for something, that is opposed by the superego. The classic example of this mechanism is the remark of the fox in one of Aesop's fables that he did not really want the grapes that he was unable to obtain because they were too sour. The sixteen-year-old girl who claims that she would not have accepted an invitation to a party even if she had received one because parties are a "silly waste of time" and that she most certainly would not have gone with Jeff if he had asked her because "he's such a creep" is probably rationalizing. So too is the student who had hoped to receive an A in a course but claims to be "perfectly satisfied" with a C because "grades don't mean anything."

Like the other mechanisms we have discussed, rationalization is an *unconscious* attempt to protect our own egos. Rather than admit, even to ourselves, our own fears or failing, we tend to expend mental energy inventing logical defenses of our behavior. One of the most common of these defenses is, of course, the claim that "everyone else is doing it."

Fixation

In the normal course of development, the individual passes gradually and imperceptibly from one stage to another, facing and dealing with the problems of each as it arises. However, the person sometimes feels so anxious about taking the next step forward that he becomes fixated at a particular point on the development continuum. Instead of moving on to the challenges and satisfactions of the next stage, he unconsciously remains where he is, clinging to his present satisfactions.

Events such as one's first day at school, first date, first day on the job, etc., ordinarily give rise to a certain amount of anxiety because they do represent a certain possibility of failure and threat to one's ego ideal. In some cases, of course, the individual really has no choice but to undertake a new venture, such as going to school. But he might do so most reluctantly, attempting to preserve insofar as possible the pleasures he knew in his preschool years. Fifteen or twenty years later, this individual might be most hesitant about, say, marrying, leaving home, or embarking on a career because he is fearful of leaving the protective, loving care of his mother. As suggested earlier in this chapter, even an otherwise normal, healthy person might, to an extent, become fixated at the pregenital stage of his development. Thus, he never really grows up and may be prevented from developing his full potential.

Regression

Regression is a mechanism whereby the individual, having attained a certain stage of psychological growth, moves backward and engages in behavior that is ordinarily more characteristic of an earlier stage of development. For example, after an emotionally upsetting experience, a ten-year-old who had apparently outgrown the habit might revert to thumb-sucking or baby talk. An older person might break down and cry when the going gets rough, or throw a temper tantrum, or blow off steam by slamming the door, breaking dishes, kicking the dog, etc. Or he might adopt a posture of helplessness, unconsciously trying to recapture the years of infancy when his satisfactions were not his own responsibility but those of his parents. Regression is also operative in various forms of nostalgia whereby the person attempts to relive the good old days.

Although normal people, in the ordinary course of events, proceed naturally through the stages of psychosexual development on to maturity and personal stability, they are usually not fully and completely satisfied in their demands for the kinds of pleasures associated with the first few years of life. Nor are their early feelings of hostility ever permanently repressed. Thus, much adult behavior can be construed as motivated by unfulfilled urges, images, and memories of the pregenital stage.

EDUCATIONAL IMPLICATIONS

Despite this rather lengthy discussion, we have touched upon only a few of the major ideas in Freudian psychology. (His entire works fill twenty-four volumes.) Freud's views are extremely controversial, of course. (Critiques of his position also could easily fill twenty-four volumes.) But, despite the criticisms of psychoanalysis, it is fair to say that no psychologist and no system of psychology has been unaffected by his views. In fact, a great deal of post-Freudian psychology has been an attempt to test, modify, or refute some of his theories or to incorporate some of his ideas into some other system. But, how has psychoanalysis affected schools, teachers, education in general, and the problem of motivation in particular?

To begin with, we must realize that professionally Freud was more concerned with the treatment of emotionally disturbed individuals than he was with normal children in regular classrooms. His greatest contributions have been in the area of clinical rather than educational psychology. He offered no theory of education per se and little in the way of practical advice to teachers on how to motivate their students toward scholastic achievement. However, his theories have had a strong impact in such related areas as child development, discipline, character formation, and mental hygiene (Hill 1971).

Students' Hidden Motives

One of Freud's most significant contributions to education is the help he has given teachers in understanding their students. Of course, we need not accept the entire psychoanalytic theory to be able to appreciate the possible effects of unconscious drives on human behavior and misbehavior. Even some of Freud's severest critics agree that a person's observable behavior might well be only a superficial manifestation of some deeply rooted emotional problem that perhaps does go back to early childhood.

In trying to interpret the behavior of your students, naturally you should not attempt to psychoanalyze them. But, as a minimum, you might be able to apply your knowledge of repression, displacement, projection, and other defense mechanisms to particular cases so that you can arrive at a deeper insight into the *why* of their behavior. Freud can help you to understand, for example, that a student who defies you does not necessarily have anything against you personally but might be using you as a target for the release of his pentup hostilities toward someone or something else. Without attempting to play the role of armchair psychiatrist, you might be able to use Freudian principles to guide the student toward an awareness of his own hidden motives for acting as he does. Along with some of the intrinsic and extrinsic strategies that we discuss in later chapters, you might also be able to use your understanding of such mechanisms as sublimation and identification to motivate your students to do what you would like them to do.

Preschool Years

Freud was not the first to recognize that the patterns of behavior and modes of adjustment acquired in the first few years of life are likely to have a profound effect on the individual's subsequent personality development. But no other individual has contributed more to bringing to public attention the point that the motivation behind a considerable amount of adolescent and adult behavior can be traced to experiences in the pregenital years. Many contemporary psychoanalysts do not share Freud's views on infantile sexuality and the Oedipus complex, or at least do not emphasize them as he did. But they do agree with him on the importance of the first five or six years as *the* most critical period of development. Freud, therefore, must certainly be numbered among those who have contributed most significantly to the early or preschool educational movement, particularly as it relates to the child's social and emotional needs (Tyler 1972).

Concern for the Whole Person

Freud has contributed significantly to the idea that schools should be concerned with the whole person and not just the development of his rational abilities. Traditionally, the main function of the school has been to cultivate what Freud called the *ego processes*— that is, the student's intellectual or cognitive potentialities. Freudian psychology has helped to broaden the concept of the school's purpose to include concern for the student's social, emotional, moral, and aesthetic development as well.

One need not be a Freudian to recognize that poor scholastic achievement and the lack of motivation toward scholastic success are not uncommonly due to frustrations, conflicts, anxieties, and other forms of personal maladjustment. But Freudian psychology certainly does give strong support to the notion that schools should be concerned with the student's mental health not only because mental health is in itself good, but also because it is a necessary means toward scholastic achievement and desirable classroom behavior.

Freud's theories also imply that a very important purpose of education is to promote the development of healthy superegos. Michael Maccoby recommends that from a psychoanalytical position schools should place less emphasis on the transmission of academic subject matter and more on the development of the student's character. In this respect, he is especially critical of what he perceives as excessive competition and overreliance on extrinsic motivation in our schools. He believes that these serve only to produce "alienated-competitive" character. Instead, the school should focus its efforts on the development of "productive-cooperative" character—that is, on the development of individual human beings who actualize their inherent potentialities and who use them for social rather than for selfish purposes (Maccoby 1972).

In short, Freudian psychology reinforces the idea held also by many non-Freudians that the school should play an active role in helping the student to form a favorable self-concept; to satisfy his personal, social, and emotional needs in a realistic, socially acceptable manner; to find a set of moral values and principles by which he can govern his own life; and to develop his particular strengths, potentialities, talents, and possibilities.

Pleasure and Reality Principles

Although Freud made no systematic attempt to apply his theories directly to the everyday work of teachers in their classrooms, several of his disciples (including his daughter, Anna) have tried to do so (A. Freud 1935). But Freud's followers have not always agreed on *how* psychoanalytical principles can or should be applied, or on which particular educational practices are or are not in keeping with Freudian precepts. Thus, educational reformers and traditionalists, progressives and conservatives, intrinsic and extrinsic motivators can cite Freud to support their own positions (Roberts 1975).

As Bruno Bettleheim, a leading contemporary interpreter of Freudian psychology, points out, when attempts were first made to apply Freudian principles to education, the major emphasis was placed on releasing the id and deemphasizing the ego and superego proportionately (Bettleheim 1969). In other words, attempts were made to base education on the Pleasure Principle. Hence, the rash of elementary and secondary textbooks that appeared with the word *fun* in the titles: *Fun with Arithmetic, Reading Is Fun,* etc. One might not have been too surprised to find a medical school textbook entitled *Fun with Brain Surgery.*

Freudian psychology seemed to support the views emanating

largely from John Dewey and his disciples that learning should be interesting and enjoyable (Dewey 1975). With all due respect to interest and fun as motivational devices, neo-Freudians such as Bettleheim maintain that such an approach is not realistic. Certain things should be learned whether the student enjoys them or not. Certain important forms of learning occur only when the student applies himself to the task at hand and makes an honest effort, even when the task yields no immediate pleasure. Thus, according to Bettleheim, classroom learning and motivation should be based on the Reality Principle.

The Reality Principle, you will recall, implies postponing one's demand for immediate gratification and working for long-range, delayed rewards. It implies doing things simply because they are expected or deemed necessary in the real world even though the individual might not particularly enjoy or feel like doing them. But, basing education on the Reality Principle should not and certainly need not entirely rule out the use of the Pleasure Principle. Nor should the Reality Principle be invoked to rationalize dull curricula or boring methods of instruction. Learning need not always be fun, but the alternative is not that it must therefore be a drag. If a teacher cannot find ways of making his class pleasant, he should at least try to arrange conditions so that it is not unpleasant.

Fear as a Motivator

For centuries, one of the most commonly used motivational devices has been fear. (Learn it, or else!) In recent decades, this approach has properly fallen into disfavor, thanks in no small part to Freudian psychology. But Bettleheim, among others, suggests that in deemphasizing if not completely abandoning this approach education has gone to the opposite extreme. While *too much* fear undoubtedly interferes with learning, a certain amount of it is helpful, if not absolutely necessary (Bettleheim 1969).

Learning, as has been suggested, can be hard work. Work of any kind often implies a sense of duty or responsibility, a belief that one should do his job simply because it is the right thing to do at that particular time. This type of attitude toward a task that is not immediately pleasurable requires strong support from the superego. But one of the requirements for the development of a strong, healthy superego is fear. The child *should* be afraid of some form of punishment, such as withdrawal of parental affection, if he does not behave as expected. Eventually, as the child matures, fear can be reduced as a basis for motivation. But, particularly in the early years, Freudian psychology most certainly does not recommend complete freedom from fear or unconditional love from parents.

Discipline

Because of his firm views on repression as a factor contributing to the development of neuroses, Freud has been interpreted as advocating a rather extreme kind of permissiveness on the parts of teachers as well as parents. Actually, while he did maintain that excessive repression and frustration could be detrimental to the child's long-range, overall personality development, he also taught that *some* repression is necessary and beneficial for the development of healthy egos and superegos. His views on the development of the superego have been either ignored or misinterpreted by some of his would-be disciples.

Freud believed that, to develop a system of inner control over one's behavior (superego strength), one must first experience a system of external controls as a child. One must learn to understand which kinds of behavior are good and which are bad. One effective way of learning to recognize and avoid bad behavior is to be punished for it. To learn inner control, one must also experience a certain amount of frustration and deprivation.

Freud did not recommend that teachers or parents go out of their way to repress or frustrate or punish children. But neither can he be held responsible for the idea that punishment or repression is always or necessarily bad. He certainly did not hold, as is sometimes believed, that frustration is inevitably damaging to children's delicate little psyches. His views do support the need for a healthy balance between expression and repression, or between freedom and control, and a more humane approach toward discipline than was in vogue at his time.

RECOMMENDED READING

Bettleheim, Bruno. "Psychoanalysis and Education." *School Review, 77*: 73–86, 1969. Best known for his work with emotionally disturbed children, Bettleheim summarizes in this article some of his insights into the behavior and misbehavior of normal children and young people. He also offers parents and teachers some recommendations for motivation, based on psychoanalytical principles.

Erikson, Erik H. *Identity: Youth and Crisis.* New York: W. W. Norton, 1968. An extended discussion of the adolescent's search for a sense of identity. More than Freud, to whom he is greatly indebted, Erikson emphasizes social interaction as a prime factor in the individual's psychosocial development. Also recommended is his *Childhood and Society.*

Freud, Anna. *The Ego and the Mechanisms of Defense.* London: Hogarth Press, 1968. Rev. ed. Written by Sigmund Freud's daughter, also a prominent psychoanalyst, this book discusses various ways in which the ego controls instinctive urges and regulates impulsive behavior. A good overview of her father's thoughts on the subject along with some valuable insights of her own.

Freud, Anna. *Psychoanalysis for Teachers and Parents.* New York: Emerson Books, 1935. A series of four lectures centering on infant sexuality and psychosexual development. Brings out the relationship she sees between psychoanalysis and teaching. Includes some recommendations, leaning toward permissiveness, for the application of Freudian principles to home and school situations.

Freud, Sigmund. *The Psychopathology of Everyday Life.* New York: W. W. Norton, 1965. There is no one book written by Freud himself in which he systematically sets forth all of his theories or summarizes his views succinctly. If you are interested in primary source material, you must therefore choose from among his several books and articles. Freud seems to have thought that, of all his books, this is the best general introduction to psychoanalysis for lay people. It deals with forgetting, mistakes, superstitions, slips of the tongue, and other nonmedical behaviors of normal people in ordinary circumstances. Several of Freud's other books are listed in the bibliography.

Gilman, Richard. "The FemLib Case against Freud." *New York Times Magazine,* Jan. 31, 1971. A critique of Freud's views on sex differences, particularly of his many disparaging remarks about women, biological determinism, and his belief that "anatomy is destiny."

Hall, Calvin S. *A Primer of Freudian Psychology.* New York: World Publishing

Co., 1954. A very clear, well-organized summary of the main facets of psychoanalysis, emphasizing the functioning of the normal rather than the neurotic personality. One of the most popular and useful books about psychoanalysis available.

Hill, John C. *Teaching and the Unconscious Mind.* New York: International Universities Press, 1971. Of the hundreds of books on Freudian psycology, this is one of the few that apply it directly to education. The author relates principles of psychoanalysis to classroom management, early education, secondary education, and various school subjects and includes a section in the Appendix on "Freud's Influence on Education."

Jones, Ernest. *Life and Work of Sigmund Freud.* New York: Basic Books, 1961. This is an abridged edition of Jones's definitive three-volume biography of Freud. A must for the serious student of Freudian psychology. The book deals with his life, associates, times, correspondence, personal problems, quarrels with Alfred Adler and others, and the development and revisions of his theories.

Roazen, Paul. *Freud and His Followers.* New York: A. Knopf, 1975. Based on hundreds of interviews with people who knew Freud personally, this book describes his personal and professional relationships with Adler, Jung, and several others who were part of his famous circle. Offers some good insights into Freud, the human being.

Roberts, Thomas B., Ed. *Four Psychologies Applied to Education.* New York: John Wiley, 1975. Part One of this anthology includes sixteen short articles that bring out what the author of each sees as the practical educational implications of Freudian psychology. The other three parts include articles on the educational implications of behavioral, humanistic, and transpersonal psychology.

Tyler, Louis L. "Curriculum Development from a Psychoanalytic Perspective." *Educational Forum, 36*: 173–179, 1972. The author outlines five educational goals derived from Freudian psychology and suggests some means of implementing them, particularly with children between the ages of three and seven.

CHAPTER 3: PREVIEW QUESTIONS

(After you have finished reading Chapter 3, you should be able to answer the following.)

1. What are some major differences between Freudian psychology and Alfred Adler's Individual Psychology?

2. What, according to Adler, is the prime motive of human behavior? How does this motive work?

3. According to Individual Psychology, when and why do feelings of inferiority originate? How and why do they develop as a person grows older?

4. Why is it that feelings of inferiority are sometimes beneficial to personality development and motivation? How and why are they sometimes detrimental?

5. What does Adler mean by a life-style? What are some factors on which an individual's life-style depends?

6. What does Adler mean by power? What is the significance of that concept in Individual Psychology? Why does Adler regard much human behavior as part of a power struggle?

7. What are some manifestations of the will to power in infancy or early childhood? In adolescence? In adulthood? In old age?

8. What are Adler's views on sexual equality and the so-called women's liberation movement? How does he account for common stereotypes of masculine and feminine behavior?

9. What does Adler mean by masculine protest? By weapons of weakness?

10. What does Adler mean by social feelings? What is the significance in Individual Psychology of Adler's belief that human beings are essentially social animals?

11. How does Adler differ from Freud in his concept of human nature? What support, if any, does Adler lend to the notion that human nature is fundamentally good?

12. What are some reasons or motives for deviant behavior in Individual Psychology?

13. What does Adler mean by the perfection toward which he believes we are all striving?

14. What are Adler's views on competition as a motivational tactic? On the practice of encouraging students to earn good grades?

15. Why, according to Adler, does everyone compensate? What are some common forms of compensation?

16. What light does Adlerian psychology shed on the behavior of people who seem to be preoccupied with image or status?

17. What is your overall reaction to Adler's theories of human motivation? How, if at all, do they help you to understand your own behavior or that of people with whom you come in contact?

CHAPTER THREE

Individual and Social Dimensions

This chapter centers on some of the main ideas of Alfred Adler (1870–1937). Early in his professional career, Adler was a colleague of Freud's and one of his staunchest defenders. Eventually, he came to disagree rather sharply with Freud on a number of points, including Freudian pansexualism, and formulated a system of his own which he called Individual Psychology (Adler 1968). Adler's theory of motivation is considerably simpler than Freud's in that it entails far fewer abstract, esoteric constructs. It also seems to be much more down to earth in that it more clearly and directly explains much of our ordinary, everyday behavior.

Because of his early association with Freud, Adler is sometimes classified as a neo-Freudian. More properly, he can be regarded as one of the major progenitors of what has come to be called humanistic psychology (Ansbacher 1971). Adler's Individual Psychology is not, as is sometimes thought, a mere spinoff or modification of Freudian psychoanalysis. It is, rather, a reaction to Freudian psychology, bearing but little resemblance to the views that Freud set forth. For example, while Freud maintained that to understand human behavior it is necessary to analyze the person's innate, instinctive, unconscious *drives*, Adler maintained that it was potentially more productive to understand the person's *goals*. It is this emphasis that he places on the person's goals or purposes as the primary factor in motivation and his views on the individual's social relationships and concern for others that link him with contemporary humanism (Adler 1964).

INFERIORITY FEELINGS

One of the key concepts in Adler's theory is inferiority. As he states very explicitly, Individual Psychology "begins and ends with the problem of inferiority" (Adler 1954). Actually, his social ideas are at least equally significant, but this, I believe, is the best point with which to begin.

According to Adler, every human being—young or old, rich or poor, male or female—has a basic feeling of inferiority. Each of us is in some respect inferior to someone else and, unless we are completely out of touch with reality, we know it. (The person who believes that he is in no way inferior to anyone in anything is probably suffering from delusions of grandeur and could be dangerous!) Inferiority feelings are normal. They are natural. They are universal. And they are potentially very beneficial. While they might not be anything to brag about, they are certainly nothing to be ashamed of!

All of us, according to Adler, not only have these feelings but we are also consciously aware of them. This does not mean that the average person spends a lot of time and energy brooding about his inferiority. These feelings are not constantly or usually in the forefront of our consciousness. But neither are they buried deep in the unconscious regions of the mind. The unconscious, in fact, plays a relatively minor role in Adlerian psychology.

Inferiority Complex

While we all have inferiority *feelings*, we do not all have inferiority *complexes*. There's a big difference between the two. An inferiority complex is a neurotic *obsession* with one's inferiority. It is a very intense, persistent, and global feeling of personal inadequacy usually accompanied by strong anxiety and depression. The normal person feels that he is inferior in certain respects only whereas the person with an inferiority complex feels very strongly that he is inferior in just about everything. The point at which normal inferiority feelings end and an inferiority complex begins cannot be easily or positively identified. This is a problem for clinical psychology, with which we need not presently concern ourselves. Suffice it to note that in this chapter we are dealing with normal people having normal feelings of inferiority.

Effects of Inferiority

A basic drive or goal of the human organism is to overcome or alleviate one's feelings of inferiority and to achieve a measure of perfection or superiority. Later in this chapter, we explore Adler's concept of perfection as well as his ideas on the individual's social orientation and social feelings. For the present, let us simply note that inferiority feelings can be regarded as *the* prime motivator, the force behind everything a person does.

Inferiority feelings, as has been suggested, are potentially very valuable. They are the source of many of our positive, constructive activities. They motivate us toward personal growth and fulfillment. They stimulate us toward worthwhile achievement in our careers as well as in many aspects of our everyday lives. But, just as they are the source of all our productive, socially beneficial behavior, so are they also the motive underlying negative, destructive, antisocial behavior as well.

Not only is the reduction of inferiority feelings a tremendously attractive goal toward which much of our behavior is directed but, as we shall see, the particular manner in which an individual copes with those feelings is the main determiner of his personality, character, and overt behavior.

Development of Inferiority Feelings

Although normal and natural, inferiority feelings are not innate. They are learned. They are acquired very early in life as they grow out of the infant's complete helplessness and total dependence on others for the satisfaction of every need, including, of course, nourishment and other requisites for physical survival. Thus, the basic structure of one's personality is formed during the first few months of life. By about age two, the child is well aware of his inferiority and dependence and begins to want to do something about it.

Dependence continues to imply a kind of inferiority throughout life. To the extent that I am dependent upon someone else to do something for me that I want but cannot do for myself, I feel inferior (because I am inferior) to that person in that respect. Although the child becomes progressively less dependent as he matures, he never becomes completely independent of others. Moreover, as the person advances through childhood and adolescence to maturity, other factors arise that contribute to the inferiority feeling.

As the child grows up, he is constantly being compared, or he is comparing himself, with others: parents, sisters and brothers, playmates, various adults, celebrities from the fields of sports or entertainment, characters in books and television, etc. The individual makes these comparisons—even if no one else does—in the family circle, in play activities, at school, and later in the world of work. Invariably, the person finds that others are bigger, or smarter, or stronger, or richer, or more popular, or more skilled, or more successful, or somehow superior to himself. Thus, despite one's growing independence, the feeling of inferiority continues and, perhaps, even intensifies.

Perhaps owing to his training as a physician, Adler perceived inferiority feelings as resulting in many cases from physical frailty or some organic deficiency within the child. His followers, however, have placed more emphasis on social factors as contributing to inferiority feelings. However, Adler was also very much concerned with the socialization process, particularly in the home, and attributed many inferiority feelings to pampering or harsh disciplinary measures on the part of parents (Adler 1963).

Compensation

Much human behavior by adults, as well as children, can be explained in terms of their trying to overcome or alleviate their inferiority feelings. One way in which they do this is through the mechanism of compensation. Compensation is one of the ego-protective processes recognized by Freud. It could have been mentioned in the previous chapter, along with displacement and sublimation to which it is very closely related. But compensation plays such an important role in Adlerian psychology that it seems more appropriate to discuss it here.

Essentially, compensation is an attempt to excel in one area as a means of making up for some real or imagined shortcoming in another. A classic example is the male adolescent who lacks (or feels that he lacks) the ability to do as well as his classmates scholastically. To compensate, he attempts to bolster his ego and gain social approval through some substitute activity, such as sports or playing the role of the class clown. Another person, who lacks (or feels that he lacks) athletic ability, on the other hand, might try to compensate by becoming a sports reporter for the school newspaper, or a cheerleader, or an outstanding student in chemistry.

Since no one can excel in everything, a certain amount of compensation is necessary for one's psychological well-being. It is largely by means of this mechanism that we develop and capitalize on our strong points and help to overcome our limitations, or what we *perceive* as our limitations. Since compensation protects the ego against needless anxiety and helps the individual to develop a favorable self-concept and a feeling of personal worth, it is in effect a psychological lifesaver. We shall return to this point shortly.

Forms of Compensation

Everybody uses the mechanism of compensation, but each in a different way. The effects of compensation—like the effects of the inferiority feelings—might be good or bad, productive or destructive, socially useful or harmful. Attempts to overcome inferiority feelings might stimulate a person to try to excel in business, one of the arts or professions, in politics, sports, scholarship, or some other worthwhile area of human endeavor. But the same attempts might lead to bullying, vandalism, mugging, dope-pushing, embezzlement, unscrupulous business practices, and other kinds of delinquent or immoral behavior. Thus, insofar as basic motivation is concerned, parents and children, students and teachers, saints and sinners, are all pretty much alike.

The particular manner in which an individual compensates depends on variables such as the person's age, sex, associates, occupation, ethnic or religious background, socioeconomic status, particular circumstances, and what Adler called the person's "life-style." More important, the form of an individual's compensatory activities depends upon his education—not only on that which he receives in school but particularly on what he learns in the home.

Life-style

Every person, according to Individual Psychology, has a unique life-style (Adler 1969). One's life-style, as Adler uses the term, is essentially a kind of life plan. Adler defines *life-style* as a consistent movement toward the goal of overcoming the feeling of inferiority and achieving control over oneself and others. All human beings have this same goal, but each individual uses a different set of means to attain it. It is by means of one's life-style that the person expresses his or her individuality.

Adler's concept of life-style is an outgrowth of his idea that a human being is an active, purposeful, goal-seeking, unified organism whose behavior is generally consistent and predictable. He maintains that one's life-style originates in infancy when the baby, in effect, begins to map out the general strategy it will employ for overcoming feelings of helplessness: through crying, aggression, docility, etc. By about the age of four or five, one's life-style has been pretty well fixed.

Adler believed that one's life-style depends to a great extent also on birth order and position in the family. He notes that no two children, not even brothers or sisters, grow up in exactly the same environment. The very presence of an older sibling, for example, means that the circumstances under which the second-born is raised are different from those under which the first-born was brought up. Similarly, the position of a middle child, an only child, youngest, or oldest in a large family is likely to have a profound effect on the individual's life-style.

STRIVING FOR PERFECTION

Like most, if not all, psychologists, Adler recognizes that the first law of human nature is self-preservation. But self-preservation implies more than the maintenance of life in the physiological sense. It includes a tendency toward the preservation and the enhancement of the *psychological* self as well. Because a human being is a unified organism and not simply a collection of parts or an aggregation of traits, every person is striving for the full development of his or her self as a whole. This full development is referred to as perfection and implies a kind of superiority as well as what Adler calls a "will to power" (Adler 1968).

Everyone, according to Adler, has the same propensity or goal—a will to power or a striving toward superiority. From this single source, all other human motives are derived. To say that every person is striving for perfection does not mean that he literally wants to be perfect in the sense of free from every conceivable defect. It does mean that he wants to develop his particular potentialities and attain something very much like what later psychologists have come to call personal fulfillment or self-actualization.

Despite the emphasis that Adler places on inferiority, some of his interpreters, such as Heinz Ansbacher, maintain that actually it is this idea of striving for perfection that is the cornerstone of Individual Psychology (Ansbacher 1970).

Goals

Far more significant than instincts or innate drives as determiners of human behavior in Individual Psychology are the individual's goals. In general, all human beings have essentially the same goals simply because they are human beings. As a means of perfecting himself, every person strives for some form of superiority. Every individual is unique and therefore has a unique goal or a unique self ideal which, for that individual, constitutes perfection. There is no single way to achieve this goal. There is no one route, no best way that every person can or should take to perfect himself. Rather, the route that a person takes, the plan that he follows, the strategies that he employs, and the particular details of the goal itself depend on the individual's unique life-style.

Superiority

Along with perfection, a term that summarizes the goal of much human behavior is *superiority*. Adler believed that people are striving not only to overcome a feeling of inferiority but also and more positively to achieve a measure of superiority over themselves and others. Thus, a great proportion of human behavior has as its purpose what we might call self-assertion, the affirmation of one's personality, self-expansion, or self-enhancement. These terms, along with competence, esteem, recognition, and a feeling of personal worth come closer to Adler's concept of superiority than does any idea of snobbishness, arrogance, or lording it over someone else. Superiority as a goal implies that every person wants to be in some respect or other, depending upon the personal goals derived from his life-style, if not literally superior to others at least not inferior.

Just as inferiority implies dependency, superiority implies independence. It also connotes a certain amount of dominance or control over others. In a word—Adler's word—self-assertion, perfection, the freeing of oneself from a feeling of inferiority implies *power*.

Will to Power

As one of the basic characteristics of human nature, Adler posited a universal tendency that he calls the will to power. The power of which Adler speaks, and the power which he maintains everyone is seeking, is not necessarily or usually physical and has no necessary implications of force or aggression. It refers, rather, to the individual's efforts to show himself and others that he is a force to be reckoned with; that he cannot be easily ignored, casually dismissed, or taken lightly; that he makes a difference in the scheme of things.

Every individual wants to feel not only that he is capable of controlling his own behavior but also that at least to a certain extent he can control the behavior of others. He wants to feel that he can influence or affect events in the world of which he is a part. As a minimum, the individual wants to be noticed, admired, respected, and perhaps even a little bit feared. Much human behavior, therefore, has as its purpose what other psychologists call the need to satisfy one's needs for esteem or self-enhancement. These kinds of social needs closely approximate what Adler refers to as the striving for power.

Power in Individual Psychology plays the kind of central role in motivation that sex plays in Freudian psychology. Power, in effect, is the all-pervasive motive underlying most, if not all, of the things we choose to do. Strictly speaking, the will to power is not an innate drive or an unalterable component of human nature. It is, however, universal in the sense that everyone acquires it and uses it (Adler 1968).

Will to Power in Infancy

The will to power, like the feeling of inferiority, begins to develop very early in life. By about the age of two, and sometimes earlier, children are well aware of their weakness and helplessness. Consequently, they want to grow, to develop, to become stronger, and to overcome their helplessness. At about the same time, they discover that they have a will; that is, they discover that if they do certain things they can cause others to react in certain predictable ways. Thus, children of age two or thereabouts go through the well-known negativistic phase of development. They begin to try out their wills to see how they work. They begin to use their wills by asserting themselves, sometimes simply for the sake of doing so, as though it were a matter of principle. At any rate, they want their wills to prevail; they want to have their own way. Although there is usually no malice or element of hostility present in the very young child, he does want to dominate his parents and other older people with whom he comes in contact.

The child soon learns that there are various means which he, as small and helpless as he is, can use to control his environment and have his will prevail. One way is through crying ("If I cry long enough and loud enough, my parents will eventually give me the cookie or whatever else it is that I want.") Another way is to throw a temper tantrum. Still another means of getting one's way is by being cute, docile and obedient, or by imitating one's elders and being rewarded for doing so. Another possibility is to capitalize on one's helplessness, to gain sympathy and an eventual reward for using what Adler calls the "weapon of weakness" (Dreikurs 1968).

One simple, but very common and tremendously important, way of exercising power over others is to gain and maintain their attention (To the extent that I am paying attention to you, I am not paying attention to anyone or anything else. If you have my full and undivided attention, you have in a very real sense a kind of control over my thoughts, my present behavior, and quite possibly my future behavior as well.) There are few human goals of more significance to parents and teachers than attention. We'll discuss this motive at greater length in later chapters. For the present, I should simply like to have you recognize how it is related to the broader concept of power.

Will to Power in Childhood

As children grow older, the will to power is often readily apparent in their peer-group relationships. The object of many of the games they play is to win, to get the better of their opponent, to demonstrate their superiority. Even in noncompetitive play activities, when a high degree of cooperation might be required, most children either aspire to a position of leadership or tend to identify with their leaders, so that the activity is conducted in accordance with their desires. When they can't have their own way, some children withdraw from the activity entirely, pretending disinterest, and might even attempt to disrupt or somehow sabotage the activity. Others might seek out some other type of activity in which they think they have a better chance of being recognized as Number One.

The will-to-power concept helps to explain much of the pushing, shoving, fighting, name-calling, and wanting to be first in line that is commonly observed among children. It also helps to explain the "my father can beat your father" syndrome and other types of childish behavior in which the individual's purpose is to impress others with his or her own superiority. It certainly helps to explain many other desirable or undesirable things children do just to get attention (Yura and Galassi 1974).

Will to Power in Adolescence

From the standpoint of Individual Psychology, the home and classroom situation can often be perceived as a tug of war, a power struggle, between parents (or teachers) on the one hand and children (or students) on the other, with each trying to impose their wills on the adversary. The battle cry in both camps seems to be, "Not thy will, but my will be done." When parents declare, "You will . . . ," their offspring are likely to respond by thinking, if not actually saying, "I will not . . ." In some confrontations of this type, what is at issue is not the prescribed (or forbidden) activity itself but the principle of *who* will decide.

This type of power struggle is likely to peak in adolescence. At this stage, of course, young people want to feel and appear big, strong, grownup, important, independent, and self-sufficient. They are eager for recognition as adults and for privileges which they perceive as a release from their inferior positions as children. They are also seeking responsibilities that imply the power to make their own decisions, control their own behavior, and thus—to a certain extent—control the behavior of others.

The will-to-power concept helps to explain why some young people so readily and firmly attach themselves to causes, and become involved in movements to change something or other. As they begin to feel their muscles, they presume—or would like to think—that, by carrying placards, making demands, or protesting government policies, the world can and will be changed to meet *their* specifications.

Will to Power in Adulthood

Attempts to compensate for a feeling of inferiority, together with the will to power, certainly do not cease at adolescence. Rather, they continue to motivate people for as long as they live. Even the senior citizen is likely to be intent on asserting himself, having his way, and exerting control over others. Resisting the very thought of returning to a state of infantile helplessness and losing the power he has accumulated, he might resort to rather devious strategems—including the "weapon of weakness"—to maintain a semblance of self-respect.

Throughout adulthood, as well as in adolescence, Adlerian psychology goes a long way toward explaining man's great preoccupation with power. This preoccupation is particularly evident in individuals or groups who have been or feel that they are being oppressed. While the slogans themselves are not as commonplace as they were in the 1960s—the decade of protest—the concepts of Black Power, Woman Power, Student Power, Latino Power, Indian Power, and Senior Citizen Power are very much with us and offer continuing evidence that Adler knew what he was talking about. Among some other instances of the will to power operative in adult society are the following. The factory worker, out on strike, intent on bringing some gigantic corporation down to its knees . . . The officers of a gigantic corporation intent on keeping its employees in their place and on business transactions that will enable them to overtake or take over a competitor . . . Jane Q. Citizen, arguing politics, maintaining that the future of the country should be placed in the hands of *her* candidate and that her proposals should be implemented immediately . . . Husbands and wives arguing about the kind of new car they should buy, or whether they should buy a new car at all . . . A hoodlum mugging an old man or raping an old woman . . . A student studying for a test—or cheating on a test—in order to receive the highest grade and the accompanying recognition . . . A mother trying to control her children by reminding them of the many sacrifices that she has made on their behalf . . . Teenagers trying to control their parents by reminding them that everyone has a right to lead his own life and do his own thing . . . And so forth.

SEX ROLES

As we have seen, Adler believed that every individual is different from every other. Each person develops a unique, individual life-style as a means of overcoming inferiority feelings and attaining a feeling of superiority. But he also recognized and distinguished between two major types of life-style: feminine and masculine. This does not mean that Adler was anything like what has come to be called a sexist, much less a male chauvinist. In fact, he might properly be regarded as just the opposite, as one of the leading forerunners and proponents of the move for sexual equality. He certainly foresaw, some fifty years in advance, many of the subsequent and ongoing developments in this area. His theory helps to explain not only the women's liberation concept but also why certain behavior is regarded as typically male or female.

Adler maintained that there is no justification in the nature of things for the stereotyped differentiations between manly and womanly personality traits. Unlike Freud, he did not believe than "anatomy is destiny." But he did see two rather different sets of traits, commonly designated masculine or feminine, that are used by different individuals to satisfy their wills to power.

Masculine Domination

"As things stand now," Adler wrote in the 1920s, "there is a constant striving on the part of men to dominate women, and an appropriate dissatisfaction with masculine domination on the part of women." All of our traditional institutions, including our laws, customs, morals, and conventional attitudes, he goes on to say, "are determined and maintained by privileged males for the glory of male domination" (Adler 1954).

Adler points out that the concept of male superiority originated in prehistoric times. It came into being with the division of labor and the invention of war. Being bigger and stronger, males assumed tasks that were considered more difficult and therefore presumably more important than those taken care of by women. As civilizations developed, laws were formulated by and for men. The myth of female inferiority began to develop and, through literature, history, philosophy, and theology, came to be perpetuated. For thousands of years, the generally accepted belief was that woman's role was to serve and be pleasing to men. In return, the male role was to protect and provide for women and children. By lumping women and children together, as is still done, the implication was that both are dependent upon and therefore inferior to the male of the species.

Development of Sex Roles

Freud, you may recall, believed that in early childhood little girls begin to feel inferior to little boys because of what he called "penis envy." Adler agreed that a sense of female inferiority begins to develop early in the life of a child, but for quite a different reason. At a very tender age, the little girl begins to perceive that somehow, for some reason she does not fully comprehend, boys are considered more valuable than girls. When her mother has another baby, for example, the little girl might overhear a conversation in which the parents reply to a question about the baby's sex by exclaiming, "Of course, we hoped it would be a boy . . ." or, "Well, it's a girl, but we're very happy." If they're so happy, the little girl must wonder, why the "but"?

As she grows older, the little girl notices that boys are not only permitted, but encouraged, to play games and participate in activities that are not considered appropriate for "little ladies." When a little girl does act like a boy (a tomboy), her behavior might be considered quite acceptable and even cute. But when a little boy acts like a girl (a sissy), his behavior is likely to be frowned upon. If the little girl (or for that matter a grown woman) expresses the wish that she were a boy (or a man), her desire is understandable and considered to be quite normal. But when a little boy (or an adult male) expresses the wish that he were a member of the other sex, he is likely to be regarded as in need of immediate psychiatric attention. Thus, little boys and little girls alike soon begin to sense that males occupy a privileged position and that it is somehow better to be a man than a woman.

However they might love their mothers, girls and boys are both more likely to look up to, respect, and envy their fathers. They might not have the slightest idea of what Father does when he is away from home all day, but his life seems to be more interesting, more exciting, and more attractive than the routine housekeeping chores that keep Mother occupied. Father, moreover, is likely to be perceived as having more authority (power) than Mother, not only in the home but in the outside world as well.

Times have changed since Adler's day of course, and in certain details his observations might not be as true today as they were five or six decades ago. For example, Adler mentions job discrimination (the restriction of certain occupational areas to men) and a double standard of morality (certain behaviors that are socially acceptable on the part of males but not of females) as factors contributing to the development of female inferiority. Despite the changes in these respects that have been taking place in recent years, there are many who insist that men still have more freedom, more opportunities, and more power than women and that the concepts of male superiority and masculine domination are still all too prevalent.

Much male activity, Adler believed, is an attempt to preserve the privileged male position, whereas much of the behavior of women is a reaction against feminine subjugation and an attempt either to overcome or to compensate for inferiority feelings or to derive power in some other way.

Female Reactions

Adler thought that women by and large are dissatisfied with the role they have been made to play. He refers to their reactions as forms of the "masculine protest." The masculine protest—that is, the woman's way of liberating herself from masculine domination—takes two main forms.

In some cases, the woman begins to act like a man, tries to compete with men, and generally takes on a stereotyped masculine set of personal characteristics. This would be the outspoken, aggressive woman who is bent on gaining personal power by achieving success, no matter the cost, in fields thought of as traditional male strongholds. Such women may have only a secondary interest, if any, in marriage and family life and may have difficulty entering into a love relationship. When they do marry, they are likely to be little interested in playing the role of the contented little housewife. A considerable part of their energy is likely to be devoted to dominating (nagging?) their resistant husbands and attempting to rule the roost themselves. Some women, using this form of masculine protest, become teachers, in which capacity they derive a certain kind of fulfillment from exercising power over their male students particularly.

In other cases, the masculine protest can take the form of a woman adopting the role of the helpless female. Such a woman tries to dominate the men in her life by using the weapon of weakness mentioned earlier in this chapter with respect to children. Using this approach, the woman seeks to get her way not by competing with men but by being meek and submissive. She might use such feminine charms as she has to captivate (enslave?) men and thereby achieve domination over them. In this category, we might include television's happy housewives (whom Adler, fortunately for him, never had to watch) who get their kicks from having cleaner, brighter, better-smelling laundry than their neighbors'. We might note, in passing, that producers of TV commercials seem often to go out of their way to find women who are singularly unattractive in physical appearance to portray the roles of good housekeepers. The message apparently is, "Maybe I'm not as sexy-looking as the woman across the street, but my floors are a lot shinier!"

As regards either form of the masculine protest, we should also note that according to Adler, those women feel inferior not only to men but to other women as well. Much of their behavior, therefore, is directed toward achieving equality with, if not superiority over, members of their own as well as the opposite sex.

Male Reactions

The male counterpart of the masculine protest is a striving for what the individual regards as full masculinity. In our culture, as well as in most others, masculinity implies strength, power, control, aggressiveness, dominance. Much behavior on the part of the male, therefore, is directed toward the development and maintenance of traits such as these. Thus, one of the major masculine motivations is for the man to convince himself and others of his manliness and to project an image of unmitigated virility.

Males feel inferior not only to other males, they feel inferior to certain females also. They may feel too that they do not measure up to their own ego ideals—that is, to their *image* of masculinity. Consequently, they are often preoccupied with beating someone at something. The something might be sports, politics, business, one of the professions, or some other form of competitive activity, depending upon the individual's particular circumstances and life-style. If the male cannot dominate other males, he might resort to dominating his wife, children, or other women. Hence, we have among the male population such characters as the wife-beater, the tyrannical father, the seduction artist, and the rapist.

Adler's theory helps to explain why men are not uncommonly infatuated with big cars, heavy trucks, guns, machinery, and power tools that give them a feeling of strength and an opportunity to dominate nature. From early childhood onward, boys are of course rewarded for identifying with and imitating their fathers. Providing them with toys and encouraging them to play games that symbolize power are among the more important ways in which they learn the sex roles that they will play later in life.

SOCIAL FEELING

In addition to striving for power, or superiority, or to express one's individuality, Adler maintains that every person has what he calls an inherent "social interest" or "feeling for community." As Adler did, we shall refer to this innate component of human nature as the person's "social feeling."

Socialization

Far more than Freud, who emphasizes the person's biological nature, Adler stresses the social aspect of the human personality. This emphasis on social feeling is in fact regarded by some of Adler's interpreters as the most distinctive and essential feature of his entire system (Ansbacher 1976). Adler asserts that there is only one absolute truth—that a human being is a "social animal." He makes much of the fact that people cannot survive except in societies and that social living is, therefore, a natural requisite for self-preservation and individual perfection (Adler 1964, 1973).

According to Adler, people not only want and need affiliation with others and social acceptance. They also want and need—and usually have—the feeling that they can somehow contribute to the good of society or the welfare of others. Thus, as part of human nature, every person is born with an inclination toward social-ization. If human beings had to be described in one word, Adler would have been inclined to use the word *social* rather than *sexual* as Freud probably would have. Adler claimed that Freud was wrong in the primacy he assigned to sex, that it is not one's sexual drives that determine one's personal and social adjustment. It is just the opposite. One's social adjustment determines one's sexual behavior and just about everything else of consequence that one does. The satisfaction of one's social needs and the exercise of one's social feeling, in fact, are essential components of the previously discussed concept of individual perfection (Adler 1973).

Selflessness

By nature, according to Adler, every human being has an innate tendency, a positive inclination toward selfless, altruistic behavior. This social feeling implies not only consideration for others and a genuine desire to help them, it implies also a need to go out of oneself, as it were, to give of oneself or part of oneself to someone else.

Adler's portrayal of human nature is certainly prettier and more optimistic than Freud's. There is reason to believe, inci-dentally, that Freud was more than a little influenced by Adler in formulating his later views on such matters as love and the superego. At any rate, love in Individual Psychology is directed outward toward others and not primarily inward toward oneself as is the case in the Freudian view.

According to Adler, it is this innate selflessness, this social feeling, that underlies the system of laws and the customs, tradi-tions, and mores that hold societies together. It is also the basis of justice, honesty, charity, and other traits of individual char-acter that are ordinarily regarded as virtuous (Adler 1954, 1964).

Character

So far, Adler tells us that we are motivated on the one hand by the goal of individual perfection, superiority, power, or the reduction of our personal feelings of inferiority and on the other by our social consciousness. As shown in Figure 5, the well-adjusted, happy, emotionally healthy individual is one who is able to achieve a *balance* between these two motivations. Such a person is able to satisfy his needs for self-enhancement, recognition, esteem, etc., *in a social context,* and at the same time respect the rights and needs of others and contribute to their welfare.

According to Adler, for an individual with well-developed social feelings, the goal of superiority or perfection results in positive and socially beneficial outcomes or behaviors. In addition to being well-adjusted, the person who attains this kind of harmony also has a "good" character. He achieves his goals without intentionally trampling on others and is relatively free of feelings of greed, jealousy, hatred, vanity, etc. He is characterized by charity, sympathy, compassion, honesty, and the like. Thus, for Adler, personality adjustment is essentially a moral concept and our main motives are essentially moral or immoral, social or unsocial, in nature (Adler 1954).

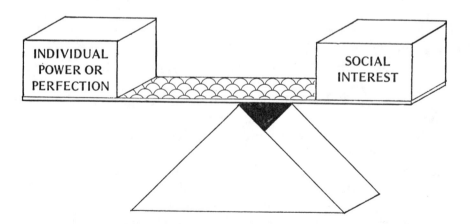

FIGURE 5. Adler's Concept of a Healthy Personality. The well-adjusted person has achieved a balance between personal desire for perfection and interest in the welfare of others.

Deviant Behavior

The two main motivations mentioned at the beginning of the preceding section are likely, of course, to come into conflict with one another. The inability to resolve this conflict is the most common underlying factor in personal maladjustment and in various forms of socially deviant behavior. For example, Adler attributes conditions such as neuroses, crime, alcoholism, drug addiction, jealousy, brutality, etc., to either underdeveloped social feelings or a misdirected striving for power, or more likely, a combination of the two. In other words, these unhappy conditions result when the individual will to power is frustrated by the demands or conventions of society. This unsuccessful attempt to liberate oneself from the feeling of inferiority intensifies one's frustration and results in feelings of hostility which lead in turn to unsocial, if not antisocial, behavior. The key to preventing or changing such behavior, according to Adler, lies in education, a main purpose of which should be to cultivate the person's inborn predisposition toward social consciousness.

EDUCATIONAL IMPLICATIONS

In line with the social orientation of his theory, Adler seems to place more explicit emphasis on education than does Freud. He discusses at length the responsibilities and opportunities that school teachers and parents have regarding the socialization, motivation, and future personality development of the young. By way of concluding this chapter, let us summarize a few of his recommendations. In later chapters, we discuss these ideas in more detail.

Competition

Competition is one of the oldest motivational devices known in the history of education. Adler was by no means unalterably opposed to it. He recognized that, along with the striving for perfection, a moderate degree of competition can serve as an effective incentive toward self-improvement and social achievement. But, he deplored what he regarded as the overemphasis on competition that he found in the schools of his day. Similarly, contemporary Adlerians (as well as a great many non-Adlerians) deplore the intense competitiveness that can be found today not only in our schools but also in the business world, the athletic arena, and elsewhere (Dreikurs 1968). They might particularly view with consternation, as Adler did, the preoccupation in our society with being the first, or the best, or with somehow excelling others, sometimes regardless of the cost (Dreikurs 1968).

By definition, most people cannot be the first or the best. Therefore, artificial, unnecessary pressures to strive for this degree of superiority can contribute only to a sense of failure for many and an intensification of their existing feelings of inferiority. Attempts to keep up with, and even to surpass, the proverbial Joneses might in some cases work to spur people onto greater effort. But, in the greater number of cases, it is more likely to contribute to needless anxieties and feelings of personal dissatisfaction.

In a classroom situation, Adler recommends that teachers deemphasize competition, that they avoid comparisons, treating each student as an individual and helping each to actualize his or her potentialities, whatever they might be and regardless of what others do or fail to do. Along with this thrust toward individualizing instruction, Adlerians are among those who would recommend developing the student's social awareness by cooperating more and fostering less a dog-eat-dog, me first, and to hell with everyone else set of attitudes.

Intrinsic Motivation

By and large, Individual Psychology supports intrinsic over extrinsic motivation. Extrinsic motivation implies the use of some sort of incentive, such as good grades, provided by an external source. Intrinsic motivation is that which comes from within the individual. Extrinsic motivation undoubtedly does serve a useful purpose and often produces good results in scholastic achievement. But the use of such incentives might have unde-sirable side effects that could cancel or even outweigh any benefits. Adler suggests that encouraging students to study *in order to* gain recognition, prestige, good grades, or some more tangible reward might serve to promote what he calls vanity or self-glorification on the part of the student. It would be better, he maintains, to try to develop the students' *interest* in the material that they are expected to learn and to stress its social value so that they will study *because they want to.*

Self-concept

Individual Psychology also lends strong support to the idea that the school should be very concerned with the student's self-concept. Teachers, counselors, and school administrators should do what they can to alleviate and not intensify the student's inferiority feeling. They should, of course, avoid sarcasm, ridi-cule, and other such motivational techniques that might serve to lower the student's image of himself. In a more positive way, they should try to build up that image and the student's self-confidence by offering acceptance, encouragement, and opportunities to ex-perience success. Toward this end, school personnel should make a special effort to help students to recognize or discover their potentialities, and then to develop them as a means of compen-sating for their limitations. Similarly, they should try to find ways of helping students to satisfy their needs for recognition or self-enhancement in ways that are productive and socially beneficial (Dinkmeyer 1975).

Democratic Discipline

With respect to the problem of motivating students toward desir-able classroom behavior, Individual Psychology supports a demo-cratic rather than an autocratic approach to discipline. Rudolf Dreikurs, one of the leading contemporary proponents of Adlerian psychology, has written extensively on this subject (Dreikurs 1968, 1971, 1972). One of his major theses is that teachers (and parents) should not allow their relationships with their students (or children) to degenerate into a power struggle. Teachers who attempt to rule with an iron hand by impressing the students with their own strength might win a few battles, he believes, but are likely to lose the war. Such teachers might find that in the long run they have actually defeated their own purposes by causing the troublesome student to feel more inferior than he did to begin with. Such a student, in turn, might become motivated to seek revenge or in some other way to regain his self-esteem or improve his peer image by behaving worse than he did originally.

Authoritarian teachers, Dreikurs suggests, are more likely to be concerned with their own power or their own status than they are with the education or the welfare of their students. The democratic approach that he prefers implies cooperation between teachers and students and rather extensive use of group processes. It also implies, of course, an understanding of and consideration for the individual student as a unique human being and a genuine desire on the part of the teachers to promote each student's over-all personality development.

RECOMMENDED READING

Adler, Alfred. *The Problem Child.* New York: Capricorn Books, 1963. A nontechnical book emphasizing practical application rather than theory. Adler uses several specific cases to illustrate the principles and techniques of Individual Psychology by analyzing the life-styles of children who have various personality or behavior problems.

Adler, Alfred. *Superiority and Social Interest.* Ansbacher, H. L., and Ansbacher, R. R., Eds. New York: Viking Press, 1973. 3rd ed. A collection of Adler's articles in which he discusses the difference between Individual Psychology and psychoanalysis, neuroses, delinquency, religion, perfection, and various other topics. The book includes a short biography of Adler and an introductory essay on his contributions.

Adler, Alfred. *Understanding Human Nature.* Greenwich, Conn., 1954. Subtitled "A Key to Self-Understanding," this book is intended for the general public rather than the specialist. It summarizes the main ideas of Individual Psychology systematically, brings out Adler's views on character formation, and includes a short section that deals specifically with education.

Ansbacher, Heinz L. "Alfred Adler, Individual Psychology." *Psychology Today,* Jan., 1970. A short overview and evaluation of Adlerian psychology. Ansbacher stresses Adler's views on human striving for perfection rather than the concept of inferiority and relates Adler's theories to those of Abraham Maslow.

Ansbacher, Heinz L. "Alfred Adler and Humanistic Psychology." *Journal of Humanistic Psychology, 11*:53–63, 1971. Shows that Adler's Individual Psychology and humanism have much in common but expresses the belief that humanism has emphasized the self to the neglect of social considerations stressed by Adler.

Dinkmeyer, Don, *et al.* "Increasing the Teacher's Understanding of Students' Self-Concepts," *Education, 96*: 180–183, 1975. Along with Ansbacher and Dreikurs, the author of this article is one of Adler's best-known contemporary interpreters. Drawing on the principles of Individual Psychology, he offers suggestions for helping teachers in the manner implied by the title of the article.

Dreikurs, Rudolf, *et al. Maintaining Sanity in the Classroom: Illustrated Teaching Techniques.* New York: Harper and Row, 1971. Intended to encourage and assist teachers who are having difficulties, this book describes practical methods of classroom management based on Adlerian principles. It stresses the use of diagnostic techniques and democratic methods and offers advice for coping with specific scholastic and behavior problems.

Mosak, Harold H., Ed. *Alfred Adler: His Influence on Psychology Today.* Park Ridge, N.J.: Noyes Press, 1973. This anthology includes seven short articles that apply principles of Individual Psychology to education, six that deal with Individual Psychology and various social issues, and nine on Adler's approach to psychotherapy.

Sperber, Manes. *Masks of Loneliness: Alfred Adler in Perspective.* New York: Macmillan, 1974. The author, a personal friend and one-time colleague of Adler's, describes Adler the man, the psychological climate in which he lived, his relationship with Freud, the development of his theories, and the influence of those theories on contemporary psychological thought.

Stacey, Judith, *et al.*, Eds. *And Jill Came Tumbling After: Sexism in American Education.* New York: Dell Publishing Co., 1974. A collection of forty-two articles from a variety of sources, showing the effects of sexual discrimination and stereotyping on the motivation and achievement of women.

Steffenhagen, R.A. "Drug Abuse and Related Phenomena: An Adlerian Approach." *Journal of Individual Psychology, 30*: 238–250, 1974. Sees drug abuse as either an attempt to protect one's self-esteem or a form of compensation expressing a pampered life-style. Also discusses pseudo-homosexuality, bisexuality, and attraction to the occult.

Yura, Michael, and Galassi, Merna. "Adlerian Usage of Children's Play." *Journal of Individual Psychology, 30*: 194–201, 1974. Shows how a child's goals, life-style, and concept of social interest or feeling for others are reflected in play activities. Discusses ways of dealing with children who are either bossy, attention-seeking, or withdrawn.

CHAPTER 4: PREVIEW QUESTIONS

(After you have finished reading Chapter 4, you should be able to answer the following.)

1. What are some basic beliefs or assumptions of behavioral psychology?
2. Why and how do some behaviorists attempt to explain motivation without using the term *motivation*? What objections do they have to the use of such terms as *id, inferiority feelings, will, goals,* and *purposes*?
3. Why is it that behaviorists are apparently not much concerned with identifying the underlying causes of behavior?
4. What is meant by the statement, "Behavior is shaped by its consequences"?
5. What is operant conditioning and how is it related to motivation?
6. What is a reinforcer? What are some of the main kinds of reinforcers? Give a few examples of each.
7. What is negative reinforcement? How does it differ from positive reinforcement? From punishment?
8. What are the two main forms of punishment? From a behavioral standpoint, what are some objections to the use of punishment for motivational purposes?

9. What is the difference between a drive and a cue? What is meant by the concept of motivation as drive reduction?

10. How do behaviorists tend to explain fear? Anxiety? Frustration?

11. Explain and give an example of four basic kinds of conflicts. How do behavioral views of conflict differ from those of Freud? Adler?

12. What are approach and avoidance gradients? How do they affect human behavior?

13. What are the behavioral views on the proposition that human beings are naturally good? Naturally aggressive?

14. What is meant by contingency management? How does it work?

15. What is meant by programming? What are some objections to programming people? What are some behavioristic responses to these objections?

16. What are performance objectives? How can they be used for motivational purposes?

17. What are some principles or assumptions of behavior therapy?

18. How do behaviorists tend to differ from humanists with respect to the use of extrinsic versus intrinsic motivation?

19. What is your overall reaction to behavioral theories and techniques of motivation?

CHAPTER FOUR

The Payoff of Human Behavior

This chapter is organized around some principles and concepts of behavioral psychology. Without stretching the point very much it could be said that motivation is what behaviorism is really all about. Yet, in many of the books about behavioral psychology, the word *motivation* is conspicuous by its absence.

Contemporary behaviorists are not as concerned with the theoretical problem of why people behave as they do as they are with the practical problems of getting people to behave in certain predetermined ways. They are certainly very much interested in motivating students toward scholastic achievement, good citizenship, personal adjustment, and self-realization. But, many behaviorsts do not find the word *motivation*, or the concept signified by that word, to be particularly useful, much less necessary. The reason for this apparent paradox lies in the basic assumption of behavioral psychology that the only thing that can be known, or need be known, about human beings is their behavior—that is, the things they do. Motivation or motives are not things that people do.

John B. Watson (1878–1958), one of the founders of behaviorism, believed that the purpose of psychology is to understand, predict, and *control* or *regulate* behavior. He maintained that, to fulfill that purpose, psychology should operate as an exact science and use only empirical data and the same rigid methodology that is used in physics, chemistry, and the other older branches of science. There is no room in his theory for mere speculation or philosophizing about human behavior. Watson said that only those things that can be studied scientifically, under controlled laboratory conditions, are deemed worthy of consideration by a psychologist. Thus, he had no use for concepts such as goals, purposes, will, intellect, human nature, self, desire, intention, ego, superego, consciousness, unconsciousness, or motive. None of these, he claims, lends itself to scientific analysis (Watson 1913).

A motive, for example, cannot be either seen or measured or subjected to experimental control. It can only be inferred from what a person *does*. Such inferences, he believed, add little or nothing to our understanding of human behavior or to our repertoire of techniques for changing or regulating behavior. To say, for example, that a person achieves in a certain area because he has something called an achievement motive really says nothing and is nothing more than so-called circular reasoning. For example:

Why does George achieve?

Because of his achievement motive.

What's an achievement motive?

It's what makes a person achieve.

How do you know that George has an achievement motive?

Because he achieves.

But why does he achieve?

Because he has an achievement motive.

And so forth.

Similarly, the assertion that a person does something because he wants to or needs to actually conceals the real reason for his behavior. We do the things we do because we have *learned* to do them. In the terminology of behaviorism, we have been conditioned to behave as we do. Even our aims, desires, intentions, social needs, etc., are simply words that describe particular kinds of learned behavior. To say that a person does something because he wants to leaves unanswered the question of *why* he wants to do this rather than that and why he chooses to satisfy a particular need in *this* way rather than another (Skinner 1971, 1974). Also, it leaves unanswered such practical questions as: How can a teacher get a student to pay attention, do his work, remain in his seat, learn what he is expected to learn, etc.?

REINFORCEMENT

Although contemporary behaviorists such as B. F. Skinner (1974), Albert Bandura (1969, 1974), and Wesley Becker (1975, 1975), to name a few, differ with Watson on a number of technical points that need not concern us here, they do tend to share the convictions that have just been mentioned. Instead of relying on such ideas as motivation, purpose, unconscious drive, inferiority feeling, or the striving for perfection or self-fulfillment, they believe that reinforcement is the only concept necessary to explain motivation.

The term *reinforcement* refers to any stimulus (or event or situation) that follows a particular form of behavior and increases the probability that that behavior will recur. Most of this chapter is devoted to an analysis of this concept and a discussion of ways it can be applied.

Motivation and Learning

One of the basic tenets of behaviorism is that, except for a few innate physiological drives (e.g., hunger and thirst) and reflex actions (e.g., blinking), all human behavior is acquired. Not only our overt behavior but also our so-called inner behavior—including our attitudes, values, interests, preferences, inclinations, predispositions, and other factors that cause us to act as we do—are learned responses. According to most contemporary behaviorists, these responses are all learned in essentially the same way: through operant conditioning.

Operant conditioning should not be confused with respondent (or classical) conditioning. Respondent conditioning is exemplified by Pavlov's famous experiment in which a dog was conditioned to salivate in response to a bell. Respondent conditioning involves the substitution of one stimulus (the bell) for another (meat) and the formation of a conditioned response. Respondent conditioning is useful in explaining much of our *involuntary* behavior, including some that is emotionally toned. Through respondent conditioning, for example, we might learn to like or dislike a particular melody or aroma as a result of the pleasant or unpleasant events with which we associate it. Operant conditioning (with which Skinner and many other behaviorists have come to be identified) is more useful in explaining our *voluntary* behavior and is considerably more relevant to the problems of motivation (Blackham and Silberman 1975).

Since this book deals particularly with motivation rather than learning, we shall not discuss the fine points of operant conditioning except as they relate to the subject with which we are primarily concerned. But, we should recognize that from a behavioral standpoint motivation and learning are practically inseparable. Motivation is not, as is sometimes thought, a process that precedes learning. It is, rather, an integral part of the learning process itself. For a more detailed explanation of operant conditioning and behavioral principles of learning, see Macmillan (1973), Craighead (1976), or some of the other Recommended Readings for this chapter.

Consequences of Behavior

The basic principle of operant conditioning is that behavior is shaped (if not actually determined) by its consequences. That is, acts having pleasant consequences tend to be repeated whereas those having unpleasant consequences are likely to be avoided. The concept of consequences implies some system of reward or punishment, some form of pleasure or pain, some type of positive or negative reinforcement. To put the matter as concisely as possible, we behave as we do to experience pleasant consequences or to avoid unpleasant consequences. This means that everything we do voluntarily either is somehow presently satisfying, has previously been satisfying, promises to be satisfying in the future, or is at least less dissatisfying than alternative courses of action.

In operant conditioning, the causes of behavior—that is, the events that *precede* the behavior—are not as critical as the events that *follow* the behavior and are *contingent upon* the behavior. The assumption here is that the causes of a particular form of behavior might be very difficult, or perhaps impossible, to ascertain. Besides, even if the underlying causes could be discovered, it might be impossible to change or eradicate or do anything about them. What's done is done and often cannot be undone. The consequences of a person's behavior, however, are subject to control. Thus, the behavior itself can be controlled.

The emphasis in behavioral psychology, therefore, is not on attempting to change some presumed underlying motive but on directly changing the behavior itself. For example, behavioral educators are not so interested in motivating a student to *want* to read as they are in teaching him *how* to read and in seeing to it that he *does* read with a certain predetermined degree of proficiency. The best way to get (or, if you prefer, to motivate) a child to read (or to do anything else) is by regulating the consequences of his reading (or whatever.) In some cases, with respect to reading or other forms of behavior, events that occur prior to the attempted or desired behavior might be significant and also subject to control. But, ordinarily, much more reliance is placed on the consequences.

Discriminative Stimuli

At this point, we should note a distinction between reinforcing and discriminative stimuli. As is shown in Figure 6, discriminative stimuli are the objects, events, or situations that precede a response; reinforcing stimuli are those that follow. Just about anything that a person sees, hears, or otherwise experiences can serve as a discriminative stimulus: a No Parking sign, the aroma of freshly brewed coffee, television commercials urging us to buy a particular brand of toothpaste, a feeling of warmth or coldness, and so

FIGURE 6. Discriminative and Reinforcing Stimuli. Discriminative stimuli determine the particular responses that individuals make initially, whereas reinforcing stimuli increase the probability that individuals will make these or similar responses again.

forth. These are called discriminative because we respond to each differently. None of these guarantees that we will respond in any particular way. However, we have learned that, in the presence of certain discriminative stimuli (such as a feeling of coldness), certain responses (such as putting on a jacket) are likely to be followed by rewarding consequences or reinforcing stimuli (such as a feeling of warmth).

In a classroom situation, discriminative stimuli include books, audiovisual aids, other instructional materials, etc. Most commonly, however, they take the form of verbal cues from the teacher.

Let's open our books to page 65.

Please take your seat and be quiet.

For your homework tonight do . . .

Who can tell me how to spell Chicago?

Note that in none of these cases do the teacher's words in and of themselves bring about the desired behavior on the part of the student. They do increase the probability that the student will do what the teacher wants him to do by indicating what he should (or must) do to experience favorable reinforcing stimuli as a consequence. It is largely through the presentation of carefully selected discriminative stimuli and the differential reinforcement of students' responses that a teacher is able to control their behavior.

Primary and Secondary Reinforcers

A distinction is commonly made between two main kinds of reinforcers: primary and secondary. Primary reinforcers include
satisfiers such as food and drink. Necessary for the preservation of
life, the reinforcing power of these is natural rather than acquired.
Primary reinforcers correspond to the satisfaction of physiological
needs. Although primary reinforcers, particularly food, are widely
used in animal training, they are relatively insignificant in human
motivation. A trainer might reward a seal with a fish after the seal
has given its performance and we might reinforce a dog's standing
on its hind legs and begging behavior by giving it a morsel of food,
but we do not ordinarily attempt to motivate human beings in
quite this fashion. Rather, we rely on secondary reinforcers.

Secondary reinforcers are learned. Therefore, they are sometimes referred to as conditioned reinforcers. Secondary reinforcers
acquire their reinforcing power by having been associated with or
substituted for primary reinforcers. For example, a mother's
smile or a hug or a word of approval as she feeds her child can become a secondary reinforcer. There is a wide variety of kinds of
secondary reinforcers that motivate us to act as we do. Among the
most important of these are social, symbolic, tangible, activity,
and intrinsic reinforcers.

Social Reinforcers

The purpose of much human behavior is to be noticed, admired,
respected, approved, etc. In the terminology of behavioral psychology, anything that contributes to the satisfaction of one's
need for approval, affection, acceptance, affiliation, esteem, or
some other social need is a social reinforcer. Just as social needs
are said to be secondary (or acquired), so too are social reinforcers.

Social reinforcers usually take the form of pleasant verbal
responses such as

That's right.	I'm proud of you.
Very good.	Right on!
Nice going.	Keep up the good work.
Beautiful!	You're really on the ball.

They might also take the form of a smile, a wink, a nod, a pat, a hug, a kiss, or some other kind of nonverbal response.

The principle underlying social reinforcement is that having done something for the first time, and having received some reward of this type as a consequence, the probability is that we will continue to act in the same or a similar way. Later in this chapter and again in Chapter 8, we offer some practical suggestions for the use of social reinforcers in home and classroom situations and consider their effectiveness. First, let us survey a few other kinds of secondary reinforcers.

Symbolic Reinforcers

Traditionally, our schools have relied heavily on symbolic reinforcers to help to motivate students toward scholastic achievement and the observance of classroom rules and regulations. Symbolic reinforcers include test grades, report card marks, gold stars, trophies, certificates, medals, honor rolls, Deans' lists, and displays of projects on a bulletin board. These are, in effect, substitutes for verbal approval that some students have learned to value. They have the advantage of being somewhat more tangible than spoken words of praise and can be highly effective.

Just as adults might work very hard to win a blue ribbon at the county fair for achievement in cooking, a trophy symbolizing the highest scores in bowling, or a document indicating superior salesmanship or excellent workmanship, so are there those students who work very hard for the coveted A or at least a passing grade. But, just as there are those adults who are unwilling to exert much effort for the sake of winning some symbol of little if any intrinsic value, so are there those students who are not impressed by mere symbols and are by no means inclined to work very hard to obtain them. For such individuals, more tangible reinforcers might be necessary.

Tangible Reinforcers

For most teachers as well as most other adults who work for a living, the principal reinforcer is usually money—or some of the tangibles that money will buy. Many adults might derive other satisfactions from their work, but the chances are that they would not (because they could not) continue in their occupations without financial remuneration. This principle, of course, is used by parents who pay their children for performing certain specified tasks such as shoveling snow, mowing the lawn, getting good grades, etc. (Kruglanski 1975, Allen, 1975).

Note that most children who are given an allowance unconditionally, without having to do anything in particular to earn it, are really not being reinforced at all or, if they are, they are reinforced indiscriminately. The reward is theirs regardless of what they do or fail to do. Thus, the allowance is not contingent upon anything and it does not serve as an incentive. However, the acquisition of tangible objects such as toys, books, or records, can be made contingent upon specific behavior and can thus become a very powerful incentive.

Later on we discuss the controversial question of paying students for good grades in connection with the token economy. For the present, let us simply note that the pleasant consequences of receiving a regular paycheck or some other tangible reward explain a great deal of ordinary, everyday behavior in the real world outside the school and that this principle has possibilities for motivating students within the school and in the home.

Activity Reinforcers

One reason why we do A is that as a consequence we will be able to do B. We work at a job that we might not particularly like to be able to afford to take a vacation, attend theatres, throw parties, go sailing, play golf, etc. These kinds of payoffs constitute activity reinforcers.

Just about any activity that a person finds pleasant or enjoyable can serve as a reinforcer: watching television, going out to play, taking a field trip. The possibilities are endless. As with other forms of reinforcers, activity reinforcers are most effective in motivating a person toward desired behavior when the rewarding activity is *contingent upon* the prior completion of the desired behavior. Parents make use of this principle when they inform their children: After you finish your homework, you may watch TV. Watching TV in this situation is not presented as something to which the child has an inalienable right guaranteed by the U.S. Constitution. It is, rather, presented as an incentive, something to be earned by finishing his homework.

In using activity reinforcers, one might be guided by the Premack principle, named after the behavior psychologist who formulated it (Premack 1959). According to this principle, any activity that is more attractive to an individual than some other activity has a reinforcing potential. For example, presumably a child would rather go out and play than solve mathematical problems. According to the Premack principle, the opportunity to go out and play can be used to reinforce the mathematical problem-solving behavior. So too can any other activity that the child would select, if given the opportunity. In the rather unlikely event that a particular child, if given a choice, would prefer solving math problems to playing in the fresh air, the Premack principle could be applied as follows: If you go out and play for half an hour, then you may work on your math problems.

Internal Reinforcers

Certain activities contain their own rewards for particular individuals. A person might write poetry, walk in the rain, or sip good wine simply out of enjoyment in doing these things. Satisfying in and of themselves, these behaviors—for that individual—require no incentive, no external system of reward and punishment. The reinforcement comes from within the person. While engaged in these activities, they are, for the individual, self-reinforcing. Of course, a particular behavior such as writing poetry or solving mathematical problems that is internally reinforcing for one person may not necessarily be internally reinforcing for another.

When internal reinforcement is operative, a person might be rewarded, for example, with a kind of inner glow, or a personal, subjective impression of accomplishing something good and having done it well. One's behavior might be reinforced by a feeling of achievement or pride or self-respect. It might be reinforced by the pleasure derived from the activity itself. Whatever might be the nature of the inner reward, the behavior is not contingent upon external incentives.

The classic example of intrinsically reinforcing behavior is play. Ordinarily, parents do not have to motivate children to play. For that matter, it is usually unnecessary to motivate parents or teachers or other adults to play. Uusually, we play a particular game simply because we like to play it. If we do not enjoy the game or derive any personal satisfaction from playing it, the game can perhaps be more accurately regarded as a work rather than a play activity, requiring social or some other form of extrinsic reinforcement (Greene and Lepper 1974).

Intermittent Reinforcement

Often, it is neither possible, necessary, nor advantageous to provide reinforcement every time a desired response is made. Instead, reinforcement is sometimes given according to a ratio or an interval schedule. When a *ratio schedule* is used, reinforcement is given only after the person has made the desired response a specified number of times. For example, the teacher who praises a student who has completed five assignments satisfactorily would be using a 5:1 ratio schedule. With an *interval schedule*, reinforcement is given only after a specified time has elapsed. In this situation the teacher might praise or otherwise reward a student who has behaved well for, say, three consecutive class periods.

Proponents of behavior modification recommend that teachers experiment with intermittent reinforcement in order to discover the ratio or interval schedules that will be most effective with their particular students in particular situations. Praise, like blame, can be overdone and in some cases too many rewards might be worse than too few. Ordinarily, the recommended procedure is to gradually decrease the frequency of reinforcement in order to lessen the student's dependence on extrinsic rewards and have him come to rely more on intrinsic satisfaction.

Imitation

Along with reinforcement, some behaviorists (such as the noted social psychologist Albert Bandura) emphasize the role of imitation as a factor in learning and motivation. Most human behavior, according to Bandura, is not regulated by immediate reinforcement from some external source. Rather, we regulate our own behavior to some extent by what he calls "self-generated anticipatory and self-evaluative consequences." That is we set certain standards of behavior for ourselves and respond to our own behavior by self-reward or self-punishment depending on whether our performance matches, exceeds, or falls short of our own self-imposed standards. These standards commonly arise from our observations of and attempts to imitate the behavior of others (Bandura 1969, 1974).

We observe, for example, the kinds of clothes others wear, or how they pronounce certain words, or react when they are threatened. We note for which of these activities others are either rewarded or ignored or punished. In this way, we experience a kind of vicarious reinforcement. But, we want to experience more concretely the rewards that others have received and so we adopt their standards and model our own behavior on theirs. If we dress or speak or otherwise act as "they" do, we expect to be reinforced externally. Even if we are not, we may be self-satisfied and reinforced intrinsically.

Imitation corresponds approximately to the Freudian mechanism of identification that is so critical in the formation of one's superego. However, identification refers to the assimilation of another individual's personality traits or values whereas imitation pertains more to the reproduction of particular ways of behaving and is, thus, more selective.

Social psychologists such as Bandura have done a great deal of research on the problem of imitation particularly as it affects aggression, moral behavior, and other aspects of the socialization process. Their findings tend to corroborate the common-sense viewpoint of many parents, teachers, and others that social as well as unsocial or antisocial behavior is acquired through imitation. But the question of the relative effects of imitation and extrinsic reinforcement is still not fully answered. Perhaps a safe principle to follow in this respect is that behavior is most likely to be imitated when it is subsequently reinforced externally as well as internally.

AVERSIVE MOTIVATION

Thus far, we have discussed positive reinforcement as an explanation of human behavior. But some of the things we do, or avoid doing, can be more adequately explained in terms of negative reinforcement. Negative reinforcement, as we shall see, is not the same as punishment although each is a form of what has been called aversive motivation. Aversive motivation is so called because it involves situations that we want to avert or turn away from. Such situations have what Lewin called negative valence. These aversive situations, then, can be thought of as negative goals or as things that "turn us off."

Negative Reinforcement

The purpose of much human behavior is not primarily to reach a goal or to experience pleasant consequences but to avoid the unpleasant consequences of *not* acting in that particular way. Thus, we do certain things to avoid the consequences of not doing them. For example, we study to avoid failing a test; obey traffic regulations to avoid being fined, etc. In situations such as these, the principle of negative reinforcement is operative.

Like positive reinforcers, negative reinforcers are objects, events, or situations that increase the probability of our doing something. The difference between the two is that negative reinforcers are aversive or noxious stimuli that we try to terminate.

A good example of a noxious stimulus is the raucous, nerve-grating sound of the buzzer that can be terminated only by fastening the seat belt in a car. The relief to our nervous system that comes as a consequence of fastening the belt is what motivates us to fasten it. The relief, the avoidance, the termination of the unpleasant noise is the (negative) reinforcer.

Another example of a noxious stimulus would be the torture inflicted on a spy to make him reveal some secret. Strictly speaking, as painful as the torture is, the spy is not being punished. According to his tormentors, the spy can terminate the torture whenever he wishes by doing what his tormentors want him to do: by making the desired response. (Whether or not they will keep their word and actually release him with no further harm if he reveals the secret is, of course, another matter.) Here, again, the relief is the negative reinforcement. A less dramatic, but more common, example of negative reinforcement would involve the young man who gets a haircut to get his father off his back or to put an end to his mother's nagging.

Punishment

The term *punishment* sometimes carries with it an implication of revenge, retaliation, or retribution. Thus, in ordinary everyday usage, people speak of punishing a criminal in terms of making him pay his debt to society. He made the lives of law-abiding citizens miserable; now they are getting even by making his life miserable. Punishment in this sense usually implies an attitude of hostility toward the offender. He did a bad thing and we don't like it, so we punish him. The expectation is that punishment will teach him a lesson and act as a deterrent to criminal behavior on the part of others. Punishment in this popular sense is not usually thought of primarily as an aid to learning or even as a rehabilitative procedure.

As used in psychology, the term *punishment* has a rather different meaning. Certainly it does not have any emotional overtones of vengeance or hostility. An experimental psychologist carrying out research in his laboratory might, for example, punish a rat with an electrical shock when the rat takes a wrong path in a maze. Let us hope that the psychologist does not dislike the rat and that he is not trying to get even with it for making a wrong turn. The psychologist, presumably, is trying to teach (or, if you prefer, train or condition) the rat to avoid that particular path. Negative reinforcement refers to a rat's or a person's *doing* something to avoid an unpleasant situation, whereas punishment implies *not doing* something to avoid some unpleasantness. Negative reinforcement *increases* the probability that we will behave in a certain way and punishment *decreases* that probability. When we are negatively reinforced, an aversive stimulus *ends*. When we are punished, an aversive stimulus *begins*. Thus, negative reinforcement is often instrumental in motivating us toward *desired* behavior (desired, that is, by the government, the school administration, an employer, or someone else in a position of authority). On the other hand, punishment (or the prospect thereof) motivates us *away from undesired* behavior. The similarities and differences among punishment, negative reinforcement, and positive reinforcement are summarized in Figure 7.

Pain and Deprivation

As Figure 7 indicates, punishment takes two main forms. It involves either pain or deprivation or both. The pain might be physical (as in a spanking) or psychological (as in humiliation). In either case, it involves the presentation or the imposition of aversive stimuli. Deprivation involves the withholding or the withdrawal of a positive reinforcer. A person might be punished by being deprived of some privilege or opportunity, of his freedom, or of anything else that he has come to value.

There is no doubt that both forms of punishment are effective means of reducing deviant or undesired behavior. Punishment alone, however, is likely to be ineffective in eliciting desired behavior. Punishment involving pain is likely to be particularly ineffective for that purpose. Suppose, for example, that a child is spanked for using the word *damn*. The chances are that he will avoid that particular word in the future. But there is no assurance that he will avoid other words that might be even more objectionable. There is even less likelihood that in the future he will use such desired words as *please* or *thank you*. Many of us, I suspect, use the word *please* not because we have been punished for using four-letter obscenities but because we have been positively reinforced for saying *please*.

The second type of punishment—involving deprivation—is likely to be more effective not only in terminating undesired behavior but also in eliciting desired behavior, especially when it is accompanied by reinforcement. Thus, a parent might withhold candy from a child who says, "Damn it, give me some candy!" but offer to give him some on the condition that he ask for it politely.

		Pleasant Stimuli	Aversive Stimuli	Effect on Behavior
"Reward"	POSITIVE REINFORCEMENT	*Presented (begin)*		Strengthens it. Increases the probability that the behavior will be repeated.
	NEGATIVE REINFORCEMENT		*Withdrawn (terminated)*	
Punishment	PAIN		*Presented (begin)*	Weakens it. Decreases the probability that the behavior will be repeated.
	DEPRIVATION	*Withdrawn (terminated)*		

FIGURE 7. Relationships among Four Basic Means of Modifying Behavior.

Side Effects of Punishment

Even though the presentation of aversive stimuli is sometimes highly effective in reducing certain forms of undesired behavior, many behavioral as well as other psychologists do not recommend its use except perhaps as a kind of last resort in emergency situations. The main objection to this form of punishment is that it, in effect, teaches people to avoid (or try to avoid or to escape) the punishing stimuli. Avoidance of pain or escape from a potential inflictor of pain is essentially a form of negative reinforcement. Thus, a person who lies or cheats or hides or runs away or blames others for his offenses to escape detection or to avoid a spanking is, practically speaking, being rewarded for acting in those ways. The probability is that he will continue to try to do so. If he is apprehended and punished even more severely for trying to escape, the chances are that the next time around he will try even harder to avoid being caught.

Another objection to punishment is that it might cause resentment or even hostility on the part of the person being punished toward the one doing the punishing. This side effect is especially likely to occur when the offender perceives the form or intensity of the punishment as unfair, too severe, unwarranted, or inappropriate for his particular offense. Along with this is the possibility that the offender will come to fear, dislike, or become unwilling to confide in the punishing agent. Thus, a potentially helpful relationship between a child and a parent, a student and a teacher, or a delinquent and a police officer might be severely weakened.

Still another undesirable side effect of punishment is that it provides the child with an aggressive-type model. Since some of our most important learning results from our imitation of others, children who have experienced a high degree of physical aggressiveness in their parents or in other adults with whom they identify also turn out frequently to be aggressive individuals. Finally, there is the argument that in addition to these and other possible undesirable side effects, punishment does not really get at the *causes* of misbehavior but merely suppresses it temporarily, thus creating a potentially explosive situation.

Uses of Aversive Control

Despite their general aversion to aversive control, a relatively small but growing number of psychologists, such as Donald Baer (1971) and R. V. Hall (1977), not only offer no strong objection to punishment, but actually recommend it not as a last resort after all else has failed but in the early stages of a behavior-modification program. Punishment involving deprivation rather than pain is the more favored method, but even physical punishment seems to be regaining a degree of respectability in certain educational and psychological circles (Ebel, 1977a). Others, such as Redl (1977) and Clarizio (1977), continue to argue against the use of physical as well as other kinds of punishment in home or classroom situations. In Chapter 9, we continue our discussion of punishment in connection with the practical problem of classroom management. But next let us turn our attention to certain personality factors as they relate to motivation.

DRIVE REDUCTION

One of the basic assumptions of behavioral psychology is that personality, learning, and motivation are all inextricably interconnected. As we have seen, motivation is not regarded as a separate process that precedes learning but as an integral part of the learning process itself. Learning, moreover, goes a long way toward determining one's personality, just as one's personality affects one's motives and subsequent learning. In the behavioral view, our personal traits, qualities, characteristics, and idiosyncrasies for the most part are not innate. They are acquired responses, the products of learning.

The concepts of learning, personality, and motivation are closely integrated in the theory formulated by Neal Miller and John Dollard (1941). In their view, the learning process is characterized by four elements: drive, cue, response, and reward. We want something, we notice something, we do something, and we get something. In the Miller–Dollard theory, the most basic of these elements are the drives. While reinforcement (reward) is central to Skinner's theory of motivation, drives occupy a central role in the theory of Miller and Dollard. The purpose of most human behavior is to reduce one or some of these drives.

A drive is any powerful stimulus that initiates behavior. It motivates a person to act until the strength of the drive is reduced. Some drives, such as hunger and thirst, are innate. Like physiological needs, to which they correspond, these drives are said to be primary. They pertain to things necessary for the maintenance of life. Other drives, such as fear, anger, guilt, and hostility, are learned. These are commonly referred to as secondary.

Drives activate behavior. They do not determine the particular form or mode of behavior. One's hunger drive, for example, activates a person to seek food. But what he eats and when and where he eats depend on the so-called cues in his environment. Cues are specific stimuli that guide a person's behavior and determine the kind of response he will make to reduce the drive. Among the cues that a hungry person is likely to notice are the eggs in his refrigerator, a sign advertising carryout chicken, the hamburger on a menu, the various items stacked on the shelves of a supermarket, etc. Through previous learning, some of these cues have become more powerful (or, if you prefer, attractive) than others. The person may, for example, have acquired a taste for pizza. It is to that cue, therefore, that he responds. His response—eating the pizza—reduces the hunger drive, and this drive reduction is his reward.

Fear

Fear is a learned response to aversive stimuli. It is commonly regarded as an acquired aversive drive. Like other secondary drives, fear is not only a response but also a cue for future behavior. A substantial portion of human behavior is aversively motivated by fear. Fear of what? Fear of failure, punishment, illness, injury, or death; fear of ridicule, rejection, humiliation, loss of status; fear of not pleasing others or of not living up to their expectations; fear of having our shortcomings brought to light, etc.

For some people, motivation to reduce fear or to avoid failure is greater than the drive to succeed. Thus, while fear often inhibits undesirable behavior, it also serves at times to stifle desirable behavior. Fear, for example, might prevent a person from even attempting certain tasks because he doesn't want to run the risk of failure. "Nothing ventured, nothing lost." Fear, on the other hand, might motivate him to attempt tasks that are unrealistically difficult and even perhaps impossible for him to complete. Here, he stands a good chance of being rewarded for his good intentions, courage, perseverance, etc.

Responses such as knocking on wood, praying, locking doors, taking vitamins, studying, etc., can all be fear-reducing. The reduction of fear, like the reduction of hunger, is highly reinforcing. With respect to an aversive drive such as fear, the reinforcement is negative. We knock on wood, study, etc., to avoid the consequences of not doing so. After doing so, we feel better. Thus, the connection between the cue (an aversive stimulus, such as the mention of F) and the response (knocking on wood or studying) is strengthened.

We are not, of course, born with particular fears. But through a process of respondent conditioning, we learn to fear this, that, or the other thing. Through conditioning, we might learn to fear practically any object or situation much as the infant in Watson's classic experiment learned to fear white rats. As psychoanalysts suggest, fears might be reasonable in that they relate to stimuli that are realistically dangerous, or they might be unreasonable as in the case of phobias. But in either situation, fear can be, and often is, a powerful activator of human behavior.

Anxiety

The relationship between the terms *fear* and *anxiety* is not clear. One distinction between the two is that, while both pertain to some threatening situation, fear refers to threats that are more immediate and identifiable. For example, a person might be anxious about his economic security in a rather general long-range sense, but he might be afraid of losing his job next week. One might be anxious about his physical or social well-being; he might fear some specific danger, such as muggers, cancer, the consequences of failing a particular test, or not being invited to a party. Quite often, however, the line between fear and anxiety (if, indeed, there is a line at all) is very fine. Consequently, the two concepts are commonly employed interchangeably. Any semantic differences notwithstanding, with respect to motivation their effects are practically the same.

Anxiety—the more frequently used term—is commonly regarded

as the source of all neurotic behavior. Compulsions (to knock on wood, for example), obsessions (with germs or death, for example), various phobic reactions, periods of intense depression and withdrawal, so-called nervous breakdowns (more properly called asthenic reactions), and mild delusions of persecution can often be traced to the individual's feeling that something dreadful lies in his future. Behaving in these neurotic ways is one way in which some people reduce their anxieties.

Freud assigns a major role to anxiety as a motivator of normal as well as neurotic behavior. So do behavioral psychologists, but for rather different reasons and without using such psychoanalytical constructs as id and superego. From a behavioral standpoint, it could be (and has been) argued that anxiety is the drive that activates much, if not most, human behavior, and that the alleviation of anxiety is a, if not the, prime reinforcer. According to this interpretation, underlying all of our so-called needs is what we might call worry, concern, apprehension, fear, or anxiety that we will not get something that we want or that we will lose something that we currently have and value. This explanation does not seem to deal satisfactorily with our striving for positive goals or even with the potentialities of positive reinforcers in determining human behavior. But it does help to explain the concept of aversive motivation and the idea that many of the things we do (from taking a shower to working for a college degree, for example) are done to avoid the anticipated consequences of not doing them. (For further information on behavioral approaches to the problem and management of anxiety, see Bernstein 1976.)

Frustration

The term *frustration* is commonly defined as being a feeling that a person experiences when he is somehow prevented from reaching a goal or satisfying a need that he regards as significant. In behavioral terms, frustration can be thought of as the nonoccurrence of an expected or desired reinforcer. Frustration occurs when a reinforcer is withheld or the situation is such that the person is unable to attain it. Frustration is not quite the same as failure. It is a feeling of failure. For example, a student expecting an A on a test might feel frustrated with the B he receives. Objectively, he has not failed. Subjectively, he feels that he has.

A distinction can be made between two kinds of frustration: those involving internal and external obstacles. External frustration occurs when the obstacle toward the reduction of a drive lies outside the person himself. Physical restraint, delay, the deliberate withholding of a satisfier, various rules and regulations that must be followed before the reward can be obtained, and consideration of the rights and welfare of others often lead to external frustration. So does the unavailability of a drive-reducer within one's environment. Mother Hubbard's dog experienced this type of frustration when it found that her cupboard was bare and she was unable to provide him with the expected bone. External frustration might also be experienced by the child who is told that he is not old enough to do something that he wants to do or that he must wait until certain other conditions are met.

Internal frustration results from subjective obstacles within the individual human organism. Fear of failure, which often deters people from even trying to get the things they want, is a common source of this type of frustration. Other sources include feelings of inferiority or inadequacy and the actual lack of the knowledge, skill, strength, or perseverance necessary to reach their goals. These inner obstacles are usually the consequence of a person's perceptions, environmental contacts, and experiences with other people. They are far more personal than external barriers and might be considerably more difficult to overcome.

Just about anything that can be done to alleviate internal or external frustration is reinforcing. Since attempts at alleviating them often spur us on with intensified effort, frustrations can be a significant factor underlying various forms of constructive achievement. But they can also strengthen aggressive drives and give rise to behavior that is physically harmful, socially undesirable, or psychologically self-destructive.

Conflicts

One of the principal sources of frustration is a conflict—a situation in which an individual is motivated to act at the same time in two incompatible ways. He finds himself pursuing or attaining one goal or satisfying one drive but unable to achieve the other. The person must then make a choice. But, whichever course of action he elects, he is likely still to be frustrated in one way or another. Figure 8 shows that a distinction can be made among four basic types of conflicts: approach/approach, approach/avoidance, avoidance/avoidance, and double (or multiple) approach/avoidance.

In an *approach/approach* conflict, the individual has two goals, both of which are equally attractive, but he cannot have or directly seek both at the same time. This kind of conflict is classically expressed in the homily, "You can't have your cake and eat it too." It is experienced, for example, by the child who is torn between wanting to please his parents by acting in one way and wanting the approval or recognition of his peers, which he thinks he can achieve only by acting in quite another way.

An *avoidance/avoidance* conflict occurs when the individual must choose between two courses of action, both of which are unattractive. His situation is such that he cannot avoid both. A student, for example, might not feel like studying for a test, but neither does he relish the prospects of failing it.

An *approach/avoidance* conflict is experienced when a particular situation has both positive and negative features. A high school student, for example, might want very much to attend a particular social event—but not with the particular individual who has invited her. Since he is the only one who has asked her, her only choice is between going with him or not going at all.

The *double approach/avoidance* conflict is one in which the individual is confronted with two complex stimuli (choices), each having attractive and aversive features. Given a choice of two jobs, for example, we might want to approach the higher salary of the first but would also like to avoid its poorer working conditions. At the same time, we might be attracted by the better working conditions that accompany the second position, but be repelled by the lower salary that it offers. Our choice is likely to depend on the relative strength of the positive and negative reinforcers that are involved.

Resolution of Conflicts

In many instances, the resolution of conflicts is actually an extremely complex process because often there are more than one or

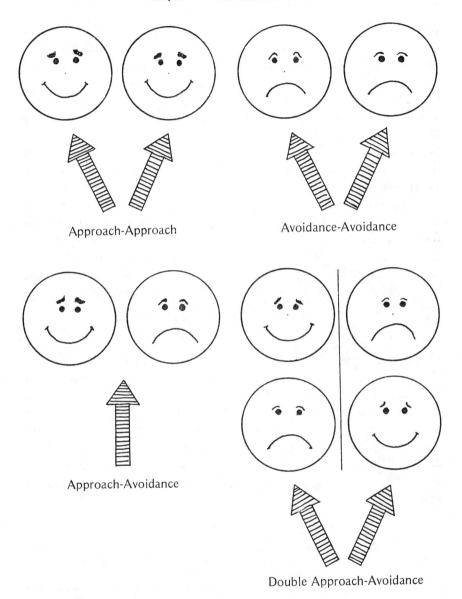

Approach-Approach

Avoidance-Avoidance

Approach-Avoidance

Double Approach-Avoidance

FIGURE 8.   Four Basic Kinds of Conflicts. Involved are combinations of attractive and repelling situations that we want to approach or avoid.

two attractive or aversive features in each choice, and there may be more than just two alternatives open to us. Our decisions in such cases, as well as in simpler choice situations, can be said to depend upon our values. In behavioral terms, *values* can be explained in terms of the relative strength of various reinforcers. Thus, a person might value leisure more than money, money more than honesty, honesty more than status, etc., because of his previous pattern of reinforcement. He has learned, in short, that this is more rewarding than that, and that is more aversive than the other thing.

The values and the corresponding drives of some people are so weak and underdeveloped that they rarely experience difficult conflicts. Easily swayed, they follow the path of least resistance, not really caring very much which way they go or what they do. Others, for just the opposite reason, seldom experience what could be characterized as a genuine conflict. These steadfast, strong-minded individuals are practically dominated by some drive or value, and conflicting alternatives have little if any effect on their behavior.

Most people do experience conflicts, of course, but some are able to resolve them quite easily. They have clear-cut goals and a hierarchy of values so that there is little doubt in their minds as to which consequences of which kinds of behavior they will find most satisfying or annoying. But then there are those whose values are so fuzzy that they seem to be incapable of deliberation and are in a continuous state of uncertainty as to what they should do or how they must proceed even in comparatively minor conflict situations.

Approach and Avoidance Gradients

Largely on the basis of laboratory research with rats, Neal Miller (whose work with John Dollard was noted earlier in this section) formulated an idea that helps to explain human behavior in conflict as well as nonconflict situations. In one of his experiments, a rat was placed in a situation where it was exposed to approach and avoidance stimuli. If the rat did one thing, it received an electrical shock; if it did another, it was rewarded with food. Thus, the rat experienced a conflict between its drive for food on the one hand and the drive to avoid pain on the other.

Miller noted that the closer the rat came to the food, the stronger was its tendency to approach it. The relationship between these two variables is called the *gradient of approach*. He also observed that the closer the rat came to the aversive stimulus, the stronger was its tendency to avoid it. This relationship is called the *gradient of avoidance*. Miller found that the strength of avoidance increases more rapidly with proximity to the aversive stimulus than approach behavior does with respect to the attractive stimulus.

As applied to human behavior, we might predict that the closer a person approaches a goal, the more highly or strongly motivated toward it he will become. When the ball is on the five-yard line, football players are likely to exert more effort than when the ball is at midfield. A student who believes that he has a good chance to earn an A in a course is likely to work harder than one who believes his chances for that grade are remote. Similarly, we are likely to be more highly motivated to avoid an immediate aversive stimulus (such as a burglar in the next room) than one at a great distance. Moreover, we are likely to be more highly motivated to avoid an immediate aversive situation than to approach an immediate positive goal. Our response, of course, depends on the relative strengths of the stimuli. While watching an enjoyable television program, if we discover that our house is on fire, there's not much doubt about how we will react. But in planning our evening's activities a few hours in advance, the approach television motive is likely to be far more powerful than a drive to avoid being caught in a fire.

Aggression

The literature on aggression is so extensive that there is no way that I can even begin to summarize it in one short section of one chapter of this short book. As you may recall, we touched upon the subject from Freudian and Adlerian points of view in Chapters 2 and 3, respectively. At this point, let us simply recall that, from a behavioral point of view, aggressive behavior is learned behavior.

People learn to behave aggressively because they have somehow been reinforced for doing so.

Recall too that anything that reduces frustration can be reinforcing. For some people in some situations, vandalism, child-beating, and other acts of violence and brutality can reduce frustrations, at least temporarily. Such behavior is therefore rewarding for them. For others, the use of verbal aggressiveness—name-calling, spreading rumors, gossiping, character assasination, tattling, lying to get others in trouble—is rewarding. These alleviate anger, reduce frustrations, help the individual to terminate an aversive situation, and make him feel better. Thus, they are negatively reinforcing.

Frustration does not inevitably lead to aggression. Nor does it follow that all forms of aggression are invariably the consequences of frustration. But the possibility of a strong causal relationship between the two should certainly be taken into account in attempting to understand antisocial behavior. So, of course, should the broader concept that aggressive behavior, like any other form of behavior, is shaped by its consequences.

EDUCATIONAL IMPLICATIONS

As noted at the beginning of this chapter, the very purpose of psychology from a behavioral standpoint is to understand, predict, and change (or improve, modify, or control) human behavior. Use whichever of these verbs you prefer. For our purposes, they all amount to the same thing: eliciting desired responses, motivating students, or simply getting them to act in a certain way. The purpose of education centers on the changing aspect (Krumboltz 1972).

In this context, the function of a teacher is to do something so that students will come to act in the desired way and avoid acting in undesired ways. The desired behaviors might involve reading, writing, driving a car, or whatever other changes or improvements the teacher has as an objective. The undesired behaviors might include stealing, misspelling, making arithmetic mistakes, using coarse language, etc. The something that teachers do to students to modify their behavior involves not only the methods and materials of instruction but also the motivational procedures that are employed.

Contingency Management

According to behavioral psychology, teaching in the classroom as well as teaching in the home can be thought of as essentially a matter of contingency management. The word *contingency* implies being subject to. Because behavior is assumed to be fashioned or determined by its consequences, one of the main functions of a teacher is to see to it not only that desired behavior is followed by pleasant consequences, but also that the pleasant consequences (reinforcers) are contingent upon the student's acting in the desired way or making the desired response.

The principle of contingent management has been used, in effect, for countless generations by parents who have said to their children, "if (or "only if") you eat your vegetables, you may have your dessert." Eating the vegetables, of course, is the desired behavior. Getting dessert is the reinforcer. According to the parents' stipulation in this situation, the only way that the child can get what he wants is to do first what his parents want him to do.

By administering or withholding reinforcers in accordance with a carefully worked-out plan or schedule, instead of in a random, haphazard manner as is frequently the case, behaviorists believe that it is possible to bring out the kinds of behavioral changes that teachers are expected to bring about: to change *non*reading to reading behavior, *un*social to social behavior, *un*polished to polished behavior, etc.

Programming

Education in this sense of behavior modification or contingency management has been criticized on the grounds that it involves programming or manipulating human beings. Even the concept of changing behavior is difficult for some people to accept. Let's be sure that we at least understand it.

If a teacher is perfectly satisfied with the way in which a child reads, one can assume that she will neither want to nor try to change his behavior in that respect. If she is perfectly satisfied with how he spells, solves math problems, obeys classroom regulations, relates to his fellow students, etc., she might be quite content to leave him as he is in those respects. But, most teachers see room for improvement in student behaviors such as these. If their attempts to bring about these desirable improvements as systematically and efficiently as possible are labelled *programming* or *conditioning,* so be it. Behaviorists feel no need to apologize for these words despite their sometimes unfavorable connotations. Programming to them simply means logical, structured, orderly, sequential, step-by-step, bit-by-bit, teaching, with frequent reinforcement along the way (Anderson and Faust 1973; Becker 1975a, 1975b). As for manipulation, in programming or contingency management, teachers do not directly manipulate students as much as they do the reinforcers in their environment.

Performance Objectives

To bring about changes in the student's behavior, it is necessary that teachers have a clear idea of the kinds of changes they wish to bring about. For this reason, behavioral principles of motivation support the use of performance objectives. A performance (or behavioral) objective is a precise description of the desired behavior, stated in terms of what the student will do, or be able to do, as a consequence of the instruction received. It does not merely suggest, but specifies—preferably in observable, measurable terms—the particular behavior toward which the student is being motivated (Kibler 1974).

Performance objectives are conspicuous by the absence of adjectives (such as *honest, reliable, courteous*) and abstract nouns (such as *knowledge, understanding,* and *appreciation*). While such words reflect the desired behavior in a vague, general way, they are regarded as too vague, too general, to be of much use. What does it mean, for example, to be courteous or be a good citizen? What must a person *do* (how must he behave) to *show* that he is a good citizen or that he understands, say, mathematics? Unless teachers have clear answers to questions such as these, behaviorists believe that they will have a difficult time trying to teach or motivate students toward the implied objectives.

The purpose of performance objectives is to make implicit objectives as *explicit* as possible. Thus, a listing of performance objectives might specify, for example, that the teacher expects each student to

> remain in his seat until given permission to leave
>
> wait his turn at the drinking fountain
>
> say "excuse me" when passing in front of another person
>
> spell correctly the words on a given list
>
> add fractions
>
> compare one poem with another
>
> admit his wrongdoings
>
> participate in group activities

For a discussion of the pros and cons of behavioral objectives, see articles by Gagne (1977) and Miles (1977), who favor them, and by Ebel (1977b) and Kneller (1977), who do not.

Behavior Therapy

The principles that we have been discussing in this chapter also underlie behavior therapy, a system of counseling people on their personal, social, and emotional problems. Performance objectives play as important a role in this area as they do in classroom management and instruction. Behavioral therapists are unlikely to use such words as *hostile, withdrawn, depressed, hyperactive,* or *neurotic* in analyzing the behaviors of clients. Instead, they will attempt to identify the specific behavior to be changed. For example, the client may

> hit other children on the playground
>
> cry when corrected
>
> suck his thumb
>
> refuse to remain seated

steal things that are neither needed nor wanted

smoke two packs of cigarettes a day

Behavioral therapists maintain that all of these behaviors have been learned, that they can therefore be unlearned and replaced by better (or more adaptive) forms of behavior. Behavioral therapists see their role as essentially one of teaching their clients new (and presumably better) ways of acting or not acting. Ordinarily, they do not attempt to discover the underlying causes of the undesired behavior, believing that to do so is unnecessary if not impossible. Neither do they have much use for the abstract concepts as id, superego, self, etc. Rather, they focus as directly as possible on changing the client's behavior. Although they are commonly criticized for dealing only with the symptoms—the surface manifestations—of maladjustment, they maintain that the symptoms *are* the problem. When the symptoms are eliminated and better behavior is learned, the problem is solved.

As with contingency managers in a classroom, behavioral therapists rely heavily, though by no means exclusively, on positive reinforcement and aversive stimulation. For a detailed discussion of the principles and techniques of behavior therapy and illustrations of various kinds of situations in which they have been used, see Craighead (1976) and O'Leary and Wilson (1975).

RECOMMENDED READINGS

Anderson, Richard, and Faust, G. W. *Educational Psychology.* New York: Dodd, Mead, 1973. A partially programmed textbook written from the standpoint of behavioral psychology. Especially recommended is Chapter 11, which deals most directly with motivation.

Bandura, Albert, Ed. *Psychological Modelling.* New York: Lieber-Atherton, Inc., 1974. A collection of nine articles on various aspects of imitation, edited by a foremost authority on the subject. Especially recommended is Bandura's article, "Analysis of Modelling Processes," which includes a good review of the literature and a discussion of various pertinent theories.

Blackham, Garth, and Silberman, Adolph. *Modification of Child and Adolescent Behavior.* 2d ed. Belmont, Cal.: Wadsworth, 1975. Especially recommended are Chapters 6 through 9, which show how operant conditioning strategies have been used in home and classroom situations with well over fifty different kinds of behavior problems.

Carpenter, Finley. *The Skinner Primer: Behind Freedom and Dignity.* New York: Free Press, 1974. Subtitled "What the B. F. Skinner Debate Is All About," this book summarizes the views of this very controversial psychologist as well as the major objections to those views and responses to those objections.

Craighead, W. Edward, *et al. Behavior Modification: Principles, Issues and Applications.* Boston: Houghton Mifflin, 1976. Chapter 13 deals with behavior modification in the classroom. Other chapters relate it to work in hospitals, prisons, and home situations, and with alcohol and drug abuse, sexual deviation, smoking, obesity, marital and other problems. Includes a good summary of research and accomplishments in these areas.

Krumboltz, John D., and Krumboltz, Helen B. *Changing Children's Behavior.* Englewood Cliffs, N.J.: Prentice-Hall, 1972. Intended for parents and teachers, this easy-to-read book is organized around thirteen principles of behavior modification. Includes several examples of how each of these principles can be applied to behavior problems in the home or the classroom.

Lindsey, Bryan L., and Cunningham, James W. "Behavior Modification: Some Doubts and Dangers." *Phi Delta Kappan, 54:* 597–598, 1973. The authors briefly summarize twelve reasons why they think that educators should proceed cautiously with the use of behavior modification techniques. Their article is accompanied by one other *con* and two *pro* behavior modification articles.

MacMillan, Donald L. *Behavior Modification in Education.* New York: Macmillan, 1973. A good overview of the subject—not too technical for the beginner but weighty enough for the somewhat more advanced reader. Briefly traces the historical development of behavior modification, explains its main principles, applies them to regular and special classrooms, and examines some criticisms and limitations of the theory.

Miller, Neal E., and Dollard, John. *Social Learning and Imitation.* New Haven, Conn.: Yale University Press, 1941. This book can properly be regarded as a classic in the literature of behavioral psychology. Some of the authors' views have been summarized in this chapter.

Psychology Today, Nov., 1972. Practically the entire issue is devoted to behavior modification. Included and especially recommended are the articles "Who's Who and Where in Behavior Shaping," "Will Success Spoil B. F. Skinner?" and "TV for Kiddies: Truth, Goodness, Beauty—and a Little Bit of Brainwash."

Skinner, B. F. *Beyond Freedom and Dignity.* New York: A. A. Knopf, 1971. One of the most controversial, widely discussed books in the field of psychology. In this book, Skinner urges us to reject the concepts of personal freedom and human dignity and recommends behavior modification as the only way of saving our civilization. Also recommended are his books *About Behaviorism* (1974) and *The Technology of Teaching* (1968).

Skinner, B. F. *Walden Two.* New York, Macmillan, 1962. Originally published in 1948, this controversial, thought-provoking, and for some readers frightening novel describes a Utopian society that is brought about and maintained through the scientific management of individual human behavior. Can be enjoyed simply as a work of science fiction or read seriously as a stimulating venture into the areas of psychology and moral philosophy.

CHAPTER 5: PREVIEW QUESTIONS

(After you have finished reading Chapter 5, you should be able to answer the following.)

1. What is the difference between cognitive and behavioral theories of motivation?
2. What does Piaget mean by assimilation and accommodation? How are these processes related to intelligence? To the concept of intrinsic motivation?
3. Compare Piaget's views on moral development with his theory of cognitive development with reference to the stages of each.
4. What is the basic principle of the attribution theory of motivation? What are two internal and two external factors to which a person might attribute his or her success or failure in a particular situation?
5. Explain the locus of control concept. What is the difference in this respect between Internals and Externals? Between Pawns and Origins?

6. What does White mean by a person who is competent? How is White's concept of competence related to motivation?

7. What are some common characteristics of underachievers? In what respect might a scholastic underachiever have a high degree of achievement motivation?

8. How can the strength of a person's achievement motivation be measured? Why is achievement motivation stronger in some people than in others? How can sex differences in achievement motivation be explained?

9. What are some differences between success-oriented and failure-oriented people with respect to their willingness to take risks?

10. What are some techniques used in training programs designed to increase achievement motivation? Under what conditions is achievement motivation training likely to be most successful?

11. What is meant by the statement that success and failure are relative concepts? Why is it that an experience or accomplishment that is satisfying to one person might be frustrating to another?

12. What is a level of aspiration? Between what two kinds of conflicting tendencies can one's level of aspiration be considered a compromise?

13. What are the two main characteristics of a realistic level of aspiration? What is likely to happen when either of these characteristics is lacking?

14. What are some findings of research studies on the effects of one's level of aspiration? What can teachers do to help their students to set appropriate levels of aspiration?

15. What is a self-fulfilling prophecy? How are such prophecies related to teacher expectations? What are some possible effects of teacher expectations on student motivation and achievement?

16. What are discovery methods of teaching and learning? Why does cognitive psychology favor them?

CHAPTER FIVE

Interpretations and Expectations

Having considered some ideas about motivation derived from Freudian, Adlerian, and behavioral psychology, let us now see what cognitive psychology has to offer. According to the model presented in Chapter 1, there are several factors about students that we should try to understand as a first step toward motivating them (or helping them to motivate themselves) toward orderly classroom behavior and scholastic achievement. Among these factors are their perceptions, beliefs, aspirations, and the modes of thinking characteristic of their respective stages of development. It is with factors such as these that cognitive psychologists, and this chapter, are largely concerned.

Cognitive theories of motivation take a variety of forms. But, as Bernard Weiner points out, they have enough in common to warrant their being grouped together and distinguished from behavioral (or, as he also calls them, mechanistic) theories (Weiner 1974). In Chapter 4, we noted that behavioral theories tend to follow a basic S–R or S–R–S model. According to that model, we respond (we behave or react) as we do because of the particular internal or external stimuli that we experience before or after acting. Cognitive theories, on the other hand, emphasize the point that our behavior is not determined by discriminative or reinforcing stimuli in and of themselves but by our perceptions or interpretations of those stimuli—by what we know, think, feel, or believe about them and by what we expect of them. For example, what we do when we hear a particular kind of bell depends to a great extent on what that particular sound has come to mean to us and on the consequences that we anticipate if we ignore it, respond immediately, delay responding, or whatever. A simplified cognitive model of motivation appears in Figure 9.

One of the main differences between cognitive and behavioral theories, according to Weiner, has to do with the extent to which the former uses higher mental processes to explain the initiation, direction, intensity, and persistence of goal-related behavior. Thus, a major distinguishing characteristic of cognitive theories is the emphasis that they place on the mental processes that intervene between antecedent stimuli (input) and the responses (output) or consequences that follow (Weiner 1974).

One of these higher mental (or cognitive) processes is expectation. We respond as we do to the particular bell because of the consequences that we anticipate. Our expectations, in turn, are the result of our own previous experience, information-gathering, data processing, judgment, evaluation, and other forms of internal behavior that are commonly referred to as thinking. Cognitive theorists are inclined to the view that our behavior depends not

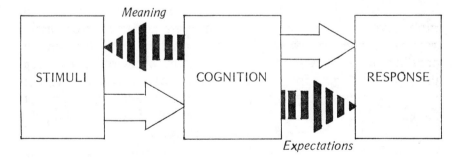

FIGURE 9. A Simplified Cognitive Model of Motivation. An individual's response to a particular stimulus depends on the meaning that he attaches to that stimulus and the consequences of the response that he anticipates.

only on what we know, think, or believe about objects, events, and situations in the world around us but also on what we know, think, feel about (and expect of) ourselves.

To help us to understand the processes by which children come to know, think, believe, and interpret their environment, we begin this chapter by summarizing some of Jean Piaget's contributions to the psychology of cognition. As a further aid toward understanding our students and because we might want to influence their moral behavior, we shall also review his ideas and the related views of Laurence Kohlberg on how children at different stages of development reason about moral problems.

In later sections, we discuss, among other things, some of the ways in which people interpret the causes of their own behavior and the expectations of themselves that they hold accordingly. We shall be concerned particularly with the expectations of those who do and of those who do not have high degrees of achievement motivation and with individuals' feelings about their successes and failures, especially as those feelings affect their subsequent aspirations and expectations.

PIAGET'S CONTRIBUTIONS

Jean Piaget's major area of specialization is not motivation but cognitive development. Nevertheless, his views on how the human mind develops and functions at different age levels from early infancy to adolescence have added considerably to our understanding of how thought processes affect behavior. They have also given strong support to the concept of intrinsic motivation and to teaching strategies designed to foster students' independent thinking. Based on more than forty years of research, Piaget's findings and theories do not lend themselves well to concise summarization. In the section that follows, therefore, we shall attempt no more than to sketch a few of his key ideas.

According to Piaget, human development and life itself is a process of continuous interaction between the individual person and his or her environment. The aspect of development with which Piaget has been most concerned is intelligence. Intelligence, he believes, is a particular form of biological *adaptation* to one's environment. Adaptation is the process by which a person changes his behavior as a consequence of interacting with the environment. We adapt ourselves to the world around us so that subsequent beneficial interactions will be likely to occur (Piaget 1952, 1973).

Adaptation involves the continuous reorganization of ideas, or of what Piaget calls the schema or structure of the mind. Through this reorganizational process, we arrange and rearrange sensory, perceptual, and cognitive data into units and patterns that have meaning for us. When we see a red traffic light, for example, the signal conveys a particular message to us and we adapt our behavior to that situation. Note that it is not the light itself that causes or motivates us to adapt. It is the meaning that we have come to attach to that signal that does so.

Assimilation and Accommodation

According to Piaget, adaptation takes place by means of two processes: assimilation and accommodation.

Assimilation is the process by which we take in new experiences and relate them to what we already know. In assimilating, we respond to a new stimulus with behavior similar to that which we have previously used with similar stimuli. For example, when a young child is given an apple for the first time, he might try to roll it as he would a ball. When he first encounters a doughnut, he might begin to eat it as he would an apple. When we read a book, listen to a lecture, or watch television, we also might be assimilating but at a higher level as we relate new to previously acquired ideas.

Accommodation refers to the process by which our ideas (or thought patterns or cognitive structure) are modified to fit ourselves to the environmental objects or situations that we experience. For example, when the child discovers that an apple not only rolls like a ball but can also be eaten like a cookie, he is accommodating. As the child takes in new information (apples are edible, balls are not) and integrates it with his existing store of knowledge (apples and balls can both be rolled), the number of possible responses that he can make to the apple are increased.

Note that in assimilation the person imposes his existing

cognitive structure on the new stimulus. The child "forces" the apple to fit his concept of a ball. Similarly, an adult might force his concept of a new politician about whom he has just read in a newspaper to fit his existing idea of what politicians are like. In accommodation, the situation is just the opposite. Here, the person is "forced" to change his existing cognitive structure to fit the new stimulus. The child does not react to a ball precisely as he would an apple. At election time, the adult might accommodate by changing his mind and deciding to vote for this rather than that candidate.

Among Piaget's major contributions are his findings about the conditions under which assimilation and accommodation are most likely to occur. One of his most significant ideas in this respect is that these two processes take place only when environmental stimuli are appropriate (or matched) to the individual's stage of cognitive development. For example, showing the apple to a new-born infant would not help it to adapt to its environment. Neither would reading a political treatise to a one-year-old child or presenting a complex abstract mathematical problem to a kindergartner.

Cognitive Development

Piaget makes an important distinction between learning (which depends greatly upon external stimulation by teachers, books, etc.) and cognitive development (which is largely, though not entirely, a function of natural maturation). Piaget stresses the point that a child's *mode* of thinking about apples, politicians, justice, causality, or anything else changes with age. The thinking processes of the ten year old, for example, ordinarily differ qualitatively from those of the two year old. It is not just that the older child *knows* more (or has learned more) than the younger one. He *uses* what he has learned in a different way. He responds to, or adapts to, the world around him differently.

Central to Piaget's theory is the idea that through interactions with their environments children construct internal models of what the world is like and respond accordingly. Through their everyday experiences, they test and revise these models while developing progressively more and more sophisticated ways of thinking (Wadsworth 1971).

Cognitive Stages

Cognitive development, according to Piaget, involves a child's passing through a sequence of fairly well defined stages. These he designates as

- sensorimotor (birth to about age two)
- preoperational (ages two to seven)
- concrete operations (ages seven to eleven)
- formal operations (age eleven or twelve and up)

Detailed discussions of children's cognitive behavior at each of these stages along with critical analyses of Piaget's methodology and findings are readily available in a number of other sources which are cited in the bibliography (Piaget 1952, 1973; Wadsworth 1971; Ginsburg and Opper 1969).

The chronological ages that correspond to Piaget's stages should not be taken too literally. They are intended only as approximations of the ages at which cognitive changes begin to occur. Wide variations among individuals in this respect are to be expected. More significant than the exact ages is the idea of the inflexible sequential order in which the stages emerge. For example, before a person is capable of performing intellectually at a mature level (the stage of formal operations), he must first have had successful experiences in the earlier, prerequisite stages.

According to Piaget, while younger children are constantly growing in their ability to think, it is not until they reach the stage of formal operations that they increase appreciably in their abilities to think abstractly. After about age eleven, they become increasingly less dependent on concrete data and come to rely more on their own abilities to make logical deductions, formulate hypotheses, grasp symbolic or abstract concepts such as justice, and solve abstract theoretical problems. Thus, Piaget's research suggests that it would be a mistake to even try to motivate a child who is in the concrete operation stage to perform the kinds of tasks or learn the kinds of material that require a more advanced level of cognitive maturity.

The evidence that Piaget presents showing that new cognitive structures are developed in an orderly fashion on or out of existing structures implies the need for careful consideration of the child's readiness for a new learning experience. His findings also support the idea that the focus of instruction should be to help the individual to make a smooth progression through the various cognitive stages. Furth and Wachs (1975), whose book is one of the recommended readings for this chapter, offer a number of practical suggestions for doing so.

The suggestions offered by Furth and Wachs for the implementation of Piaget's theories include 179 games intended to help to develop eight modes of thinking. From the simplest to the more complex, these are

1. General Movement Thinking (e.g., reflex control, bodily balance and control)
2. Discriminative Movement Thinking (e.g., ocular tracking and convergence; finger, lip, and tongue control)
3. Visual Thinking (e.g., noting similarities and differences just by looking)
4. Auditory Thinking (e.g., noting similarities and differences by listening)
5. Hand Thinking (e.g., learning through touching, feeling, manipulating)
6. Graphic Thinking (e.g., drawing, tracing, coloring, cutting)
7. Logical Thinking (e.g., classifying, sorting, rearranging, predicting consequences, manipulating symbols)
8. Social Thinking (e.g., dramatizations, group activities requiring cooperation or social interaction)

Although these games are primarily intended for use at the kindergarten and first-grade levels, where Piaget's findings have had the greatest impact, they can also be used in the upper elementary grades.

Moral Development

Paralleling his theory of cognitive development, Piaget has also set forth a theory of moral development. It can be summarized in terms of changes in a child's attitudes toward rules such as those governing a game or behavioral standards necessary for social living.

During the first stage of moral development, from birth to about two years, the only rules that apply in play activities are those determined by his neuromuscular development. Since play activities are usually solitary during these years, there are for the child no set procedures to be followed.

During the second stage, between the ages of about two and five, the child begins to imitate rules that are followed by others. During these years, children still tend to play by themselves and when playing with others they are not particularly interested in competing or cooperating. Following rules, therefore, is still not especially important.

During the third stage, beginning at about age six or seven, the child is less egocentric and more socially oriented. He tries either to cooperate or to win and so begins to pay more attention to the rules of the game. Although his ideas of these rules are likely to be vague, he is quite willing to try to follow them. At this stage, according to Piaget, rules come to be regarded as "sacred and untouchable, emanating from adults and lasting forever." Attempts at changing the rules during this stage are unthinkable since they are perceived of as emanating from some higher authority.

In the fourth and final stage, beginning at about age eleven, rules come to be fixed in detail. The person is capable of understanding not only the rules, but also the reasons behind them. The rules, however, are no longer necessarily inviolable but subject to scrutiny, criticism, and, if necessary, change. Behavioral standards now come to be regarded as matters of mutual agreement. While they must be respected while in effect, they can be modified when those playing (or working or living) together agree (Piaget 1965).

Kohlberg's Theory and Strategy

Building on Piaget's findings, drawing heavily on the views of John Dewey, incorporating some Freudian ideas on the emergence of the superego, and adding some important insights of his own,

Laurence Kohlberg has formulated what he calls a cognitive-developmental theory of moral development and a corresponding strategy for moral education (Kohlberg 1975). Kohlberg identifies three levels of moral development: the preconventional, conventional, and postconventional. Each of these levels includes two stages, as is shown in Figure 10.

At the *preconventional* level, the person has not as yet formulated any general principles or moral standards that he can apply to particular situations. Rather, he interprets good and bad behavior in terms of its expediency or immediate consequences.

At the *conventional* level, the individual is mainly concerned with supporting the existing social system. He therefore begins to develop moral principles that center on conformity to the rules and regulations that are generally accepted in his family and community.

At the *postconventional* level, the person begins to think critically about these social conventions and accepted standards of moral behavior. Here, he begins to form abstract moral concepts and to act in accordance with internalized principles arrived at through his own intellectual efforts.

According to Kohlberg, to teach moral principles (or to motivate a child toward moral behavior), we should begin at the highest stage that the student has already attained. Then, he believes, instruction should center on helping children to learn to solve moral dilemmas or to think about moral problems at progressively higher levels.

At Stage 3, for example, a person believes that it is wrong to take something that belongs to someone else because to do so would displease other people and result in their disapproval. Good boys and girls do not steal and at Stage 3 they do want to be thought of as good. At this stage, the teacher does not preach about the abstract concept of honesty or attempt to explain the abstract underlying principle of justice. She does help the student come to realize that there is a higher reason for their not stealing, that social living requires honesty for reasons above and beyond that of personal approval or disapproval, and that it would be wrong to steal even if one had the chance to do so with impunity.

When Stage 4 is attained, the law-and-order level of moral development, the individual is ready to begin to learn to think

Stage 1	**PRECONVENTIONAL LEVEL** *Punishment-Obedience Orientation* (obeys parents and others in order to avoid punishment)
Stage 2	*Instrumental-Hedonistic Orientation* (does what is expedient in order to receive rewards)
Stage 3	**CONVENTIONAL LEVEL** *Interpersonal Concordance Orientation* (conforms to expected standards of behavior in order to be regarded by others as good)
Stage 4	*Authority or Law-and-Order Orientation* (complies with the requirements of legitimate authority in order to maintain the social order)
Stage 5	**POSTCONVENTIONAL LEVEL** *Legalistic Social-Contract Orientation* (observes most laws and social conventions but examines them critically and recognizes that they can be changed)
Stage 6	*Universal Ethical Orientation* (follows own conscience in formulating abstract moral principles such as justice, human equality, and respect for others)

FIGURE 10.   Kohlberg's Stages of Moral Development.

at the Stage 5 level. There, he critically examines the concept of honesty. He begins to perceive *why* society values it so highly. He also begins to relate it to the concept of individual rights and to think about what honesty means in particular situations. According to Kohlberg, not until he has attained Stage 5 is the individual ready to grasp abstract moral principles. Then and only then is he able to move upward to Stage 6 where he can function consistently as a morally autonomous individual, doing what he thinks is right because he has a deep inner conviction that it *is* right.

Since space limitations and the nature of this book do not permit a more extended discussion of Kohlberg's views on moral development and moral education, you are urged to read his article, which is one of the recommended readings for this chapter (Kohlberg and Turiel 1971).

PERCEPTIONS OF CAUSALITY

One of the more significant cognitive variables that affects a person's behavior is his or her concept of causality. Do *we* cause our own behavior or does someone or something else "cause" it? Indeed, the nature of a person's response in a variety of situations depends in part not only on his beliefs about the causes of that particular situation but on his beliefs about causation itself.

Piaget's research has shed much light on the question of how the concept of causality develops from early infancy onward. In the earliest stages of cognitive development, the child is egocentric, viewing himself as the primary cause of all activity. Gradually, he begins to develop an awareness that other people can cause things to happen. Eventually, he develops the ability to make logical cause-and-effect relationships and to distinguish between situations which he himself can or cannot control. Other psychologists have investigated the problem of how people *perceive* of causality. From their research, there has evolved a cognitive theory of motivation that centers on the idea of attribution.

Attribution

Fritz Heider, the founder of attribution theory, noted that an important part of an individual's cognitive structure is how and to what he attributes the causes of things that happen to him. Note that the emphasis here is not on the real objective causes per se but on the individual's *perceptions* of the causes. A basic assumption of attribution theory is that human beings want and need to find out why things happen. But causes cannot be directly observed. They can only be inferred from behavior or events that are observable. Thus, our inferences might be at variance with objective reality. Although our perceptions of other people's motives or the causes of their behavior might not be true, nevertheless we are still likely to respond in terms of those perceptions (Heider 1958).

Suppose that someone bumps into you and knocks some books out of your hand. Your reaction, according to attribution theory, will depend on your perception of the other person's motives. Was the bumping an accident? Did the person bump you deliberately? If so, why? Out of sheer meanness? As a joke? To assert his superiority? Because he is naturally aggressive? What you do is interpret the event, make a judgment about its cause, and react accordingly.

Of particular concern to Bernard Weiner (1972), the best-known representative of attribution theory, is the question: to what do we attribute our own successes and failures? Why, for example, do you think you received the grade you did on the last test you took? Weiner identifies four factors to which you might attribute your performance. Two of these are internal: (1) your own ability and, (2) the amount of effort that you put forth. The other two are external: (3) the degree of difficulty of the task and (4) just plain luck.

Locus of Control

The judgments that we make about the causes (or sources) of events that we experience, including our successes and failures, as well as our assignment of credit or blame for those events depend on our idea of how much control we have over the things that happen to us. Here, of course, we are raising the age-old question of free will versus determinism. In more contemporary terms, we are introducing the concept of locus of control (Solomon and Oberlander 1974). Is our behavior freely chosen, self-initiated, autonomous, and subject to personal or internal control? Or is it determined by external factors (luck, chance, fate, the environment, the juxtaposition of stars and planets, the behavior of others) that we cannot control? For present purposes, the critical question is not where in objective reality the locus of control *is*. Rather, it is where a person *thinks* it is.

Several instruments have been devised to measure people's beliefs or attitudes in this respect. Typically, these instruments include a list of statements such as the following with which the individual is asked to indicate whether he agrees or disagrees.

1. The grades I receive depend primarily on how hard I study.
2. My grades depend primarily on my teacher's whims.
3. I can contribute, at least in a small way, toward the solution of national problems.
4. Those who run the government could not care less about what I think or want.
5. What becomes of me is mainly up to me.
6. Whatever will be will be.
7. No matter how good I am at something, I believe that I can always improve.
8. Success is mainly a matter of getting the breaks in life.

Those who tend to agree with the odd-numbered kinds of items have been categorized for research purposes as Internals, whereas those more in agreement with the even-numbered items are regarded as Externals.

Research by Rotter (1966), Phares (1957), and others suggests that Internals, who believe that their acts are primarily voluntary, are more likely than Externals to accept responsibility for their activities and are more highly motivated to carry them out. Internals have also been found to receive higher grades and achievement test scores than Externals and their overall attitude toward education is more favorable. Externals, who see little relationship between what they do and what happens to them, are likely to regard their own efforts as futile. Consequently, they are disinclined to put forth much effort.

An individual might, of course, be Internal in some respects and External in others. As Weiner and Kukla (1970) point out, we tend to attribute our successes to ourselves and our failures to others. Consider, for example, the student who says,

"I pulled an A in math."

"He gave me a D in English."

Those with high levels of achievement motivation are especially likely to regard success as resulting from their own abilities or effort and their failures as due to luck or some other factor outside themselves. Here we might do well to recall the Freudian mechanisms of rationalization and projection.

Pawns and Origins

Richard de Charms (1971) uses the terms *Pawns* and *Origins*, respectively, to refer to Externals and Internals. Pawns believe that either someone or something outside themselves is in control of their destiny. They feel that they act as they do because they have, in effect, been forced to do so. Perceiving that external forces determine their behavior, the Pawns neither carefully formulate personal goals nor have especially high levels of aspiration. Also, they do not concern themselves much with attempts at self-improvement. Rather, they tend to be docile and apathetic and allow themselves in a classroom situation to be manipulated by their teachers—which is why many teachers like them and wish they had more of them in their classes.

Origins, on the other hand, feel that what they do is the result of their own free choices. They act as they do because they want to. Unlike Pawns, they are very much concerned with formulating realistic goals and are confident of their abilities to attain them. They are also likely to be more independent, assertive, and self-reliant and to have greater or more positive self-expectations than Pawns. Origins are very much like the people White refers to as competent.

White's Idea of Competence

Drawing on, but reinterpreting, some insights derived from Freud, Piaget, and others, Robert White has developed the concept of *competence* as a prime factor in motivation. White believes that human beings by their very nature have a basic need for or tendency toward competence, or as he sometimes calls it, *effectance* (R. W. White 1959).

The competent person, according to White, is not simply one who possesses certain skills or is able to do something well. Rather, a competent person perceives himself as the master of his own destiny. He is able to relate to his environment effectively and is confident of his ability to cope with it. White sees people not simply as the products of external influences but as reasoning organisms who can help to shape the course of their own development. The term *competence*, then, refers to a person's ability and willingness to take the initiative and act upon his environment instead of passively allowing the environment to control him.

Along with the tendency toward competence, White postulates natural curiosity. The wide range of exploratory behaviors in which young children notoriously engage constitutes their first attempts to interact with, manipulate, and, to a certain extent, control their environments. The very process of mastering the environment affords the child a great deal of satisfaction. As he learns more about himself and his world, he is pleased with his accomplishments and is motivated toward further exploration. Thus, White supports the view of Piaget, Bruner, and other cognitive psychologists that learning and subsequent achievement are in and of themselves rewarding.

White maintains that such simple activities as walking or playing, as well as higher mental processes such as thinking, grow out of the person's need to deal with his environment effectively. We do not always or necessarily engage in these activities to *master* the environment, but to *understand* it—that is, to find out what the world is like. According to White, it is not so much the subsequent knowledge or mastery that follows discovery which is rewarding as it is the process of discovery itself that constitutes what behaviorists call intrinsic reinforcement.

Taken together with the ideas of attribution, locus of control, Origin versus Pawn behavior, and cognitive development, White's contribution to motivational theory helps to explain why and how it is that our behavior depends so often on our knowledge, perceptions, expectations, beliefs, and feelings about ourselves and the world around us. White further suggests that the need to know—and to be competent—is not something that has to be created or implanted in an individual. It is already there, as it were, waiting to be developed.

ACHIEVEMENT MOTIVATION

Closely related to White's concept of competence is what David McClelland, John Atkinson, and others refer to as the need for achievement. Everyone has a need for achievement (or competence) in some area or other, but this need is stronger and deeper in some people than it is in others. Moreover, a person might have a rather high *need* for achievement but, unless that need is somehow aroused—unless the person is somehow challenged or stimulated to activity—it might remain dormant or submerged and have little or no effect on his behavior. For example, a student who gives every appearance of being bored, listless, inattentive, and unmotivated might actually have a high degree of achievement need. But for any one of a number of possible reasons, he might not perceive *scholastic* achievement as particularly desirable or attainable. On the other hand, his need for achievement in the scholastic or some other area might be relatively low as compared with his need for, say, affiliation—or even for food.

Underachievement

Achievement motivation, or the lack of it, seems to be particularly relevant to the so-called underachiever. An underachiever is usually regarded as one whose scholastic performance (as reflected by his grades) is not commensurate with his ability (as inferred from intelligence-test scores). Thus, an underachiever might be a very bright, high-IQ student who is doing only average work, or an average-ability student doing below-average work. Educators seem to think of underachievers as a breed apart and perhaps they are. In a sense, though, just about everyone is an underachiever in that very few, if any, of us ever completely realizes his or her full potentiality. As we noted in an earlier chapter, no matter how successful we are in any given area, no matter how highly we achieve, there is always the possibility that we could have done better.

There is no specific degree to which a person's achievement level must fall below his ability level for him to be formally categorized as an underachiever. In certain research studies or special-help programs, students whose percentile rankings or standardized achievement tests were more than thirty points below their intelligence-test scores have been arbitrarily designated underachievers. In other cases, for other purposes, other cutoff points have been used. The important consideration, of course, is not to label a person as an underachiever. The important problem is to recognize and help the student who is capable of doing better work than he has been doing.

Characteristics of Underachievers

A number of studies have been conducted in order to discover the common traits or characteristics of underachieving students at the elementary, high school, and college levels. Ringness (1965), for example, compared two groups of ninth-grade boys with IQs of 120 or higher. Those in the first group had grade point averages of 3.0 or above; those in the second group, 2.0 or lower. Using interviews and special tests, he found that the underachieving boys had a higher need for affiliation than achievement—that is, they tended to value popularity with their peers more than they did good grades. Ringness attributed the difference in the performance of the two groups to differences in their motivation.

After reviewing a number of other such studies, the Wellingtons (1965) concluded that underachievers as a group tend to be low in achievement motivation, to have certain personality problems, or both. They found that underachievers tend to be low in self-confidence, sense of responsibility, seriousness of purpose, capacity to function effectively under pressure, and their concern for others. They are also likely to have negative attitudes toward school, little interest in reading, and a tendency to procrastinate, withdraw from competition, and rely excessively on external influences. In another survey, Taylor (1964) found that underachievers are characterized by a high degree of anxiety, feelings of personal inadequacy, hostility toward others, negative interpersonal relationships, and unrealistic goal orientations.

Measurement of Achievement Motives

Two of the main requirements for scholastic success—or, for that matter, success in any other area—are ability and desire. In most areas, if the person has the necessary ability to succeed and a determination strong enough to persevere until he does succeed, the chances are that he *will* succeed—provided that his level of aspiration is realistic. Most students have the necessary ability to do well in school, but they do not always have the desire to use that ability for that purpose. Hence, the motivation problem in classrooms and attempts on the part of experimental psychologists to learn about achievement motives.

Building on pioneering research in the 1930s by Henry A. Murray (1938), David McClelland began in the 1950s to investigate achievement motivation experimentally. His pioneering efforts in this respect are still being carried on throughout the world and attempts are being made to put his findings to practical use.

To measure the strength of their subjects' achievement motives, McClelland and his associates had them tell a little story about each of a series of pictures they were shown. For each of these pictures, they were asked to respond to four questions:

What is happening in the picture?

What led up to the situation that is pictured?

What is the person in the picture thinking or feeling?

What is likely to happen next?

It was assumed that, in responding to a picture, the subjects would fantasize about it and project some of their own motives into the situation, attributing them to the person depicted. Each response was recorded and later scored in such a way that would indicate the subject's "achievement-need imagery."

One picture, for example, showed a boy seated at a desk with an open book in front of him. If, after looking at the picture, the response was something like, "The boy is studying because he wants to get a good grade on a test the next day," or, "He wants to become a famous writer," the subject would be given points for achievement imagery. On the basis of responses such as these, he would be credited with being success oriented. If the response were something like, "He doesn't want to fail the test," it would be regarded as indicative of failure orientation. A simple response such as, "He's reading a book," with no explanation of why, would be regarded as neither success- nor failure-oriented, but neutral, and would be interpreted as showing a lack of achievement imagery.

Those subjects whose stories tended to emphasize success were classified as having strong achievement motives. When later given the task of solving word puzzles, they were indeed found to achieve at higher levels than their counterparts whose stories showed less concern with success. Presumably, the need or desire to achieve contributed to their actual achievement (McClelland 1955).

Risk-Taking

McClelland and his followers noted the differences between subjects with high and low (or strong and weak) achievement motives. Many of these differences centered on risk-taking. When we are attracted by a goal and know that there is a chance of failure in attaining it, we face a risk. Whether or not we take the risk depends to a considerable extent on whether we are motivated primarily by the expectation of success or the dread of failure (Atkinson 1957, 1966).

Subjects who are motivated primarily by fear of failure tend to take a chance if the odds of being successful are very great or very small. If the odds are moderate, such subjects tend to abandon the goal. For example, the high school or college student who is fear-oriented might be expected to elect courses that he believes will be either very easy or very hard. The reason for selecting easy courses is obvious enough. But why select courses that are known to be difficult? The answer seems to be that if he fails them, he can always rationalize failure on the grounds that the course was unreasonably difficult and that anyone might have failed it. He might expect to be recognized for his courage in undertaking so difficult a course, but has protected himself in advance against any feeling of shame or frustration if he should not succeed in it. In this respect, he is similar to the student who, after repeated failures, sets a level of aspiration for himself that is higher than the one he had before his failures (Maehr and Sjorgren 1971).

Similarly, in the economic world, an executive whose main motivation is to avoid financial failure might be very conservative with investments and very cautious with the money he already has, or he might be inclined to take wild financial risks, gambling that he might just possibly strike it rich. But, since realistically his expectations or prospects of doing so are so remote, he will probably not feel too disappointed if his venture does not pay off.

Success-oriented people, on the other hand, tend to avoid both high-risk and low-risk situations, preferring those with a moderate risk. Their moderate risk situations provide them with goals that are sufficiently challenging to satisfy their needs for achievement, but not so difficult that they seriously threaten them with the prospect of failure.

A person can, of course, be motivated simultaneously by a fear of failure and a desire for success. In such a situation, the individual experiences what we have referred to as an approach-avoidance conflict. The person with a high degree of achievement motivation might be willing to risk failure—provided that the risk is not perceived as too great.

Motivation Training Programs

Since the mid-1960s, a number of formal programs have been established for increasing achievement motivation. Although these programs differ from one another in the specific methodology employed, their general purpose is to help individuals to become ambitious, to set realistic goals for themselves, and to persevere and strive for excellence in attaining them. The program conducted by D. A. Kolb (1965) is fairly representative of other such attempts.

Kolb devoted a six-week summer program to working with a group of underachieving high school boys. These students had high degrees of intellectual ability but had been doing poor schoolwork. Presumably, they were low in achievement motivation. Kolb himself exhibited high need-achievement behavior to provide the boys with a model. He communicated to them his own high expectations of the program. He explained the purpose of the program, the concept of achievement motivation, and the characteristics of people with a high degree of success orientation.

As part of the training program, the boys played a car-racing game to give them an opportunity to see how risk-taking is related to the achievement need. They discussed their behavior while playing the game and analyzed their thinking with respect to such matters as orientation toward the future and delay of gratification. They discussed stories that involved achievement motivation and learned how to score their own stories. They discussed conflicts between achievement and affiliation needs, risk-taking, goal planning, decision making, and the importance of knowing one's own abilities.

Using a somewhat different procedure, S. W. Gray and others (1970) devised an achievement motivation program for preschool disadvantaged children. Their program was based on the assumption that achievement motivation includes two basic components: persistence and gratification delay. The program centered on training in these two areas. Persistence training included activities such as having the child throw a ball into a wastebasket from a challenging but attainable distance. The child received encouragement whenever he made the attempt, whether successful or not. Gratification delay was taught by giving the child frequent opportunities to choose between an immediate or a delayed reward, with the clear understanding that the delayed reward would be greater.

McClelland (1972), Alschuler (1972), and others have reported on motivation training programs that involved the use of a variety of games, simulations, exercises, case studies, tests, discussion procedures, audiovisual aids, programmed textbooks, and other kinds of instructional materials. None of these programs has been 100% successful with all the subjects, but practically all of them have had *some* success with *some* of the subjects. McClelland suggests that attempts to strengthen the achievement motive are most likely to be successful when the subjects

- clearly understand the nature of the motive
- believe that they can and should and will develop it
- can relate the motive to their everyday lives
- perceive the motive as an improvement in their self-images

- commit themselves to achieving concrete goals that are related to their newly formed motive
- keep records of their progress toward these goals
- work in an atmosphere where they feel supported and respected.

Development of Achievement Motives

Most of those who have studied the achievement motive seem to believe that it is acquired through learning. Hence, the recommendation that teachers adapt some of the principles and techniques that have been mentioned for use in their own classrooms. There is a possibility, however, that certain components of achievement motivation are inherent in human nature. Jean Piaget offers evidence that certain aspects of achievement motivation are innate. He notes that by the third year of life children demonstrate their achievement orientation by wanting to do things for themselves. But ordinarily the tasks that the young child wishes to carry out independently are relatively easy tasks that he has already mastered quite well and do not offer a great deal of challenge.

Whether or not individuals have an innate propensity toward achievement, the strength of their motives to succeed and the areas in which they try to succeed are unquestionably learned responses. Heckhausen and others who have investigated **the** matter believe that achievement motivation is correlated with the individual's home and family background, his particular culture, his religious affiliations, and other environmental factors. It has been found, for example, that in the United States, achievement motivation is likely to be lower in children who have been raised in fatherless homes; that it is likely to be higher in children who come from homes in which independence and responsibility, rather than strict obedience and conformity, are encouraged (Heckhausen 1967).

Sex Differences

Numerous studies conducted over the period from the 1950s to well into the 1970s suggest that males tend to exceed females in the need to achieve at practically all age levels. In her studies of the fear of success in women, Matina Horner (1972, 1973) found that the majority of her subjects felt that academic success would threaten their femininity and possibly lead to social rejection. They also expressed reservations about the overall desirability of women excelling men in the business or professional worlds. The fear of success was found to be especially strong in the more intelligent women. They seemed to be experiencing a conflict between a need for high achievement on the one hand and to maintain a kind of stereotyped feminine image on the other.

As we noted in considering the views of Alfred Adler in Chapter 3, one of the more common explanations of the sex differential in this respect is that girls and women have been conditioned from early childhood to believe that in our culture competitiveness, self-assertion, and striving to get ahead are somehow more appropriate to the male of the species. Consequently many, but certainly not all, females might have a tendency to repress this need. Janice Gibson, among others, believes that males develop a stronger need to achieve than females because they are taught from an early age to be competitive, to value independence, and to be self-reliant, etc. (Gibson 1976). In the 1950s and 1960s, she points out, such was usually not the case with women. She also notes that "not unexpectedly" more and more research findings, such as those reported by Alper (1974), seem to show a decrease in differences between the sexes in achievement motivation.

Maccoby and Jacklin regard the idea that "girls lack motivation to achieve" as one of several common myths about sex differences that they challenge. Among some other such myths are that girls are more social than boys and more susceptible to persuasion, that they have lower self-esteem than boys, and that boys are more analytical. After studying more than 2000 books and articles on the subject of sex differences in motivation, social behavior, and intellectual ability, they found that the available evidence does not support these stereotypes. They conclude that males in general are more aggressive than females, that girls have greater verbal ability than boys, and that boys usually surpass girls in visual/spatial and mathematical abilities. But with respect to such questions as, "Is one sex more active or passive or competitive or dominant or compliant than the other?" they find that the evidence is either ambiguous or insufficient to warrant the drawing of any generalizations (Maccoby and Jacklin 1974, 1977).

FEELINGS OF SUCCESS AND FAILURE

Male or female, young or old, rich or poor, bright or not so bright, all of us want in some way to experience success and avoid failure. Whether in a classroom, on an athletic field, in the business world, or elsewhere, we are often motivated to behave as we do to achieve what we regard as success or to avoid shame, ridicule, deprivation, the lowering of our self-esteem, or some other aversive concomitant of failure. As Atkinson points out, for some people in some situations the hope of avoiding failure might be an even more potent motive than that of positive achievement. For example, a student who is not particularly interested in As or Bs might be highly motivated to avoid an F. In any competitive situation, he might have no delusions or expectations of coming in first, but he might set forth a great deal of effort to avoid the humiliation of coming in last.

Cognitive as well as behavioral psychologists are generally agreed that the prospects as well as the consequences of success are likely to be more productive than those of failure. This is why they believe that teachers should hold to a minimum any threats of failure as well as the actuality of failure. They recommend that teachers place more reliance on means of ensuring each student an opportunity to enjoy at least a small degree of success. Presumably, a taste of success here and now with relatively simple tasks will whet the student's appetite and motivate him to try harder than he otherwise would with increasingly more demanding tasks in the future.

Relativity of Success and Failure

Success and failure are not absolute but relative concepts. An experience that is perceived as rewarding by one person is not always or necessarily similarly perceived by another. Sam might be quite thrilled with a bowling score of 150 or a C on a chemistry test. Judy, however, might be disappointed with the same scores and feel that she has failed to do well, having set her sights on at least a B in chemistry and 170 in bowling. Success and failure, then, depend not only on one's actual objective achievement but also on one's expectations.

When we fail to attain the goals that we have set for ourselves, we feel frustrated. One reason why we sometimes experience this feeling of frustration is that our goals simply have been set unrealistically high. Perhaps Judy had never in her life earned a bowling score above 90. While we might admire her determination to roll a 170 on this particular occasion, we might also recognize that for her that goal might not be realistic. On the other hand, if she had been doing A work in chemistry right along, we might be disappointed to note that she had lowered her aim in that course and is now trying to buy success too cheaply.

Levels of Aspiration

The goals that we set for ourselves or the standards of performance that we think we can accomplish and are willing to try to achieve are referred to as our levels of aspiration. One's level of aspiration is a kind of compromise between two conflicting tendencies. On the one hand, we want to succeed at the highest possible level. On the other, we want to avoid failure. If our level of aspiration is too high, failure is all but inevitable. If it is too low, we might not actualize our potentials or do as well as we are capable of doing in a given area. Moreover, we will be deprived of the feeling of achievement that accompanies the successful completion of a challenging, worthwhile task.

One's level of aspiration depends in large part on how one perceives oneself. Part of your job as a teacher will be to help the individual student to perceive himself realistically and to set a realistic level of aspiration. A realistic level of aspiration has two main characteristics: it is high enough to be challenging and low enough to be attainable.

Personal growth is largely a matter of striving, seeking, stretching, extending oneself, of reaching from something that is presently just barely beyond one's grasp. If, with a little extra effort and a little more determination, we can attain whatever it is that we are striving for, well and good. But, if we literally reach for the stars, we're letting ourselves in for a disappointment.

A good rule of thumb to follow in this respect is to give the student the benefit of any doubt regarding his capabilities. A common mistake of teachers is not that they expect too much but too little of their students. These expectations, as we shall see shortly, are likely to affect not only the student's level of aspiration but also his overall achievement as well. A teacher most certainly should never discourage a student from aiming high by conveying to him in advance any idea that he will never make it. While keeping in mind both the challenging and attainable aspects of an appropriate level of aspiration, the teacher should assign a greater priority to challenging the student. In short, a level of aspiration that is a little too high is to be vastly preferred over one that is a little too low.

Effects of Success and Failure

Recent past performance is one of the most important factors affecting a person's level of aspiration. This point has been brought out clearly by Sears in a well-known study involving three groups of students in grades four through six. One group was composed of children who had a consistent history of success in their academic subjects. The second group included those who had consistently experienced failure. The third group was made up of boys and girls who had been successful in reading but unsuccessful in arithmetic.

The subjects in Sears's experiment were given a series of twenty speed tests in reading and arithmetic. After the first test, they were asked to estimate how long it would take them to finish the next. Then, half of the children in each group were exposed to a success condition. They were praised for their performance on most of the remaining nineteen tests. The other half of each group exposed to a failure condition was criticized for their poor work. After each test, all of the children were asked to estimate the amount of time that they would need to complete the next.

Sears found that students working under the success condition (even those with a previous record of failure) tended to set future goals that were realistic and slightly higher than their previous level of achievement. But those who had worked under the failure condition (including those with a previous record of success) tended to set goals that were either unrealistically high or unreasonably low.

Some of the unsuccessful students set goals lower than their previous level of achievement apparently to assure themselves of some measure of success in attaining them and to protect themselves against a feeling of failure if they did not measure up to their earlier level. Other unsuccessful students set goals that were higher than before but practically out of their reach. While they might have had no real expectation of reaching these higher goals, they probably experienced a feeling of self-satisfaction because of their good intentions, and felt that they would somehow be rewarded for aiming high (Sears 1940).

Studies by Child and Whiting (1949), Atkinson (1974), Moulton (1965), Bryan and Locke (1967), and others confirm Sears's findings. They have shown that

- Success usually leads to a raising of one's level of aspiration.
- The greater an individual's success is, the higher the subsequent increase in his level of aspiration is likely to be.
- Self-confident people set higher and more realistic goals than do those who lack self-confidence.
- Self-confident people prefer fairly difficult tasks where there is some risk of failure.
- Success with a particular kind of task and the expectation of further success with similar tasks increases the individual's interest in those kinds of tasks.
- The effects of failure on one's level of aspiration are more varied and, hence, less predictable than the effects of success.
- Failure sometimes results in withdrawal and an unwillingness to set any level whatever of aspiration in the area where the failure had been experienced.
- Failure and the expectation of failure tend to diminish the interest in and appeal of other tasks similar to those in which failure had occurred.

Self-Confidence

An individual's level of aspiration and degree of self-confidence are so closely interrelated and mutually reinforcing that either can be properly regarded as both a cause and an effect of the other. The more confident a student is about his ability to succeed, the higher he is likely to aim. The higher he can realistically aim, with a reasonable expectation of success, the greater his self-confidence is likely to be in return. As we have seen, if a student's sights are set too low, he might slough off, neglect doing the kind of work he is capable of doing, and have no real opportunity to develop his self-esteem or self-confidence.

To help to develop the student's self-confidence and gradually raise his level of aspiration, a teacher might begin by assigning work that is readily attainable (but not insultingly easy), thereby allowing the student to get off to a good start, experience success, receive reinforcement, gain confidence in his abilities, and savor a feeling of personal worth. Then, the teacher might *gradually* increase the difficulty of the assigned work and encourage the student to try to do just a little bit better the next time. In using this principle of gradualism along with systematic feedback, encouragement, and reinforcement, the teacher can contribute to raising the student's level of aspiration realistically and at the same time help him build up his own self-confidence.

Teacher Expectations

Among the factors that are likely to have a pronounced effect on the student's self-concept, level of aspiration, motivation in general, and subsequent achievement is what he perceives as the teacher's expectations of him. Ordinarily, when teachers show that they expect a high level of achievement on the part of their students and manifest their belief that the students are capable of achieving that level of performance, the students are likely to rise to the occasion and achieve accordingly. But when teachers' expectations are obviously low, their students' levels of aspirations and achievement are likely to be correspondingly low.

The effects of teacher expectations on student motivation and performance have been brought out by Rosenthal and Jacobson in a much-publicized study involving the so-called Pygmalion effect and the concept of the "self-fulfilling prophecy." As part of their study, all the children in a particular elementary school were given a test that purported to measure general intelligence. The teachers in each class were given the names of five students whose superior scores (they were told) showed that they were likely to make unusually high intellectual gains in the year ahead. Actually, these superior students were selected at random. There was no real difference between their performance on the so-called intelligence test and that of the other students (Rosenthal and Jacobson 1968).

Rosenthal and Jacobson claimed that the students who had been arbitrarily labeled superior showed significant gains in IQ. They attributed this increase to the fact that teachers had *expected* more from these students, somehow communicated their faith and confidence in them, and perhaps unconsciously favored them over other students from whom they had expected less. The conclusions of the Rosenthal–Jacobson study have been criticized rather severely by Thorndike (1968) and others mainly on the technical grounds pertaining to research methodology. As Finn (1972), Zanna (1975), and others have found, a number of attempts to replicate their procedure have failed to yield results substantiating their findings. Still, it is commonly believed that self-fulfilling prophecies do play an important part in explaining the achievement or lack of achievement of certain students, particularly those who are disadvantaged. Beginning with a prophecy (actually a prejudgment) that certain students are incapable of achieving at a high (or even an average) level, a teacher might somehow convey to those students his low expectations of them, treat them accordingly, and thus find that his prophecy has indeed been fulfilled (Rosenthal 1977).

For a further discussion of this controversial subject, see Bellamy (1975), Elashoff and Snow (1971), Good and Brophy (1974), and Rosenthal (1977).

EDUCATIONAL IMPLICATIONS

From the standpoint of cognitive psychology, human behavior depends largely on what we know or think or believe about the world we live in and on what we know or think or believe about ourselves. In a classroom situation, this implies that learning depends not only on external environmental stimuli such as the explanations, requests, demands, and expectations of teachers but more significantly on what those stimuli *mean* to us personally.

From this consideration, the function of a teacher is not simply to transmit information, dole out rewards and punishment, or program students to make certain predetermined responses. Equally, if not more, important are such tasks as promoting the student's cognitive development, helping him learn to discover personal meaning for himself, and developing his self-confidence and sense of personal responsibility for his own education. The emphasis, therefore, is not so much on changing the student's verbal responses or outer behavior as it is on helping to develop such inner behaviors as knowing, understanding, thinking, feeling, believing, valuing, perceiving, and so on.

In short, cognitive psychology places a greater stress on the *process* of learning than it does on the *products* or outcomes and tends to rely more heavily on intrinsic rather than extrinsic forms of motivation (Bruner 1960, 1973).

Piaget's Views

Piaget's theory of cognitive development lends strong support to the idea that a major purpose of education is to facilitate the student's cognitive development—that is, to help him to learn how to think more clearly and logically. Although Piaget himself has not dealt extensively with the problem of motivation as such, his views have also given strong support to the concept of intrinsic motivation. He has little if any use for the idea that knowing or thinking or understanding is motivated primarily by external factors or extrinsic reinforcers. He believes, rather, that human beings have an intrinsic need to engage in cognitive activities, a need that arises from within the organism itself. In other words, human beings by their very nature have an intrinsic tendency to assimilate and accommodate and thus to grow intellectually.

As Furth and Wachs point out, Piaget's theory does not entirely rule out the moderate use of incentives or external controls as aids to learning. In some cases, they concede, the use of extrinsic motivational techniques in conjunction with Piagetian principles has been remarkably successful. Still, an educational program such as they conducted in an attempt to implement Piaget's views relies much more heavily on motivation from within. The uniform growth in intelligence of all children from birth until at least age 12, they claim, cannot be attributed to external stimuli but is, rather, a natural characteristic of the human species. Thus, the external stimuli to which children respond are controlled or mediated by internal human mechanisms including the need to know (Furth and Wachs 1975).

Because they are convinced of the importance of the inner forces that govern the child's cognitive development, Piaget and his followers do not try to push children beyond the level of thinking that is characteristic of their stage of development. Instead of insisting upon adult-imposed standards of performance, they believe that a major function of a teacher is to provide appropriate kinds of activities and opportunities that will facilitate cognitive development, independent thinking, discovery, creativity, and, in behavioral terms, self-reinforcement.

Discovery Methods

Perhaps the best-known application of cognitive theory to educational practice involves the use of discovery methods of teaching and learning (Kersh 1962). Discovery methods are those that require the student to restructure information and induce, deduce, or intuit new insights from previously acquired data. In other words, they challenge the student to find things out or figure things out, by and for himself. Discovery (or inquiry) methods involve relatively little in the way of teacher guidance or direction or extrinsic reinforcement. Rather, they are characterized by reliance on the student's own first-hand observations and experiences, explorations growing out of his own curiosity, his own independent thinking, and his intrinsic need or tendency to know (Morine 1975).

Jerome Bruner, one of the foremost proponents of this approach, claims several advantages for discovery as compared with more traditional teacher-centered methods. He maintains, for example, that discovery methods of teaching and learning help students to learn how to learn—that is, how to acquire new information that they might want or need. He also believes that discovery methods help to develop the student's curiosity, sharpen his powers of observation and reasoning abilities, and make him more self-reliant and less dependent upon teachers, textbooks, or other external sources (Bruner 1960).

Not only behavioral psychologists such as B. F. Skinner (1968) but also certain cognitive psychologists such as D. P. Ausubel (1968) have strong reservations about the value of discovery as a means of teaching and learning. But proponents contend that one of its major values from the standpoint of motivation is that it involves the individual student more actively and more directly in his own learning experience and gives him more personal responsibility for his education. Through discovery, proponents such as Bruner contend, learning becomes not only more meaningful, personally relevant, and valuable but much more interesting and challenging than simply sitting, listening, taking notes, and reciting.

Discovery methods, like the other concepts and principles of cognitive psychology that we have considered, are by no means incompatible with reinforcement or extrinsic motivation. But they are more in keeping with intrinsic motivation, a subject with which we deal at greater length in Chapter 7.

Developing Self-Confidence

Another of the more important educational implications of cognitive theories has to do with the role of the teacher in helping the student to develop confidence in his abilities to reach the kinds of goals he wants to reach. In this regard, a big part of the teacher's job is to help the individual student to set for himself goals high enough to challenge him but realistic enough for him to attain. As we have seen, if a person's level of aspiration is too high, he might be inviting needless frustration. If it is too low, he might fail to do the kinds of things he is capable of doing and, thus, miss a good chance to build up his self-confidence.

Among the main factors on which a person's self-confidence depends are his own previous record of success and failure and his perceptions of what certain other people whom he regards as significant expect of him. Not uncommonly, when a teacher shows that he expects a high level of performance on the part of a particular student and indicates that he has confidence in his ability to reach that standard, the student will come through. But when teachers' expectations are low, their students' levels of aspiration might be even lower.

As a means of helping students to gain and grow in self-confidence, cognitive psychologists recommend that teachers begin by assigning work that their students will find rather easy—but not, of course, too easy. Thus, they can get off to a good start by experiencing a feeling of accomplishment or of competence. Then, of course, the teacher moves on toward assignments that are gradually more difficult. It is extremely important, from this standpoint, that students be able to, and actually do, complete task A before they are confronted with task B. Leaving unfinished any task that a person undertakes and considers significant is one effective way of diminishing that person's self-confidence. An effective way of increasing self-confidence, on the other hand, is to experience the feeling of having done something that one has set out to do and to see that one's own efforts do indeed make a difference.

Individual Responsibility

As Richard de Charms has observed, while teachers expect their students to act as Origins when they are adults, they are all too often inclined to treat them as Pawns while they are in school. Thus, many students come to feel that they have little control over, and therefore little if any responsibility for, their own education or their own futures. Consequently, their attitude is often one of apathy and their behavior largely passive. Along with many other cognitive psychologists, de Charms believes that too much reliance on extrinsic reinforcement and behavior modification techniques intensifies the student's feeling that he is being manipulated by others (de Charms 1971).

Internals and Externals—or inner-directed and outer-directed individuals—are made not born. They learn their respective attitudes toward themselves and others largely as a result of the way they perceive themselves as being treated by others. From a stand-point of cognitive motivational theory, one of the main purposes of education is to help young people to develop a sense of inner direction, self-reliance, and personal responsibility. Recognizing the need for a balance between the extremes of strict teacher control on the one hand and gross permissiveness on the other, cognitive psychology supports the principle that students should be treated as originators of their own behavior. This implies the use of democratic procedure with respect to classroom discipline. It also implies that students should be given more responsibility for planning their curricula, directing their own learning experiences, and for evaluating their own work. Most importantly, perhaps, it implies that the teacher should help the individual student to realize that what he learns and what he becomes is principally up to him.

RECOMMENDED READING

Atkinson, John W., and Raynor J. O., Eds. *Motivation and Achievement.* New York: V. H. Winston, 1974. A collection of articles, most of them rather technical, summarizing twenty-five years of research on differences among individuals in achievement motivation and the effects of those differences on their behavior.

Canfield, Jack, and Wells, Harold C. *100 Ways To Enhance Self-Concept in the Classroom.* Englewood Cliffs, N.J.: Prentice-Hall, 1976. Clear, detailed descriptions of 105 tested classroom activities for improving the student's self-image, for fostering character development, citizenship, and self-knowledge, and for humanizing education in other ways. A very practical book.

Coopersmith, Stanley, and Feldman, Ronald. "Fostering a Positive Self-Concept and High Self-Esteem in the Classroom" In Coop, Richard H., and White, Kinnard, Eds. *Psychological Concepts in the Classroom.* New York: Harper and Row, 1974. Discusses the significance of the self-concept in the educational process and suggests some methods that teachers and parents can use to help to build self-esteem in children. Emphasizes the child's need for acceptance and trust, encouragement, opportunities to choose within realistic limits, and authoritative enforcement practices.

Covington, Martin V., and Beery, Richard G. *Self-Worth and Social Learning.* New York: Holt, Rinehart and Winston, 1975. Among the major topics considered in this short book are institutional causes of success and failure, strategies that students use to avoid failure, attribution, and success-oriented learning structures.

de Charms, Richard. "From Pawns to Origins: Toward Self-Motivation." In Lesser, G. S., Ed., *Psychology and Educational Practice.* Glenview, Ill.: Scott, Foresman, 1971. This article includes a summary of research findings on the Pawn-Origin concept and shows how Pawns can be helped to perceive themselves as Origins.

Furth, Hans, G., and Wachs, Harry. *Thinking Goes to School.* New York: Oxford University Press, 1975. Subtitled "Piaget's Theory in Practice," this book shows how Piaget's principles of cognitive development were implemented in an experimental school program that the authors conducted. It includes a description of 179 games, exercises, and activities used for this purpose.

Kolhberg, Lawrence, and Turiel, Elliot. "Moral Development and Moral Education." In Lesser, G. S., Ed., *Psychology and Educational Practice.* Glenview, Ill.: Scott, Foresman, 1971. A good, clear discussion of what the authors call the "cognitive-developmental" approach. This article includes a description of the six stages of moral development and shows how an understanding of these stages can be used in a moral education program that avoids the pitfalls of indoctrination on the one hand and relativism on the other.

McClelland, David C., and Steele, Robert S., Eds. *Human Motivation: A Book of Readings.* Morristown, N.J.: General Learning Press, 1973. A collection of twenty-eight articles on the measurement of motivation, the relationship between motivation and performance, the affiliation motive, the achievement motive in women, the power motive, unconscious motivation in everyday life, achievement motivation training programs, and related subjects.

Nardine, Frank E. "The Development of Competence." In Lesser, G. S., Ed., *Psychology and Educational Practice.* Glenview, Ill.: Scott, Foresman, 1971. This article centers on the concept of competence developed by Robert White. It includes an explanation of four different kinds of teaching strategies for the development of competence, each of which is recommended for use with a particular type of student.

Piaget, Jean. *To Understand Is to Invent.* New York: Grossman, 1973. Unlike many of Piaget's other books, this one is easy reading, intended for the general public. Here, he sets forth his views on the cognitive stages through which children pass and on a variety of commonly used educational techniques. Also recommended are his books, *The Origins of Intelligence in Children* and *The Moral Judgement of the Child.*

Wadsworth, Barry J. *Piaget's Theory of Cognitive Development.* New York: David McKay, 1971. Of the many books that attempt to summarize Piaget's theory, methodology, and research findings, this is one of the clearest and most useful. While Furth and Wachs emphasize practical applications, Wadsworth's book is organized around Piaget's stages of cognitive development.

Weiner, Bernard. *Theories of Motivation: From Mechanism to Cognition.* Chicago: Markham, 1972. A comparison of attribution theory, which the author clearly favors, with other theories of motivation. Somewhat historical in nature, the book traces the development of cognitive theories and summarizes research findings in its defense. Includes informative chapters on drive, field, and achievement theories.

CHAPTER 6: PREVIEW QUESTIONS

(After you have finished reading Chapter 6, you should be able to answer the following.)

1. Why is humanism sometimes referred to as Third Force psychology? What are some of the distinguishing features of humanism as compared with the other two major systems of psychology?

2. Why is it, according to humanistic psychology, that people are never completely satisfied? What are some implications of that principle?

3. What are some effects on human behavior of our needs for affiliation? Self-esteem? Independence? What are some other human needs or goals?

4. What is meant by the statement that much of our behavior is multimotivated? Give a few examples of multimotivated behavior.

5. What is the difference between purposeful and expressive behavior? Give a couple of examples of each.

6. What do humanists mean by the self? What is a self-concept? What are some factors on which a person's self-concept depends?

7. What is the difference between one's personal and physical environments? What is a phenomenal field?

8. What does Lewin mean by an individual's life space? By the terms positive and negative valence?

9. What are three basic kinds of conflicts? Give a couple of examples of each.

10. What does Maslow mean by his statement that human needs are arranged in a hierarchy of prepotency? How does he classify human needs and in what order does he think they emerge? How or why does the satisfaction of some needs cause other needs to arise?

11. What does Maslow mean by self-actualization? What are some characteristics of self-actualizing people?

12. Why, according to Maslow, do so few people become self-actualizers?

13. How does Maslow's theory of self-actualization relate to humanistic assumptions about the individual's capacity for personal growth?

14. What are metaneeds? What is the difference between deficiency needs and being needs?

15. What are some implications of Maslow's theory of motivation for education?

16. What is intrinsic motivation? How do humanists tend to feel about intrinsic, as opposed to extrinsic, motivation?

17. What is your overall reaction to humanistic psychology in general and humanistic principles of motivation in particular?

CHAPTER SIX

Toward Self-Fulfillment

In this chapter, we consider some insights derived from humanistic psychology. For nearly a half century, the two dominant forces in psychology, not only in the United States but throughout the world, had been behaviorism and psychoanalysis. Because it arose largely as a reaction against what were regarded as the mechanistic-deterministic features of those two forces, humanism is still commonly referred to as Third Force psychology.

Although its roots can be traced much further back than that, humanism began to emerge as a recognizable system in the 1940s. Among those who contributed significantly to its development are Abraham Maslow (1943), Carl Rogers (1961), Gordon Allport (1955), Arthur Combs (1959), and, as we have seen in Chapter 3, Alfred Adler. While these psychologists differ among themselves on a number of particular details and on the terminology that they employ to denote their ideas, they share certain basic assumptions that warrant their being grouped together. They are certainly united in their belief that neither Freudian nor behavioral psychology deals satisfactorily with the *why* of human behavior (Schlosser 1976).

Among the distinguishing features of humanism is the emphasis that it places on personal freedom, the individual's capacity for self-determination, and our striving for personal growth and development. Humanists do not regard a human being as simply a highly developed beast, an intricate piece of machinery, or as the helpless victim of innate unconscious drives. Rather, they regard each person as a unique individual, a unified *self*, who is motivated by and toward certain goals. Foremost of these goals is to become a complete, authentic, autonomous, "congruent" or "fully functioning" person—to achieve what has variously been called self-fulfillment, self-realization, self-actualization, or self-enhancement. Although some writers on the subject have attempted to make fine distinctions among these terms, they are all close enough in meaning so that we can use them interchangeably.

By and large, humanists tend to be in general accord with many of the principles of cognitive psychology. Maslow, Rogers, Allport, and Combs, for example, are very much interested in the individual's aspirations, perceptions, beliefs, and feelings about himself. They also rely heavily on the concept of intrinsic motivation to explain human behavior and to favor student-centered strategies centering on discovery, individual responsibility, and the principle of self-determination. Thus, humanistic and cognitive psychology tend to support and supplement one another.

With reference to the model presented in Chapter 1, this chapter focuses on factors such as students' needs, goals, and potentialities—and their growth toward self-actualization. Let us begin by considering some humanistic views on the purposes of human behavior.

PURPOSEFUL BEHAVIOR

One of the basic assumptions of humanistic psychology is that most human behavior is, in a word, purposeful. By *purposeful*, we mean here that most human behavior is directed toward satisfying some need or attaining some goal. As Figure 11 shows, purposeful behavior involves at least three elements and, usually, a fourth.

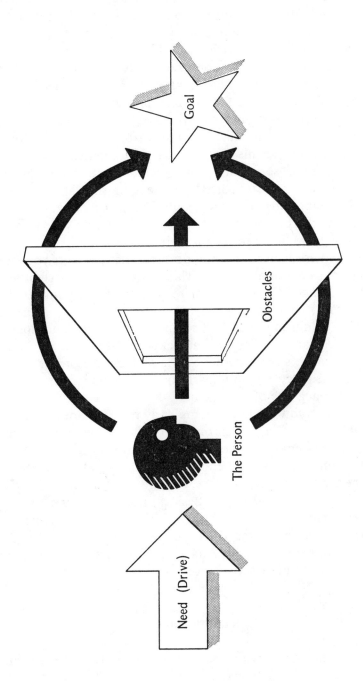

FIGURE 11. A Model of Purposeful Behavior. Experiencing a particular need, the person attempts to overcome obstacles that stand in the way of attaining the goal that will satisfy that need.

First, there is *You,* the individual human being, as you exist here and now. Although you are unique and distinct from every other person, one thing can be said about you with certainty: *You* are not perfectly satisfied with yourself or your condition in life. But neither is anyone else, so don't feel badly about it.

Second, there is some need that you have. This need makes you aware of your dissatisfaction and motivates you to act in a certain way to improve your situation. Actually, you have several needs operating simultaneously. You probably are not consciously aware of all of them at this or any other given moment.

Third, there is something "out there," some goal that you think or feel will at least partially or temporarily satisfy a need. This goal is something that you would like to have, be, or do. As is the case with the corresponding needs, you have several goals, some of which are likely to conflict with one another.

Fourth, there is usually some obstacle that prevents you from attaining your goal immediately. This obstacle, the source of your frustrations, might lie in external reality or within yourself. For example, you might be blocked in reaching a goal by some environmental condition such as prevailing economic conditions or rules and regulations that you are expected to observe. Or the obstacle might be some internal factor such as fear or a feeling of personal inadequacy on your part that keeps you from even attempting to reach one of your goals.

To say that you are never completely satisfied does not imply that you are a grouchy, chronic complainer who sits around cursing fate or bemoaning your lot in life. But it does mean that your situation can be improved, and you know it. No matter how happy, healthy, wealthy, or wise you are, you *could be* happier, healthier, wealthier, and wiser. Besides, there is always the possibility that you might lose your health or wealth, or something that you value even more. Thus, you are likely to experience a certain amount of anxiety. Anxiety, of course, implies something less than complete satisfaction with the status quo.

Needs and Goals

Such commonplace activities as eating lunch, studying, brushing your teeth, watching television, going to work, and taking a vacation indicate your lack of complete satisfaction with an existing situation and your belief that it can somehow be improved. The reason that you do these things, and just about anything else, is that you are trying to satisfy some need. You have your reasons (or purposes or motives), whether you are fully aware of them or not. You might not particularly like some of these activities, such as going to work, but you perceive them as a means toward some goal that you do have in mind.

A need can be thought of as any type of deficiency in the human organism or as the absence of anything that a person requires, or thinks he requires, for his overall well-being. A goal, as has been suggested, is something that the individual believes will contribute to the satisfaction of a need. Several attempts have been made to enumerate and classify human needs. One such list, for example, includes forty items, another twenty. One mentions eight basic needs and another only five. The differences, of course, are due to the system of classification that is used and the degree of specificity that the compiler wishes to attain. The listing that follows, therefore, is purely arbitrary and is hardly the final word on the subject. It does indicate the kinds of goals toward which most of our day-to-day activities are directed.

Physiological Needs

Just about every system of classifying human needs begins with those that are physiological or organic in nature. Undoubtedly, those are the most basic of all. Clearly, the purpose of much of our everyday behavior is to satisfy such needs either directly or indirectly. This is particularly true of routine, habitual behavior such as eating and drinking, working and resting. Because they are innate and essential to the preservation of life, physiological needs are sometimes referred to as *primary*. This is to distinguish them from all other needs, which are thought to be acquired or secondary.

Most physiological needs are universal. Among these we might mention food, clothing, shelter, water, air, sexual release, and freedom from pain and extreme temperatures. Although every human being has these needs, different people try to satisfy them in different ways. For example, although everyone has a need for food, the type and even the amount of food that a particular individual craves is an acquired characteristic. In addition to the *universal* physiological needs that have been mentioned, such things as alcohol, tobacco, and particular kinds of drugs operate as physiological needs for certain people at certain times. But, as is the case with a craving for, say, steak, rice, or whale blubber, the physiological need for alcohol and narcotics is at least in part a product of learning. So is the particular manner in which an individual attempts to satisfy his sex, clothing, and other physiological needs.

Need for Affiliation

We cannot, of course, satisfy all our physiological needs by ourselves. Hence, our need to associate with others and to feel that we belong to some group. This need for affiliation can be thought of as our most basic *social* need. As has just been suggested, social needs are sometimes referred to as secondary or acquired. However, certain social needs—such as the need for affiliation—are so vital that, for all practical purposes, they are as essential to life as our physiological needs. As we noted in Chapter 3, there is reason to believe that the socialization need is an innate component of human nature.

Because human beings are by nature social animals, they have a need for companionship as well as mutual assistance. Early in life, this need is ordinarily satisfied, to some extent at least, by association and identification with members of one's immediate family. As the child grows older, he develops a need for affiliation with a peer group, including persons of both sexes. As he approaches maturity, one of his developmental tasks might be to try to find some individual with whom to affiliate "until death do us part." Throughout life, the need to feel that one belongs to or is part of some social structure continues. Thus, at all stages of development, much of our behavior has as its purpose the formation and maintenance of close interpersonal relationships (Fromm 1963).

Need for Affection and Approval

We not only need to feel that we are affiliated with others. We also have a need to feel that we are *accepted* and *valued* by others.

We need more than a feeling of acceptance in the sense of being tolerated. We want to feel that someone loves us, or at least cares about us, for what we are, regardless of whatever shortcomings we might have. We want to feel that other people have faith, trust, and confidence in us, are favorably impressed by what we do, and regard us as somehow worthy of their favorable attention. Since most, but certainly not all, people in our culture are reasonably well satisfied with respect to their physiological and affiliation needs, much of their behavior is intended to gain approval or affection of parents, peers, teachers, neighbors, business associates, employers, and others.

Need for Self-Esteem

Besides wanting others to think well of us, we want and need to think well of ourselves. While approval comes from an external source, self-esteem comes from within. Self-esteem refers to our need to feel significant, to have a sense of personal worth, through being looked up to, respected, admired, and possibly even envied a bit. It implies such things as the need for attention, recognition, status, self-confidence or faith in ourselves, and a favorable self-concept or a feeling that we measure up to the standards that we have set for ourselves. Although self-esteem is largely a subjective quality, a feeling we have about ourselves, it depends to a great extent on the responses (including the affection and approval) that we receive from others. Thus, the purpose of much human behavior is to impress other people so that we will be able to think more highly of ourselves. Self-esteem, as I am sure you recognize, is very much in line with what Adler referred to as a feeling of superiority (Adler 1973).

Need for Independence

Although we are dependent upon others for the satisfaction of most of our needs, we also have a need to feel free and independent, to lead our own lives, to set our own immediate goals, and to decide how we shall strive to attain them. This need, which involves gradually lessening our dependence upon others and extricating ourselves from their control, implies such things as self-assertion, self-expression, the release of one's creative energies, and the establishment of a personal identity. But most of all it pertains to the individual's capacity for self-determination.

This concept of self-determination or personal autonomy is central to the thinking of most humanists. They believe that freedom to choose is one of the most distinctively human characteristics and one of the most important. It is implicit in the very ideas of personal integrity and responsibility, justice, love, morality, and good citizenship. It is central to the notion of freedom to be oneself. The manner in which an individual uses his freedom is, of course, dependent upon a variety of environmental factors, including education. But to be free, or at least to feel free, is certainly one of our major goals (Rogers 1961, 1977).

Need for New Experiences

Along with our need for independence, we also have a need to move around and branch out mentally, to explore our environments and to satisfy our curiosity. This need is apparent in young children who ordinarily want to see and touch and maybe taste and feel whatever they come near. They want to find things out and try things out for themselves. But, while this need for new experiences is commonly associated with childhood, it helps to explain some of the behavior of many adults as well. It ties in with what we referred to earlier as a kind of general dissatisfaction with one's existing condition—that is, a kind of restlessness that, according to the humanists, is practically a universal trait. Hence, the desire on the part of many individuals to travel, meet new people, see new places, try new foods, attend theatres, museums, sporting events, etc., to alleviate their boredom or at least to break up the monotony of everyday living. In some cases, this desire for new experiences is satisfied rather easily—by reading, for example, or by watching television. In other cases, it underlies bizarre and sometimes antisocial behavior as the person (particularly the young person) seeks what he might refer to as "kicks."

Multimotivated Behavior

Many of the things that we do cannot be neatly attributed to one particular need. Therefore, much of our behavior is said to be *multi*motivated. This means that many of our activities have as their purpose the simultaneous satisfying of several needs or the attainment of several goals. Frequently, we are unaware of all the motives that are operating in a given situation, and if some of them were brought to our attention we might deny them.

Consider, for example, a young man who takes his date to the most exclusive restaurant in town and orders the most expensive items on the menu. If satisfying their hunger is his *only* purpose, why does he choose that particular restaurant and make those particular menu selections? Chances are that in addition to satisfying his physiological need for food, he is also trying to satisfy a few social or psychological needs. He might be trying to impress his friend with his affluence. He might be trying to create an image as a man about town who knows the "in" places. He might be trying to identify with the kinds of people who ordinarily patronize that establishment. His goals, in short, might include bolstering his self-esteem, winning the approval and affection of his companion, satisfying his need for new experiences, and perhaps a few other satisfactions that we have overlooked.

Expressive Behavior

Abraham Maslow (1970) makes an important distinction between behavior that is purposeful and that which is expressive. Purposeful behavior can be thought of as intentional. It is intended to fill some need, overcome some deficiency, or attain some goal. While most human behavior is of this coping, striving, goal-seeking variety, some of our most important, most personal, and most distinctively human behavior is expressive. Expressive behavior is so called because it expresses the way that a person feels or reflects the kind of person that he is. It is not always easy to classify a particular act as purposeful or expressive (and some of our behavior is a combination of both), but a few examples might help to clarify an important distinction between the two.

A person who writes a poem, or reads a poem, simply because he feels like doing so is engaging in expressive behavior. One who writes a poem to fulfill a class assignment or impress somebody is acting purposefully. A person who walks in the rain because there are not other means of transportation to get something needed from the store is also acting purposefully. One's behavior is more expressive when he walks in the rain simply because he enjoys walking in the rain. Expressive behavior, in short, is not a means to some further goal. It is an activity that is satisfying in and of itself. Strictly speaking, expressive behavior serves no useful purpose. It is simply a way in which an individual expresses his personality.

Laughing or crying when you are happy or sad, hugging or kissing a person to express your feelings toward that person, listening to music or playing a musical instrument for your own enjoyment, looking at a sunset, helping someone else and expecting nothing in return, and studying history simply because you like to study history are examples of expressive behavior. Much of the behavior of a self-actualizing person is of this type (Maslow 1970).

PERSONAL GROWTH

One of the basic assumptions of humanistic psychology is that human beings by their very nature are endowed with a tremendous potential for growth. There are, of course, limitations to what a person can become. But, according to the humanists, these limitations—whether imposed by heredity or environment or by the interaction of the two—are nowhere nearly as confining as they are sometimes thought to be. In fact, very few if any human beings come anywhere near to realizing their full potential. But the main source of their motivation is to do so.

As we noted at the beginning of this chapter, humanistic psychology claims that a person's most distinctively human goal, the one toward which all other intermediary goals are directed, is what has been called congruence, self-actualization, personal fulfillment, self-realization, etc. This goal also has been referred to simply as personal growth or development and in somewhat more sophisticated terms as "preservation and enhancement of the phenomenological self." Whatever terminology they might use, humanists are strongly inclined toward the position that a human being's paramount goal is to discover, develop, and express one's true self; to actualize one's potentialities; to become to the fullest extent possible what one is capable of becoming; and to lead the richest, fullest, most personally satisfying life possible (Rogers 1977, E. C. Kelly 1977).

Self-Preservation and Enhancement

In one of the earliest important books on humanistic psychology, Combs and Snygg (1959) develop the idea that the basic, constant, all-pervasive life purpose of every individual and the sole motive of all human behavior can be summarized in a few words: self-preservation and self-enhancement.

Just about everyone would agree that self-preservation is the most basic and fundamental of all human needs. But, as Adler pointed out, self-preservation for a human being involves something more than mere physical survival. A human being is a constantly changing person living in a constantly changing environment. We must, therefore, not only maintain ourselves in the present, but also enhance ourselves so that we will be able to maintain ourselves in the future. To live, we must grow. Maintenance or preservation and growth or enhancement of the self involve not only the organic but also the psychological aspects of our being.

Self-preservation and self-enhancement can be subdivided into four classes of more particular kinds of needs: physical security, emotional security, mastery, and status. While the needs for physical and emotional security correspond to self-preservation, the needs for mastery and status pertain more to self-enhancement. Each of these four can be broken down into even more specific kinds of needs, including some of those that we have already discussed. All of these needs taken together, moreover, add up to what Adler calls *perfection*, and their fulfillment is presumed in what Maslow calls self-actualization.

The Self

Since the self is such a central concept in humanistic views of motivation, let us examine this concept a little more closely. What exactly *is* this self that we are presumed to be striving to actualize?

The self is so utterly simple yet so tremendously complex that it does not lend itself to easy definition. Trying to explain in words what the self is is something like trying to define the personal pronouns I, my, or me. As the term is ordinarily used in humanistic psychology, the *self* refers to the aggregate of everything that you, for example, regard as distinctively yours. Thus, your self includes your body, your existing store of knowledge, your memories, your attitudes, your potentialities, your aspirations, feelings, experiences, and values. In short, your self includes whatever it is that distinguishes you from me or from anyone else.

In a very real sense, even your friends and relatives, your personal possessions, and other physical objects are among the components of your self. When a person states, for example, that music, or basketball, or Chicago, or his wife "will always be a part of me," he is expressing what humanists regard as a profound psychological truth.

The self, however, is more than a mere collection of parts. It is, rather, the synthesis, the organization, the interrelations of all the traits, qualities, characteristics, and experiences that go to make up an individual human being—the binding spirit, so to speak, that ties them together and gives them meaning.

According to the humanists, the individual self is, or should be, the beginning and the end of the educational and developmental processes. Since a person has only one life to live and one self to develop, his self is something that he must learn to respect and cultivate. Each individual, as well as those who have the responsibility for guiding his development, should realize that whoever he is, he is something special. He is someone who has never existed before and will never exist again. His purpose in life, as well as his overriding need, is to become to the fullest extent possible what he and he alone is capable of becoming, and to do what he and he alone is capable of doing (Bonney 1974; Rogers 1961, 1977).

Self-Concept

The self can be thought of as having two dimensions: what one really is and what one thinks or feels that one is. The latter is the person's self-concept—that is, one's personal, subjective impression of one's self. One's self-concept includes his feelings about himself, his attitudes toward himself, his evaluation of himself, and his ideas of how he fits into the general scheme of which he is a part.

A person's self-concept is both a *cause* of his or her present behavior and an *effect* of past experiences. It is an effect in that one's feelings about himself depend to a great extent on his previous history of success and failures, on the quality of his interaction with other people, and on what he thinks other people think of him. It is a cause in that one's self-concept is likely to have a greater bearing on his behavior than his objective status has. For example, a child who feels that he is too dumb to learn how to read will, in all probability, have a difficult time with reading even though his readiness test scores and general learning abilities are quite high. Similarly, the child who has been told repeatedly that he is bad can be expected to come to think of himself as bad, and continue or begin to act accordingly.

Much of our behavior is determined not so much by what we are, in objective reality, but by what we feel that we are. From the standpoint of personal adjustment and happiness, the individual who perceives himself as capable, intelligent, popular, and good looking—even though by any available objective standards he is dull, inept, ugly, and rejected—has a distinct advantage over his counterpart who objectively has these desirable characteristics but subjectively feels that he lacks them. Similarly, whether a person actually *is* loved (or accepted or inadequate or inferior) is not nearly as critical a factor as whether he *feels* loved (or inferior, etc.) In such areas as counseling and psychotherapy, as well as in home and classroom situations, humanistic psychologists regard the individual's self-concept as a primary consideration, maintaining that a change in the self-concept is often an essential first step in motivating the student toward more desirable forms of behavior.

The Self and Its Environments

Personal growth or self-fulfillment depends to a great extent on one's interaction with one's environment. At this point, we should recognize the distinction between physical and psychological environments. According to some humanistic psychologists, every person in effect inhabits two worlds. First there is the so-called public world of objective reality; this is the physical environment. Second, there is the individual's own largely subjective private world; this is the personal or psychological environment. The relationship between the two is shown in Figure 12.

A person's physical environment includes everything that exists outside himself whether he is aware of it or not. Your next-door neighbor and the inhabitants of China are parts of your physical environment. So are your TV set, the stores in your community, the pyramids of Egypt, and the moon. Your

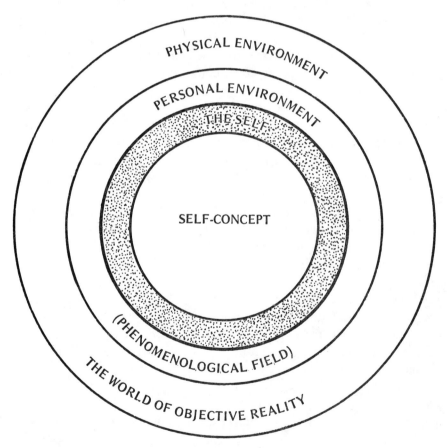

FIGURE 12.   The Self-Concept, the Self, and Its Environments.

psychological environment is that part of the total environment that affects you or concerns you or has meaning for you. It includes only those elements in the real (physical) environment that you perceive as having some bearing on you personally. For example, a fly in your room would be part of your physical environment, but if you are unaware of its presence, it would not be part of your psychological environment. The moment it lands on your forehead or otherwise distracts you, it enters your personal environment. At that point, it takes on a *meaning* for you that it previously did not have.

Personal Environment

Ordinarily, in a typical classroom all the students present share approximately the same physical environment. But their psychological environments might all be at least slightly different. Certain elements of the physical environment, such as the presence of a dictionary on the bookshelf, might not be part of a particular student's personal environment at all. He might not understand its purpose. He might never have even noticed it. As far as he is concerned, the book might just as well not be there. From a phenomenological standpoint, for him the book does not exist. It is not part of his phenomenological field, which is just another name for his personal environment. The student's phenomenological field might extend far beyond the classroom. It might include a number of things pertaining to football, for example, or horses, or volcanos, or other things in which he is interested. But it does not include the dictionary.

While one's physical environment usually remains fairly constant over a period of time, his psychological environment is constantly changing. A few words from the teacher, for example, might bring the dictionary right into the student's phenomenological (or perceptual) field. Once he perceives the relationship between the book and himself, once he comes to see how he can use it and how it can help him, the book becomes a part of his psychological environment. In a sense it becomes a part of himself and of his *life space.*

Life Space

The concept of life space is central to the theory of motivation formulated by Kurt Lewin (1890-1947). A person's life space, according to Lewin, includes all the factors that determine his behavior at any given moment. Objects or situations or other variables in the physical environment that do not affect his behavior are not part of his life space. Occupying a kind of central position in a person's life space is the self, the individual person, with his particular set of characteristics, including his memories, abilities, tensions, drives, needs, etc. Also present in the life space are goals which the person wants to attain; objects or situations that he wants to avoid; barriers that restrict his movements toward his goals and paths that he must follow to get what he wants (Lewin 1936, 1951).

To understand and predict a person's behavior, Lewin held that we must picture the person on a kind of map, such as the one shown in Figure 13. Such a map, which is a representation of the person's life space, shows the individual's position in relation to the goal toward which he is striving. As we have noted, the life

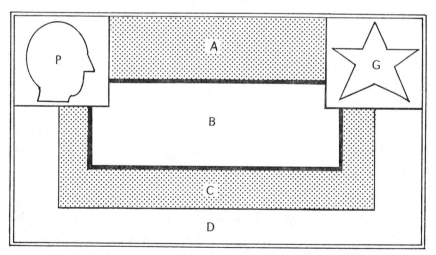

FIGURE 13. A life space. In this situation, a person (P) wants to reach a certain goal (G). Since he wishes to avoid areas A and C, which he perceives as repellent, and because the barriers around area B seem to be too difficult to overcome, he takes the route through area D.

space includes all the forces that are acting upon him at a given moment. It is to this pattern or field or configuration of forces, rather than to any one single element in the environment, to which the person reacts.

A person's goals are said to have *positive valence*, a term that Lewin adapted from topological mathematics. People tend to move toward areas in the life space that they expect will reduce their tensions or satisfy their needs. The objects and situations in the life space that the person wants to avoid have *negative valence.* In Figure 13, which is highly simplified for purposes of illustration, the person (P) wants to achieve a certain goal (G). To reach that goal, he must do either A, B, C, or D; that is, he must pass through one of those four areas. A and C have negative valence. If at all possible, he would like to avoid them. B has neither a strong positive nor a negative valence, but the barriers to B as represented by the thick boundary are very difficult to overcome. By taking route D, so to speak, the individual will have to travel somewhat farther, but he can reach G without going through A or C, and will only have to contend with the easier barriers between P and D and between D and G. The individual's problem is greater and more complex, of course, when he has two or more goals that are apparently exclusive or require two different paths.

Conflicts

In striving for personal growth, we frequently experience situations in which we are motivated simultaneously toward two or more goals that are incompatible with one another. Our life space or our phenomenological field is so structured or is perceived in such a way that we cannot always have everything we want. Conflicts arise because the forces in our personal environment have attractive features that we want to approach as well as repulsive features that we would like to avoid. Thus, there are the four basic kinds of conflicts that we discussed in Chapter 4: approach/approach, avoidance/avoidance, approach/avoidance, and double approach/avoidance.

The manner in which an individual resolves or attempts to

resolve any of these conflicts depends on a number of variables in his own background and personality. But perhaps more than anything else a person's behavior in a conflict situation depends upon his own set of values and the priorities that he assigns to his various needs or goals. The relative strength of various goals and the conditions under which certain needs take precedence over others are matters to which a great many humanistic psychologists have addressed themselves. Among the best known of those who have done so is Abraham Maslow.

MASLOW'S THEORIES

Few, if any, recent psychological theories have had a greater impact or a wider acceptance than those formulated by Abraham Maslow (1908–1970). Maslow was not only one of the founders of humanistic psychology but for many years remained one of its acknowledged leaders and respected spokesmen. So closely was he identified with the movement that he came to be called Mr. Humanistic Psychology. He has also been referred to as Mr. Self-Actualization. Maslow was influenced considerably in his thinking by the views of Alfred Adler (Ansbacher 1970). But Maslow's theory of motivation is far more than a mere extension or modification of Individual Psychology.

Prepotency of Needs

Like his fellow humanists, Maslow believed that every person is constantly striving for either growth, self-expansion, or self-enhancement. Growth, as Maslow saw it, is essentially a matter of need gratification. That is, growth is achieved by progressively satisfying higher and then still higher kinds of needs. As Figure 14 shows, Maslow identified five basic human needs which he arranged in a hierarchy of prepotency as follows:

1. Physiological well-being
2. Safety

3. Love
4. Esteem
5. Self-Actualization.

These needs and the corresponding goals or purposes of behavior are not acquired, but are innate components of human nature. Because they have varying degrees of potency, higher needs do not emerge until the lower ones are reasonably well satisfied. As we suggested earlier in this chapter, people are apparently never satisfied. No sooner is one need satisfied than another (higher) need is, as it were, clamoring for our attention and demanding its satisfaction. This is how we grow (Maslow 1970, 1977).

Physiological Well-Being

The most prepotent of all human needs are those which are physiological in nature. Among these, of course, are the needs for

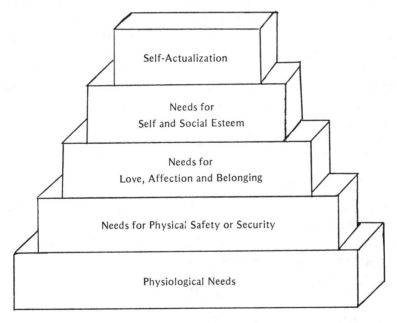

FIGURE 14. Maslow's Hierarchy of Needs. To attain self-actualization, the individual must first satisfy the four lower-order needs.

food, shelter, etc., that were mentioned earlier in this chapter. They are said to be the most prepotent because they are absolutely essential for self-preservation in the strict biological sense of the term. Chronologically, they are also the first needs to affect behavior; for an infant, they might well be the only needs. If they are not satisfied, the person dies (in which case there is not much point in discussing his needs for security, affection, status, or self-fulfillment).

As long as physiological needs are unfulfilled, they literally dominate the human organism. The other needs remain dormant, as it were, and have relatively little effect on behavior. If, for example, a person is desperately hungry, having had nothing whatsoever to eat for the past week or so, the chances are that he is not much concerned about love or esteem or self-enhancement. The only thing that he really needs is food; everything else is secondary. All of his behavior is likely to be directed toward that one end.

Maslow suggests that very few people in the United States ever find themselves in the situation of being so extremely hungry that their continued existence is seriously threatened. In our culture, when a person claims to be hungry ("I'm dying for a pizza"), he is probably expressing something less than a genuine life-or-death need for food. Still, we must keep in mind the fact that even in the affluent United States there are far too many children (and adults) who go to bed hungry and come to school hungry.

When one's physiological needs are satisfied, they cease to function as needs. They no longer motivate us. But we are still far from being perfectly satisfied with our overall situation. ("Not by bread alone does man live.") Once the physiological needs are met, a second set of needs begins to emerge. These are the safety needs. In a very real sense, according to Maslow, the satisfaction of the lower need *causes* the next higher need to become operative. Thus, it is not only the deprivation or the lack of something that motivates us. Gratification of a need is equally important as a motivator in that it releases the individual from the domination of a lower need and permits him to direct more of his energies toward a higher goal.

Safety

The second set of needs to emerge—the safety or security needs—refers to the individual's need to feel assured that his physiological needs will be satisfied in the future. Safety needs are apparent in very young children who naturally want and need someone whom they can depend upon to help them and to protect them. They want and need to feel that they can rely on certain people (particularly their parents) to do certain things (to provide them with food and comfort, for example) with a fair degree of regularity. This need for security is manifest in the child's fondness for routine, rhythmic activities with consistent, predictable outcomes. Such activities help him to feel that he is living in an orderly world and that he can count on certain things occurring in the future because they have happened in the past. For example, although he may have heard a particular story dozens of times in the past, a child ordinarily enjoys hearing it again and again. As any storyteller will testify, the child is likely to become upset when even a minor detail is changed or omitted, or when the teller changes the story so that it does not end exactly as he had anticipated.

Although the safety need is not always so readily discernible in the behavior of adults, people never outgrow their needs for stability, consistency, protection, order, freedom from fear and uncertainty, etc. As is the case with physiological needs, to the extent that these safety needs are not fulfilled, they practically dominate the person and become his main if not only concern. For example, for a person who is seriously ill or frightened because of a rash of recent burglaries in his neighborhood, self-preservation is likely to be of far greater moment than self-enhancement. The same might be true of an individual who foresees the loss of his job, what he regards as an impending financial disaster, or some other threat to his well-being.

According to Maslow, a person who is experiencing great fear or anxiety is likely to direct most of his physical and mental energies toward the satisfaction of his safety needs. Just as a person who is desperately and dangerously hungry might eat or try to eat just about anything, so might a person who feels extremely insecure resort to drastic measures to alleviate that feeling. When and only when the safety needs are reasonably well satisfied does the third need begin to have much of an effect on one's behavior. Again, it is the gratification of a lower need (Need Number 2) that brings about a higher need, the need for love. Maslow recognizes that a person does not satisfy any one need permanently and completely before going on to the next, but as one level of needs becomes relatively satisfied, the next becomes proportionately more potent.

Love

Assuming that our physiological needs are taken care of and that we feel reasonably secure about the future, we are still not satisfied. We still want and need to grow. At this stage, the need for love begins to make its appearance as a major determiner of human behavior. The term *love* in this context refers to the need for affection, for a feeling of affiliation, for a close relationship with at least one other person, for a feeling that someone else cares about us and values us for what we are.

Since most people in our culture are reasonably well satisfied with respect to their physiological and safety needs, Maslow believes that the frustration of the love need is the most common cause of maladjustment and severe psychopathology. It is also the goal toward which perhaps the greatest part of a person's behavior is directed. Maslow's belief in this regard is borne out by a survey in which a group of college students were asked to indicate on a checklist what they wanted most out of life. Heading the list of their responses were the kinds of things presently under discussion—love, friendship, affection, a feeling of belonging, etc. Further down on the list, and in the opinion of the respondents of less personal concern, were such things as money, material possessions, job security, etc. A similar survey of senior citizens yielded approximately the same results. While economic insecurity and concern for one's physical well-being are unquestionably major problems for many older people, like younger people they seem to perceive loneliness and the lack of close personal ties as among their chief concerns.

As we suggested earlier, whether or not a person *is in fact* loved or unloved, accepted or rejected, is not as critical as his *feeling* that his love needs are or are not being fulfilled. Innumerable individuals of all ages who, by any objective standards, *are* loved, do not feel loved or loved enough. Consequently, a large portion of their day-to-day activities are geared, directly or indirectly, toward satisfying this need and attaining the corresponding goal.

Esteem

Adults, adolescents, and older children want not only the kind of warmth and affection and protection with which a young child might be satisfied, they want also to be looked up to, respected, and admired. Thus, satisfaction of the love need gives rise to the need for esteem. Under this heading, Maslow includes the need for self-esteem and the esteem of others. The need for self-esteem implies the needs for self-respect, self-confidence, personal adequacy, a sense of achievement, competence, mastery, independence, etc. Esteem from others implies the needs for status, recognition, approval, attention, domination, prestige, and the like. These needs, of course, are those which play such an important role in Alfred Adler's Individual Psychology. Once the need for love is satisfied, most human behavior is directed toward these kinds of goals.

Maslow recognized that departure from, or reversals in, the hierarchy of prepotency do sometimes occur. To some people, for example, esteem seems to be more important than love. Or the need for love might take precedence over the need for security. Moreover, we should remember that most behavior is multi-motivated, directed toward the simultaneous satisfaction of more than one need, and that no need is ever permanently or perfectly satisfied. Still, Maslow believed that personal growth toward self-actualization ordinarily does follow the steps that he has mentioned and in the order that he mentions them.

Most people, according to Maslow, never advance much beyond what we might call Step Number 4 in their psychological development. Life for them is either a struggle for survival or security, or a constant striving to satisfy their needs for love and esteem. Most of their behavior, therefore, has as its purpose the satisfaction of one or some of these four lower-order needs. Since the satisfaction of these needs depends on other people, most of their behavior is said to be outer-directed. Most people, in other words, are so preoccupied with their needs for security and affection and recognition, and expend so much of their energy trying to satisfy these needs, that they never really have a chance to fulfill themselves or even to *be* themselves.

Self-Actualization

When (and usually *only* when) an individual is reasonably well satisfied with respect to his lower-order needs does self-actualization begin to emerge as a major motivator. As we have already suggested, it is in fact the very satisfaction of those needs that brings on this highest need or causes it to be felt. This, of course, is in keeping with the principle that we are never completely satisfied but want to keep growing.

Self-actualization represents what humanists regard as our loftiest and most distinctively human aspiration. It refers to a person's striving to become what he is capable of becoming, or to be that which he truly is: namely, himself. The idea here is that having satisfied one's four basic needs, the individual no longer has to channel the biggest part of his activities in those directions. He is now free to concentrate, as it were, on the development of his own potentialities, or the expression of his own individuality. He is ready, in other words, to begin living life to the fullest.

Because his lower-order needs have already been fairly well satisfied, the person at the self-actualizing level is no longer so dependent upon others. Consequently, he is inner- rather than outer-directed. His behavior is intrinsically rather than extrinsically motivated. Having satisfied his needs for love and esteem, for example, he does not have to go out of his way to impress others or to try to win their acceptance or approval. He is now free to be himself, and to live life in what for him is the most satisfying way possible.

Whether or not he is consciously aware of it, every person, according to Maslow, wants to "make something" of himself. Just exactly what it is that he wants to make is, of course, a highly individual matter. Similarly, every person wants to get something out of life and attain what is commonly referred to as happiness. But precisely what it is that happiness means to a person is again an individual matter. Thus, while everyone is striving for self-actualization, everyone has a different self to actualize. Every person has a unique combination of potentialities to develop. Depending upon a variety of circumstances and conditions, a person might try to find fulfillment as a teacher, student, musician, bricklayer, American, Muslim, or in any one of countless other ways. A woman might achieve a degree of personal fulfillment by having a baby, painting a picture, running for political office, planting petunias, or in just about any other way that she finds personally satisfying. Self-actualization, then, is not so much a matter of what a person does, but how that person feels about it.

Metaneeds

Earlier in this chapter, we noted the distinction Maslow makes between purposeful and expressive behavior. As you may recall, purposeful (or, as he also calls it, coping) behavior is a means to some end. It is directed toward overcoming some deficiency and reaching some goal or solving some problem. It is largely determined by the external environment and depends on circumstances outside the individual. Expressive behavior, on the other hand, is often unmotivated or purposeless in that it is not intended to fill any particular deficiency or to reach any particular goal. It is, rather, open, spontaneous, unaffected behavior that reflects the individual's personality and expresses his feelings. Insofar as a person is striving to satisfy one or some of his lower needs, his behavior is likely to be purposeful. One whose lower needs have been sufficiently satisfied, as we have noted, is motivated principally by the need to find fulfillment as an individual and to become a genuine, authentic self. His behavior, therefore, is likely to be largely expressive.

To distinguish the needs underlying self-actualization from those that motivate us toward purposeful behavior, Maslow has coined the term *metaneeds.* Metaneeds do not represent any specific deficiencies. They pertain to a person's *being* in the sense of personal fulfillment rather than to a person's *becoming* in the sense of coping, striving, goal-seeking. Metaneeds are essentially values that give meaning and richness to a person's life. Among them are such things as the person's need for truth, goodness, and beauty, as well as the need to transcend himself, to give of himself to someone else, to devote himself to something outside of himself, and to have experiences of a somewhat mystical nature. As Maslow puts it, it is, in a sense, as necessary for a person to live in beauty rather than ugliness as it is to have food and rest. Although everyone has these metaneeds, many do not recognize them and do not satisfy them because of the greater potency and urgency of the lower needs (Maslow 1971).

Being and Deficiency Needs

Maslow refers to the lower needs as D (for deficiency) needs, and to the higher or metaneeds as B (for being) needs. He makes a distinction, for example, between what he calls D-love and B-love. D-love has already been discussed. This is the third of the lower-order needs. It represents a deficiency that the individual tries to overcome. It implies wanting to *receive* affection. B-love, which is more characteristic of a self-actualizer, is more a matter of *giving.* It implies having affection for another person and wanting to help that person while expecting nothing in return. B-love is expressive rather than purposeful. With B-love, we are not attracted to another person because he or she can do us some good but because we can do him or her some good. With B-love, unlike D-love, we do not perceive the other person as an instrument that we can use to fill our needs. Rather, we love them for themselves, unconditionally, and with no strings attached. We love them for what they are, for their very being.

A similar distinction is made between D- and B-cognition. Deficiency cognition refers to a person's need to know something as a means of attaining some goals. The knowledge is perceived as a tool for satisfying one's physiological, safety, D-love, or esteem needs. It implies learning for the sake of putting one's knowledge to some more or less practical use. B-cognition, on the other hand, involves learning as an end in itself, the seeking of knowledge for its own sake. It implies learning for personal satisfaction or enjoyment regardless of any use to which the knowledge might be put.

EDUCATIONAL IMPLICATIONS

From the standpoint of humanistic psychology, classroom motivation is largely a process of helping the student to perceive that certain learning experiences can help him to become what he is capable of becoming and what he wants to become: a fully functioning, happy, self-actualizing person. Motivation is not so much a matter of creating new goals for the student as it is one of building on existing goals. It is largely a process of helping him to help himself with respect to his various needs. But these needs, according to Maslow, must be met sequentially.

Until and unless the child's physiological needs are met, it is unlikely that he will be motivated by the need for approval or self-esteem. If a child comes to school without breakfast because his parents are too poor to give him any, or if he arrives very sleepy because his parents kept him awake the night before with their fighting, it is doubtful that he will set forth a great deal of effort to please the teacher or to gain the recognition of his peers. Similarly, if the child feels insecure because his parents are seriously discussing divorce, or if he feels rejected by his parents and peers, it is perhaps unreasonable to expect him to focus his attention on the subject matter that the teacher would like him to learn.

The policies of particular schools with respect to providing free or inexpensive breakfasts and hot lunches vary from place to place of course. While school officials might be limited in the help that they can give to a child in satisfying his physiological needs, they are in a much better position to render assistance in helping him to meet his personal, social, and emotional needs. Humanistic psychology, therefore, lends strong support to the notion that teachers and school administrators should be very much concerned with the student's needs for affection, self-confidence, self-respect, a feeling of belonging, etc., if for no other reason than that the satisfaction of these needs is a kind of prerequisite for optimum scholastic achievement.

Unmotivated Students

We sometimes speak loosely of the student who is unmotivated or who lacks motivation. Strictly speaking, there is no such thing as an unmotivated student or a human being who lacks motivation. Every person is motivated in that he has needs that he is trying to fill and goals that he is striving to attain. All human beings, moreover, are motivated by essentially the same kinds of needs and goals. We differ in the means that we employ to satisfy these needs, in the priorities that we assign our various goals, and in our perceptions of what constitutes satisfaction. But simply because we are human beings, the purpose of much (but not all) of our behavior is to satisfy the same kinds of needs that everyone else is trying to satisfy.

For example, everyone has a need for attention. But the manner in which a particular student attempts to gain attention is not necessarily the means that the teacher would prefer to have him use for that purpose. Moreover, the goal that a student wants to pursue here and now (e.g., attention) is not always the goal that his teacher wants him to pursue in her classroom (e.g., achievement). Thus, classroom motivation problems arise from the fact that the students are not always motivated to learn or do what their teachers would like them to. The students are motivated, and maybe highly motivated, but toward something other than scholastic achievement.

Highly Motivated Students

To help the student who is *not* motivated toward scholastic achievement, we should try to understand the goals of students who *are* so motivated. Consider, for example, the student who studies diligently and tries hard to do well in all his schoolwork. What are his motives? Chances are that he has several, which are operating simultaneously. He might, for example, be intent upon pleasing his parents and winning their approval. He might also be trying to gain the recognition of his peers. At the same time, he might be trying to satisfy a need for achievement and self-esteem. He might be trying to prove to himself that he can do as well as anyone and better than most of his classmates.

Our highly motivated friend might also perceive the practical value of the material that he is learning as a long-range means toward satisfying future security and social needs. He might recognize learning as a necessity toward a chosen career or as a stepping stone toward financial independence and social success. Finally, he might be attempting to satisfy his own curiosity, to expand himself mentally, or simply because he enjoys learning for its own sake and derives personal satisfaction from the subjects to which he has been introduced.

Self-Motivation

According to humanistic psychologists such as Carl Rogers (1969), Arthur Combs (1974), and Abraham Maslow (1968), the highest and most desirable form of motivation is that which comes from within the individual. Such motivation is said to be intrinsic and the consequent behavior self-motivated.

Humanists maintain that learning is a natural and a normal process. It is something that a person wants to do to attain his goals. Humanists are disturbed by what they see as the preoccupation of teachers with forcing, bribing, threatening, or shaming students as a means of motivating them to learn material that the students do not particularly want to learn and see no value in learning because it apparently has no significance or meaning in their own lives. Instead, the humanists believe, teachers ought to focus more of their attention on helping students to learn the kinds of things that they want to learn and feel that they should be learning here and now. If the students see the value of the material that they are expected to learn, if they perceive how it will help them to become the people they want to become, then they will want to learn it and will learn, without any coaxing and, perhaps, even without much direction from the teacher. Otherwise, they will have to be motivated by some artificial system of reward and punishment. In such a situation, humanists fear, students might come to regard the inherently meaningless subject matter to which they are exposed as an obstacle rather than an aid to their individual self-fulfillment (Schmuck 1974).

Self-Development

Humanistic educators insist that teachers should capitalize on, rather than frustrate, the student's drive to realize his own potentialities and to develop the most adequate self possible. They believe that teachers should devise ways of helping each student to come to perceive learning as a means of attaining *his* goals rather than goals that have been imposed on him by school administrators. In this respect, teachers should provide opportunities for the student to come to think of himself as a responsible, contributing member of a little democracy and not as an object to be manipulated (motivated) by an authority figure.

The humanistic ideal is a classroom where each student can and will develop a favorable self-concept, a sense of personal worth, and a feeling of responsibility for his own education. He should be given sufficient freedom to plan, carry out, and evaluate his own educational program without fear of criticism or failure. He should, moreover, have ample opportunities for experiencing success and a feeling that he is accomplishing something that he himself considers worthwhile.

The humanistic views of motivation and human nature have been criticized as romantic. Perhaps they are. But they do suggest a set of ideals toward which students and teachers alike might well be encouraged to move (Read and Simon 1975).

RECOMMENDED READING

Bonney, Merl. "Self Becoming as Self Growth." *Theory into Practice, 13*: 329–334, 1974. A short, easy-to-read article on the concept of self-actualization and its applicability to the areas of education and human development.

Buhler, Charlotte. "Human Life Goals in the Humanistic Perspective." In Avila, Donald L., *et al.*, Eds., *The Helping Relationship Sourcebook.* Boston: Allyn and Bacon, 1971. This article is organized around twelve behavior patterns that contribute to the goals that individuals set for themselves and to their personal fulfillment.

Frankl, Viktor, E. *Man's Search for Meaning.* Boston: Beacon Press, 1962. Develops the thesis that the main concern of human beings is not to experience pleasure or avoid pain but to find a system of values that will give meaning to life. Maintains that the purpose of life is not simply self-actualization but self-transcendence: the giving of oneself to something outside oneself.

Fromm, Erich. *The Art of Loving.* New York: Bantam Books, 1963. One of the most popular of Fromm's books and one of the most widely read books on the subject. Deals with what he regards as the "only satisfactory answer to the problems of human existence." Combines Freudian with humanistic insights.

Kolesnik, Walter B. *Humanism and/or Behaviorism in Education.* Boston: Allyn and Bacon, 1975. Summarizes the basic principles and classroom applications of humanism, compares them with those of behaviorism, and shows how these two systems can be integrated.

Maslow, Abraham. *Motivation and Personality.* New York: Harper and Row, 1970. 2nd ed. Commonly regarded as the most authoritative book available on self-actualization, this book centers on Maslow's theory of motivation and psychological growth.

Maslow, Abraham. "Some Educational Implications of the Humanistic Psychologies." *Harvard Educational Review, 38*: 685–696, 1968. As the title of this article suggests, Maslow shows how teachers can use humanistic principles in the classroom. The article includes a discussion of the relative merits of intrinsic and extrinsic motivation.

Purkey, William. *Self Concept and School Achievement.* Englewood Cliffs, N.J.: Prentice-Hall, 1970. A short, nontechnical book centering on the relationship between self-concept and success in school. Discusses the nature and growth of the self and includes some practical suggestions for teachers.

Read, Donald A., and Simon, Sydney B., Eds. *Humanistic Education Sourcebook.* Englewood Cliffs, N.J.: Prentice-Hall, 1975. A collection of articles on the basic theory and practical implications of humanistic education. A convenient source of information about the views and recommendations of several humanistic educators and psychologists.

Rogers, Carl. *On Becoming a Person.* Boston: Houghton Mifflin, 1961. In this book, one of the founders of and best-known representatives of humanistic psychology sets forth his views on human nature and the process of becoming what one is capable of becoming. Rogers is perhaps best known for his work in the areas of nondirective counseling and encounter groups. This book is a useful introduction to his theories and recommendations.

Rogers, Carl, and Skinner, B. F. "Some Issues Concerning the Control of Human Behavior: A Symposium." In Glock, Marvin D., Ed., *Guiding Learning: Readings in Educational Psychology.* New York: John Wiley, 1971. Originally published in *Science* (74: 1057–1066, 1956), this article presents the contrasting views of Skinner and Rogers on the ways in which science can and should be used to influence, change, mold, or control the behavior of human beings. A classic of psychological literature.

Schlosser, Courtney, D., Ed., *The Person in Education: A Humanistic Approach*. New York: Macmillan, 1976. Part I of this book of readings includes a series of articles on the historical, philosophical, psychological, and sociological foundations of humanism. Part II, dealing with the educational implications of humanism, includes articles on teaching and learning, the curriculum, and the kind of environment recommended for humanistic education.

CHAPTER 7: PREVIEW QUESTIONS

(After you have finished reading Chapter 7, you should be able to answer the following.)

1. What is the difference between intrinsic and extrinsic motivation? How are they related to work and play? To interests and incentives?

2. Does interest necessarily imply enjoyment? Why or why not? Can a person be interested in something that he actually dislikes? Why? How?

3. What are John Dewey's views on interest? On making schoolwork interesting? On the relationship between interest and effort? What does he mean by *genuine* interest?

4. What is the source of our interests? How do they develop? What are some factors on which they depend? How are they related to maturation? To learning?

5. What are some common interests of children in general? Of adolescents in general?

6. What are some means of ascertaining the particular interests of particular individuals?

7. Is interest in a subject necessary for learning? Why or why not? What are two basic strategies for trying to interest a student in a subject?

8. What are Dewey's views on the relationship between subject matter and problem-solving? What kinds of classroom activities does he recommend?

9. What are pros and cons of fun and games in the classroom?

10. Why do individuals differ from one another with respect to curiosity?

11. What are some classroom conditions that are conducive to the development of healthy curiosity?

12. What happens when we pay attention to something? What are some means of attracting or maintaining a person's attention?

13. How are interest and attention related to the mechanism of identification? To the concept of personal involvement?

14. What are psychophysical factors that affect attention? Ecological factors? Collative factors?

15. What is cognitive dissonance? Why are teachers advised to create doubts or tensions in their students deliberately under certain conditions?

16. What are inquiry or discovery methods of teaching? What are their alleged advantages with respect to classroom motivation?

17. Select a school subject in which you are very much interested and which you might want to teach. Explain as you would to a person who claims to have no interest whatsoever in that subject why she should study it or what good it will do her.

18. Recall the elementary or high school subject you found most interesting. Was it the subject matter itself or the way in which your teacher presented it that accounted for your interest?

CHAPTER SEVEN

Intrinsic Motivation

In the last five chapters, we have drawn on Freudian, Adlerian, behavioral, cognitive, and humanistic psychology for some insights into the why of human behavior. We noted some classroom implications of each of these systems, but the major emphasis has been on understanding such factors as the goals, needs, perceptions, and unconscious motives of our students. In this and the next chapter, we shift our attention to strategies or techniques that can be used to influence student behavior. Although we cannot neatly classify every possible motivational strategy as either intrinsic or extrinsic, for purposes of analysis and discussion we can group some of them into one or another of these two categories.

Extrinsic motivation, you will recall, involves a goal or a reward external to the behavior itself. It implies the use of incentives such as money, recognition, or good report-card grades that an individual expects to receive from some outside source as a consequence of performing certain specified tasks in a satisfactory manner. A classic example of extrinsically motivated behavior is working at a job that one does not particularly enjoy primarily for the sake of financial remuneration.

Incentives, of course, are the motivational device on which our schools, as well as our national economy, have traditionally relied most heavily. Educators who are inclined toward a behavioral system of psychology continue to recommend the judicious use of incentives, otherwise_ known as reinforcers. But even many behaviorists, as well as most other educational psychologists, would prefer to have teachers make more use of intrinsic motivation. In behavioral terms, intrinsic motivation can be thought of as essentially a matter of reinforcement from within.

Extrinsic motivation is treated more fully in the next chapter. In this one, we examine some principles and procedures of intrinsic motivation, beginning with the concept of interest.

INTEREST

Ask the first ten experienced teachers or educational psychologists that you meet how to motivate students or attract and hold their attention and the chances are you will be advised to make your classroom work interesting. Ask them how to prevent the occurrence of classroom misbehavior and you are likely to get the same answer. Surely, this is a very good answer as far as it goes. But what do we mean by interesting and how can teachers *make* schoolwork interesting?

Interest and Incentives

Interest is related to intrinsic motivation much as incentives are to extrinsic motivation. A person is said to be interested or intrinsically motivated when he recognizes the value that is inherent in a particular activity in and of itself. The activity is automatically self-rewarding. A person acts because of motives from within when he derives pleasure or some sort of satisfaction from the very process of engaging in the activity. Thus, an intrinsically motivated person does not need any external pressures or inducements, promises or threats, to behave as he does.

The classic example of intrinsically motivated behavior is free, spontaneous play. Parents ordinarily do not have to go out of their way to motivate their children to play. Children—and for that matter adults—play because they want to. They like to. They enjoy the activity. They are interested in it.

Actually, the line between play and work is not always clear. Neither is the corresponding distinction between extrinsic and intrinsic motivation. For example, professional athletes, musicians, actors, and others who play for money are motivated extrinsically. So are children and adults whose main preoccupation in playing a game is to win for the sake of the accompanying prize or other incentive. Such individuals, however, might still derive enough personal satisfaction from their activities so that their motives for playing well are at least partly intrinsic.

Most of the things that we do cannot be neatly categorized as either intrinsically or extrinsically motivated. Most human behavior involves a combination of the two. A person might work primarily for the money needed to keep himself and his family alive but still enjoy his job very much and be greatly interested in the work that he is doing. The difference between the two basic forms of motivation, therefore, is often simply a matter of degree or relative emphasis. Consequently, there is no dichotomy between interest and incentives in classroom motivation. Teachers are well advised to think of the two, not in either/or terms but as complementing one another (Avila and Purkey 1971).

Intrinsically Motivated Students

In a classroom situation, intrinsically motivated students want to learn—not primarily to please their parents or teachers and not primarily for the sake of gaining a reward or avoiding punishment, but simply because they want to. Such students do not perceive learning primarily or exclusively as a stepping stone to economic or social success, or as a means toward some further end. For such people, learning is its own reward. It is satisfying in and of itself. It is something like looking at a beautiful sunset, or swimming, or listening to one's favorite music.

Students who are motivated from within might *incidentally* win recognition or approval for their accomplishments, and they might someday put the knowledge and skills that they have acquired to practical use. But these extrinsic benefits are not their first or main consideration. The intrinsically motivated student reads novels, for example, or works out mathematical problems, or tries to learn how to cook because he finds these activities interesting, enjoyable, and personally fulfilling. Since he neither wants, expects, nor requires any external reinforcement for doing these things, his behavior is said to be inner- rather than outer-directed. In terms of the distinction made in Chapter 6, his behavior is more expressive than purposeful or goal-seeking (Maslow 1970).

Role of Interests

Intrinsic motivation or interest in a subject is by no means absolutely necessary to the learning of that subject. Through selective reinforcement and the wise use of incentives, as we shall see in the next chapter, students *can* and often *will* learn material even though they do not especially enjoy it or see any value in learning it. Some teachers believe that students should be required to learn material that is uninteresting, not only because it will be good for them in the future, but also because of the disciplinary factors involved. Learning to do things that you do not enjoy doing and that you might find positively boring, difficult, or downright unpleasant, it has been argued, is a good preparation for Life in the Real World.

Down through the centuries, however, from the time of the ancient Greeks and Romans onward, great educators have recognized the value of interest as an aid to learning and an effective motivational tool. Most contemporary educationists and psychologists would, I believe, agree that, whereas interest might not be a *necessary* condition for learning, it is potentially one of the most useful and desirable means of stimulating scholastic achievement.

Pleasure Factor

Interest is commonly thought of as somehow involving amusement, enjoyment, or fun. Though this is frequently the case, it is not always or necessarily so. Certainly the pleasure factor might help to explain our interest in music, art, good food, or the opposite sex. But some of the things in which we might have a strong interest are really not very pleasant at all. In fact, we might be very much interested in certain matters that are actually quite repugnant. For example, I believe that most of us are genuinely interested in the threat of war, crime, disease, poverty, inflation, unemployment, natural disasters, accidents, pollution, corruption, and other matters that are hardly a source of enjoyment. The reason for this interest is our feeling that somehow these events or situations might affect us personally. Somehow, we believe, these matters could have some bearing on our own welfare or happiness.

Interest, then, seems to depend not so much on the pleasure that we derive from an experience as on the perception of a relationship between ourselves and some object or event or situation or possibility outside us. We'll return to the fun factor in interest and motivation shortly. For the moment, let's focus on the idea that the more critical factor in interest seems to be personal involvement in, and concern with the consequences of, some activity.

Personal Consequences

Even though he might not enjoy being blocked or tackled or thrown for a 10-yard loss, a football player is ordinarily very much interested in the game that he is playing. He is interested because he is involved in the activity and because he cares about the outcome. He perceives a relationship between what he is presently doing and what he would like to have happen. He feels that winning the game (or playing it well) will somehow be to his advantage or will contribute to his personal satisfaction. Perhaps his image or his self-concept is at stake. Perhaps he is counting on the outcome of the game to help to satisfy his needs for recognition, approval, power, or superiority. In any event, he is interested because he *cares* how the game turns out.

The avid spectator in the stands is also interested in the outcome of the game, very likely because he somehow identifies with one of the teams and is thus involved vicariously. Because his team represents his school or city or state, he wants them to win. The closer this identification, the more the fan cares, the more strongly he feels that he has something at stake in the outcome, the more attentive, absorbed, and excited he is likely to become. Similarly, the person who identifies with some of the characters in a movie or a television program or a novel cares how their activities turn out. He is interested in what they are doing because he feels that somehow what happens to them happens to him. Vicariously, he has a stake in the outcome of their activities.

If a fictional character with whom we identify experiences some tragedy or disappointment, we might feel bad—but we *are* interested. We are likely to be even more interested in the fortunes and misfortunes of our flesh-and-blood friends and relatives. But most of all, I suspect, we are interested in situations the consequences of which do or are likely to touch us personally. Although we might differ from one another with respect to our interest in sports, literature, politics, etc., there is one thing in which each of us has a strong and lasting interest: namely, our selves.

Dewey's Views

John Dewey conceives of interest as primarily a unified form of self-expressive activity. To him, the concepts of personal growth or development and interest are practically inseparable. To him, interest has no necessary implications of pleasure or entertainment. Rather, the critical element is the identification of one's self with some end, goal, or purpose and with an activity that serves as a means to that end. Anything that is initially neutral or even repellent to an individual becomes a matter of interest when it is perceived as a means to some desired end. According to Dewey, any impulse, habit, or experience that generates a purpose having sufficient force to move a person to strive for its realization becomes an interest (Dewey 1975).

With respect to education, Dewey rejects the traditional notion of trying to make schoolwork interesting by the use of what he called "external attractions" or what we today might call gimmicks. He also rejects the idea that teachers should first select the subject matter to be learned and then try to develop the students' interest in it. Instead of having teachers try to *make* subject matter interesting, Dewey preferred to have them teach subject matter that already is interesting to the students. In other words, he recommended that the subject matter be selected in relation to the students' present experiences, abilities, needs, concerns, and problems. He believed that the material should be presented in such a way as to enable the students to appreciate its bearing on, relationship to, and value for something that they already regard as significant.

Opposed to the artificial, transitory, superficial, interests that temporarily capture the attention of students because of their novelty, sensationalism, or entertainment value, Dewey preferred the use of "genuine" interests. Such interests arise from the individual student's natural tendencies toward physical, constructive, intellectual, and social activities. Genuine interests are directed toward something of value to the individual, as the individual recognizes that his personal well-being is somehow tied to or dependent upon the outcome of the activity. According to Dewey, interest is legitimate in education only when it fosters the students' development. Whatever the individual perceives as contributing to his development or to the attainment of his goals *is* interesting and need not be artificially made so (Dewey 1975).

DEVELOPMENT OF INTERESTS

If teachers are to build on and expand students' existing interests, they need to know what their present interests are. Individual students differ as widely among themselves with respect to their interests as they do in the other aspects of their personal development. One's particular interests depend upon such factors as age, sex, mental abilities, socioeconomic background, family and peer-group interests, the kind of community in which one lives, and the opportunities one has had for developing new interests or cultivating old ones.

We are not born with particular interests; they are learned.

They are acquired as a consequence of our experiences, of our interaction with our environment, especially with other people. Still, at various stages of human development, there are certain interests that are practically universal among children and young people in contemporary American society. To a certain extent, such interests might be regarded as a function, or at least a concomitant, of normal, natural processes of maturation.

Interests, Maturation, and Learning

As their experiences broaden and they approach maturity, children's interests change. The particular interests of a fifteen year old are likely to be different from those of a five year old simply because the one has lived ten years longer than the other and some significant biological changes have taken place in the interim. During that ten-year interval, the individual has not only been growing up in accordance with the natural laws of human development in a physiological sense but he also has been learning. Thus, by the age of fifteen—or, for that matter, by a much younger age—the individual might have learned through selective reinforcement, systematic modeling, and other instructional techniques to be interested in sports or cars or music or what have you.

It is not always possible to disentangle the effects of maturation from those of learning on the development of interests. Undoubtedly the two go together. But, whatever the reason might be, the interests of most children at a particular age or grade level are similar enough to permit valid and useful generalizations.

Children's Interests

Developmental psychologists, such as Elizabeth Hurlock (1975), have identified several common interests of human beings at various stages of their development from early infancy on, through and beyond middle age. For example, during their elementary school years, children are likely to enjoy group games involving competition, cooperation, or both. They are likely to be interested in constructive play activities (making things), collecting things (stamps, rocks, butterflies, you name it), watching television, attending movies, reading comic books, imitating their elders, finding things out for themselves, having new experiences, and daydreaming about themselves in some romantic or heroic role.

Since they are beginning to care about what others think of them and are beginning to feel the need for peer as well as parental approval and acceptance, their particular interests are likely to be imitative. As they attempt to identify with their parents, teachers, or—perhaps more likely—other children, they ordinarily display at least a transitory interest in the kinds of things in which their associates are interested. In the early elementary school years, children's interests, like their friendships, tend to be short-lived. Yesterday, it was animals. Today, it's outer space. Heaven only knows what it will be tomorrow. As children become older, their interests, like their friendships, ordinarily become somewhat deeper. By the time a person leaves childhood, his interests are ordinarily not stabilized but still developing.

The main concern of children is usually with the here and now. They are likely to be particularly interested in matters that affect them or their families directly and immediately. In this respect, they are not greatly different from their parents or grandparents. But, of course, they perceive things differently. While his parents might be very much interested in today's high cost of living, Junior might perceive something like a picnic or a birthday present as far more relevant.

In addition to their interest in matters that they perceive as directly affecting their welfare, children in the early elementary grades are likely to be interested in and have a healthy curiosity about a broad variety of things: the world of nature, dinosaurs, faraway lands, Indians, other planets, and so on ad infinitum. Their wide range of interests is indicated by the kinds of questions they ask: "Why is this?" "Who did that?" "What is this for?" "How does that work?"—and so forth ad infinitum. Teachers, of course, are well-advised to capitalize on their students' interests, to try to relate their subject matter to those interests, and to try to keep their students' curiosity alive.

Adolescents' Interests

As young people approach adolescence and pass through that stage of their development toward young adulthood, some of the interests of childhood continue. But, ordinarily, certain common new interests arise and previous interests take on a new form. With the onset of puberty, for example, boys and girls alike develop a strong interest in matters pertaining to their new bodies, to sex in general, and to their own sexual capabilities in particular. They are likely to be very much interested in such related matters as their personal appearance, health, size, and physical attractiveness. They also begin to show a marked interest in activities that they perceive as appropriate to their future adult sex roles. Hence, their interest in dating, sexual experimentation, career planning, marriage, and alternative life-styles.

The adolescent's interests are usually narrower and more specific than those of childhood. Transitory, superficial interests in a broad range of subjects are gradually replaced by deeper interests in a relatively few matters that the individual begins to perceive as more closely related to his life goals. When the adolescent sees the value in particular school subjects, for example, he might be highly motivated to excel in them. But he is likely to be critical of those parts of the curriculum whose bearing on his present status or future is not readily apparent.

Although recreational and social interests seem to be paramount at this stage of development, more mature and serious interests begin to manifest themselves. Since they are approaching maturity and will soon be expected to find a place in the adult world, adolescents are likely to take an avid interest in selected aspects of that world. Older teen-agers, for example, might be highly idealistic about changing the world and dedicate themselves (at least temporarily, but enthusiastically) to some cause with that end in mind. They might also be interested in formulating their own moral codes, philosophies of life, sets of values, and questions of right and wrong as they pertain to themselves. Adolescents are likely to be particularly interested in finding their real selves and in developing their own personalities.

Individuals' Interests

The generalizations that have just been made about the common interests of children and adolescents might be useful to teachers in formulating motivational strategies for *groups* of students, but they do not tell a great deal about the *particular* interests of particular *individuals*. The odds are that in a typical high school, for example, most of the male students (and some of the females) will be interested in cars. There is good reason to believe that, if mathematics, for example, can be related to cars, the students' interest in the latter will spread to the former. But certain members of a particular class, possibly a majority of them, might have little or no interest in cars at all. Thus, their teacher cannot always safely assume that interests common to people of a certain age group in general will necessarily apply to her particular students.

Teachers can often make inferences about the interests of individual students by casual observation, conversation, and noting the kinds of questions that they ask or the kinds of extracurricular activities in which they participate. Somewhat more systematically, they can learn a lot about their students' current interests by having them write or tell about such topics as their hobbies, collections, or vocational plans; how they spend their leisure time; the kinds of books that they enjoy reading; the television shows that they especially like; places that they like to visit; people they would like to meet; things they wonder about or would like to learn about.

Interest Inventories

The interests of older students can be ascertained through the use of interest inventories such as the Kuder Occupational Interest Survey or the Strong Vocational Interest Blank. Though primarily intended for guidance and counseling purposes, particularly with respect to career planning, these inventories can be used by classroom teachers to obtain a clearer idea than they might otherwise have of the general areas in which their students have the greatest interest.

Intended for use with adolescents and adults, the Kuder Survey consists of 300 items arranged in groups of three, such as: Visit an art gallery; browse in a library; visit a museum.

From each triad, the student selects the activities that appeal to him the most and the least. His selections indicate his patterns of interest with reference to several occupations such as accountant, automobile mechanic, beautician, carpenter, dental assistant, engineer, insurance agent, journalist, lawyer, librarian, teacher, truck driver, and X-ray technician.

The individual's scores on the Kuder are used to bring to his attention the occupations that he might not have considered but which involve the kinds of activities for which he has expressed a preference. They also indicate whether his choice of occupation is consistent with the kinds of things he ordinarily likes to do. The scores can also be used to help students to select college majors that are in line with their expressed interests.

The Strong Vocational Interest Blank serves essentially the same purpose as the Kuder but employs a somewhat different format. With the Strong, the individual is asked to indicate whether he likes, dislikes, or is indifferent to various school subjects, occupations, forms of amusement, personal characteristics, and miscellaneous activities. He is also asked to rank order certain activities according to his interest in them. As with the Kuder, the Strong has a dual scoring system for the two sexes. Thus, it might indicate, for example, that the interest of a particular girl in engineering is very high "for a girl."

CLASSROOM STRATEGIES

As we have seen, students are interested in their schoolwork (even though they do not especially enjoy it) when they perceive how the subject matter that they are expected to learn relates to them as individuals, when they see how it affects them, how it can satisfy their needs or serve their purposes. They are interested when they recognize that the learning of this material is a means to the achievement of one of their goals and that the results of the learning experience will make a difference to them personally. Students are interested in learning when they appreciate that they have something at stake in the learning experience and that the learning will have a direct bearing on that which they value above all else, their selves.

To interest a student in a subject, a teacher must know a great deal about (A) the subject and (B) the student. He must understand the student's problems, needs, goals, tendencies, and existing interests. He must also know the subject well enough to help the student perceive how it can or will contribute to his welfare. Then he must relate A and B. In helping the student to become aware of the relationship between himself and the material to be learned, the teacher might follow one or another of two basic strategies. He might begin with (A), the subject matter, or with (B), the student. When beginning with the subject matter, his task is to develop *new* interests. When he begins with the student, he builds on previously acquired, already established interests (Kolesnik 1970).

Subject-Centered Strategies

Teachers using what we might call a subject-centered strategy begin with a preplanned syllabus specifying the body of knowledge or skills that is assumed to be good or necessary for the students whether they like it or not. The job of the teacher is to make them like it. He is expected to create an interest in the subject matter, to convince his students of its value, to persuade them that it is worth learning; to do, in short, a kind of *selling job*. With some students and some subjects, this kind of selling job is no easy task. Even the most experienced teacher might have a hard time demonstrating the utility or the relevance of nineteenth-century poetry, for example, or fifteenth-century history to a fourteen-year-old boy living in the twentieth going on the twenty-first century.

Classroom motivation problems ordinarily arise because students do not see the value of what they are expected to learn. In all honesty, we might recognize that some material either has no value or its value is so remote that students cannot realistically be expected to perceive and accept it. Students often ask, for example, what good literature or mathematics will do them. Questions such as these should not be suppressed but encouraged. One of the jobs of the teacher is to answer such questions or to help the student to answer them himself.

If the subject matter *will* do the student any good, it would seem that he has a right to know the nature of that good. If it will not, the teacher, along with the student, might wonder why he is required to learn it in the first place and whether his time might not be put to better use learning things that he wants to learn and needs to learn to become a responsible, productive, self-actualizing citizen.

The relevance and the practical value of certain subjects (such as the 3 Rs) is fairly obvious and easy to demonstrate. But one of the major difficulties with the subject-centered type of strategy is, of course, that the value of some of the school subjects lies in the distant future. Trying to convince a junior high school student that literature or science, for example, will provide him with a well-rounded background and that someday he'll be glad that he learned these things might not prove to be very effective. Still, the main thrust of this approach to the motivation problem is to help the student to understand how this particular subject matter will help him to satisfy his needs, attain his goals, and become the kind of person that he really wants to become.

It has been argued that attempts to justify a subject in terms of its usefulness is essentially a matter of extrinsic rather than intrinsic motivation. When the strategy succeeds, the student perceives the subject matter not as something intrinsically valuable but as an instrument, a means toward some other goal, such as a good-paying job. Thus, he might be persuaded to study mathematics because he will need it to become, say, an automobile mechanic. Even apart from the question of how much mathematics a person really needs to know to repair automobiles, the individual is presumably being educated to become something more than a mechanic.

When using the subject-centered approach to motivation, teachers are well advised not to rely excessively or exclusively on the practical value of the material that they teach, particularly when *practical* is construed as immediately useful or financially rewarding. In a broad sense, every subject is potentially useful as a means of helping a person to lead a richer, fuller, happier, more satisfying kind of life regardless of occupation or profession. Ordinarily, when a student perceives this kind of value, he is interested and will want to learn it.

Student-Centered Strategies

Using the second strategy for making schoolwork interesting, the teacher begins with the student as he is here and now and builds on his existing interests, problems, and needs. The task in this situation is not to make the student fit the course syllabus or the day's lesson plan, but to make the subject matter fit the student. This approach involves an attempt to teach subject matter that is meaningful or can be readily made meaningful to the student in his existing circumstances. Instead of beginning with a package of knowledge that he tries to sell to his students, the teacher in this situation looks at the students and asks himself, "What do I know, what can I do, that will help my students to become what they want to become and are capable of becoming?"

Contrary to cartoonists' caricatures, the student-centered approach to motivation certainly does not imply a teacher's walking into a classroom and asking, "Well, boys and girls, what would you like to do today?" But it does involve a larger measure of spontaneity, flexibility, student planning, and individual responsibility for one's own learning than is usually found with a subject-centered approach (Silberman 1972). John Dewey and many of his followers believe that a student-centered strategy is particularly valuable for helping students to learn how to think for themselves and solve their own problems.

According to Dewey, the purpose of education is far broader and deeper than one of simply transmitting knowledge. Education, he maintained, should prepare young people for social living in a democratic society. It should be concerned not only with the individual's future, and with the preservation and strengthening of democracy, but also with the individual's welfare here and now. From his standpoint, the concepts of education and student-centered intrinsic motivation are inseparable (Dewey 1914, 1975).

Subject Matter and Problem-Solving

Dewey believed that a very important part of a student's education consists of his mastering the methods of reflective thinking in order to enable him to deal intelligently with real problems that he will encounter in the social situation of which he is a part. Dewey would have the student learn how to think reflectively and thus grow in intellectual power, but not by the teacher's imposing upon him meaningless, uninteresting problems devised in advance. Dewey would have the teacher engage the student in meaningful, interesting activities that are intrinsically worthwhile to him. As an outgrowth of these activities, genuine problems would emerge which the learner would want to solve. To do so, he would draw on his existing background of knowledge or seek out the necessary additional information. Then the student would formulate hypotheses or tentative solutions to the problem, which he would be responsible for developing in an orderly way. Finally, he would test these hypotheses to discover their validity for himself. In this way, the student would develop and have an opportunity to practice habits and attitudes that could be applied to new situations as the need arose.

The role of the teacher, according to Dewey, is to arrange for kinds of experiences that will engage the interests and activities of the student. These experiences, however, must be more than simply enjoyable. They must promote the student's having desirable future experiences and lead out into fields previously unfamiliar to him. Otherwise, no problems will arise, and without problems there can be no thinking or intellectual growth since such growth depends upon the presence of difficulties to be overcome by the exercise of intelligence. A big part of the teacher's responsibility, then, is to see to it that the student is confronted with problems that grow out of his present experiences, are within the range of his capacity, and arouse in him an active quest for information and the production of new ideas.

From Dewey's standpoint, the educative process should move toward, but not begin with, organized bodies of subject matter. The primary value of subject matter, he maintains, is for the teacher, not the pupil. Organized bodies of knowledge represent the goal toward which education should continuously move. However, the logically arranged knowledge of the specialist cannot provide the starting point of the instructional process. Rather, the starting point must be some ongoing activity in which the student has a genuine interest. As a result of his schooling, Dewey maintains, the student should arrive at socially useful and personally satisfying knowledge, but the quality of his mental process is a far more important educational outcome than the production of correct answers (Dewey 1924, 1975).

Games and Simulations

Although interest does not necessarily imply fun, having fun is one way of making an activity interesting. Applying this principle to the classroom, we might suggest that teachers try to make schoolwork as pleasant and as much fun as possible without sacrificing the quality of the work that they expect their students to accomplish.

Some imaginative teachers have invented, and other teachers borrowed, games and other instructional materials and techniques of teaching to make learning fun. A rather simple example is baseball arithmetic. When this game is played, the students are divided into teams. As each player takes his turn "at bat," he is given a problem to solve. If he answers correctly, he is credited with a hit and advances to first base. If he answers incorrectly, he is out. As in a regular baseball game, after three outs the other team comes to bat. Hits by subsequent batters advance the base runners so that four hits in an inning give the team a run. And so forth. The rules, of course, can be as simple or complex as the teacher wishes to make them. To add to the interest, some sort of prize might be awarded the members of the winning team, but commonly the fun of playing the game is its own reward.

Within the past few years, a broad variety of educational games and simulations have become available to teachers. These commercial products have been devised not only to help to make learning enjoyable and to arouse and maintain students' interests but also to promote their social interaction, present vivid portrayals of real-life situations, and to involve them directly in worthwhile learning experiences. While educational toys and games have long been used at the kindergarten and primary levels, more challenging and sophisticated games are being used more and more at higher grade levels.

One game, for example, simulates Wall Street and the workings of the stock market. Students of economics are given an opportunity to play the role of brokers, investors, and industrial tycoons. Another simulates life in a ghetto. Its purpose is to help middle-class students to learn about the problems and frustrations that poor people experience as they try to improve their situations. Another game simulates the Constitutional Convention. Here, through role playing and research activities, students can learn about some of the individuals who helped to bring our Constitution into being, as well as their political philosophies and the particular concerns of the thirteen original states. Other games are directed toward the learning of vocabulary, science, linguistics, art appreciation, and many other subjects (Cratty 1971; Stanford and Roark 1974).

Games such as these should not be regarded simply as a coat of sugar on the bitter pill of learning to make it more palatable. They should be looked upon as teaching strategies that are based on the students' existing interests in playing, competing, cooperating, imagining, and socializing. Such strategies are recommended not only because they facilitate learning but also because they build favorable attitudes toward the process. While the school is not primarily a recreation center and the teacher's main role is not that of an entertainer, a fun-and-games approach can be a very effective means of motivating students who might not otherwise be interested in what the curriculum has to offer.

Interest and Effort

Objections have been raised to fun-and-games strategies on the grounds that students should be taught, among other things, to set forth effort and try to succeed in activities that they do not find particularly enjoyable. As John Dewey points out, however, interest does not preclude effort, and the two are certainly not mutually exclusive. On the contrary, it has been argued that the intensity of a person's effort is likely to be in direct proportion to his interest in the activity. Ordinarily, the more interested a football player is in a game, the harder he plays. Similarly, the more interested a student is in a subject, and the more he enjoys it, the harder he will try to learn it.

Involvement

Ordinarily, the intensity of our interest in an activity as well as the amount of effort that we expend on it depends on our feeling of personal involvement in that activity. For this reason, small group discussions in which every member has an opportunity to participate might be more interesting than, say, listening to a lecture. Whether or not it is more productive may, of course, be quite another matter. Moreover, even the interest factor in discussions versus lectures depends on other variables, not the least important of which is the particular topic being explained or discussed. For the moment, we are focusing only on the interest factor and are suggesting that a lively, well-conducted discussion is one way of stimulating and maintaining student interest. Role playing is another, not only because it can be fun but also because it directly involves the participants –and vicariously their friends in the audience—in the learning situation (Stanford and Roark 1974).

Ordinarily, we tend to have a strong interest in activities that we help to plan. When we are personally involved in deciding the goals of an activity and in planning the means of attaining those goals, we feel that we have some responsibility for the outcome of that activity. We feel that we have something at stake. Another means of arousing and maintaining interest in classroom activities, therefore, is to allow, or require, students to participate in planning, organizing, and evaluating those activities.

As we shall see in the next chapter, student cooperation does not guarantee superior scholastic achievement, but it does seem to be a significant factor in developing and strengthening student interest. Various forms of teacher/student planning, group methods of learning, and student cooperation on projects of their own choice are sometimes effective ways of making schoolwork interesting because they afford students an opportunity to become active participants in classroom activities rather than mere spectators or members of an audience. For much the same kinds of reasons, well-designed competitive activities can also be used as means of arousing and maintaining interest. The pros and cons, the uses and misuses or abuses, of competition are discussed in Chapter 8.

Creativity

Another means of motivating students intrinsically is to capitalize on their propensities toward creative self-expression and to give them opportunities to develop their creative-thinking abilities. Creative thinking is commonly referred to as divergent thinking, as distinguished from convergent thinking.

Convergent thinking takes place when we restructure our ideas so that they converge at or point unequivocally to *the* one right answer to a question, *the* one best solution to a problem, or *the* only valid conclusion that can be drawn from a body of data. In convergent thinking, if X is true and Y is true, it follows that Z must therefore be true. Convergent thinking involves logical reasoning or the deduction of inferences. It occurs only in situations where there *is* one and only one right answer, as in the area of mathematics for example.

Divergent thinking takes place in situations in which there is no one right or best answer. It occurs when we formulate two or more possible conclusions or solutions, none of which is necessarily any better than another. Ordinarily, the more possibilities that a person can suggest, the more creative he or she is thought to be. The following are a few of the activities that are commonly use to stimulate divergent thinking.

1. List as many items as you can think of that are green (or some other color or specified shape or quality).
2. List as many words as you can that mean about the same as *big.*
3. List a number of specific things a person might do that would lead you to consider that person to be honest.
4. Formulate as many sentences as you can, the words of which begin with the letters T__ r__ i__ g__ t__ d__ s__ c__ b__ .
5. What are some things that you cannot do now that you could do if you were invisible (or ten feet tall or six inches tall)?
6. Give as many unusual uses as you can think of for a paper clip (or some other common object).
7. "Tom, Tom, the piper's son,
   Stole a pig and away he run."
   Give as many possible consequences of this act as you can imagine.

E. Paul Torrance, one of the country's recognized authorities on the subject of convergent/divergent thinking, used activities such as these in his research as a means of measuring creativity.

Some people unquestionably have more creative potential than others. But every person has some degree of creative ability as well as what Torrance calls built-in motivation toward creativity (Torrance 1975). While extrinsic incentives can be helpful in bringing about the kinds of responses called for in these activities, he believes that they are by no means necessary and might serve only to inhibit rather than foster originality and divergent thinking processes. Where the possibility of receiving external rewards exists, there also exists the possibility of not being rewarded or of being punished. Such conditions are likely to be detrimental to free, spontaneous, creative self-expression.

Although creativity is often associated with the fine arts, it can also play an important part in business and industry, engineering, homemaking, teaching, athletics, and just about any other field of human endeavor. Thus, creative thinking need not result in a painting, a poem, or a musical composition. Something as commonplace as a new salad, a bulletin board display, a figure of speech, or a means of balancing a budget might also be a product of creative problem-solving.

Promotion of Creativity

Torrance, among many others, believes that every individual has a need and a desire to find new and better ways of doing things, to discover or invent things that they can properly regard as their own, to put something of themselves into new products, and to share their original ideas or creations with others. We have, in short, a need for self-expression just as we have a need to organize our knowledge about our environment and to seek and enjoy what we perceive as beauty (or structure or order) in that environment. As a means of making schoolwork interesting, therefore, it would seem to follow that students at all levels should be given opportunities to satisfy these needs from within and to practice creative self-expression (Lytton 1972).

The following are a few examples of the kinds of activities that you might adapt to your particular grade level or subject area and assign to your students for this purpose.

1. Make as many specific suggestions as possible of things that you [*i.e. students*] can do to reduce pollution, conserve energy, beautify the environment, etc.

2. Draw a poster or make up some slogans that could be used to further some cause in which you are interested.

3. Write an on-the-spot newspaper account of some historical or current event as though you were there observing it.

4. Suggest some possible means of improving television (or your school or the government, etc.).

5. Discuss what the consequences might have been if England had won the Revolutionary War.

6. Think up some original, clever, appropriate titles for a familiar poem, picture, novel, short story, etc.

7. List some questions that you would ask your favorite sports celebrity (or politician or entertainer) if you had the chance to interview him or her.

8. Describe what you would regard as Utopia or as heaven on earth.

9. Write a letter to an imaginary (or, better yet, a real) penpal in a foreign country, asking about the kinds of things that you would like to know about everyday life in that country.

10. Pretend that you have a chance to visit Mars. What are some questions that you would want answered before deciding whether or not to go?

Some of these activities, you will recognize, not only call for original, divergent thinking but also presume, or are intended to stimulate, the student's curiosity.

CURIOSITY

Psychologists do not agree on whether curiosity is either an innate drive, an acquired response, or both. It is apparent, however, that human beings, like animals, are motivated by an inclination to explore their environments. We want to satisfy our curiosity and find out more about the world around us even when there is no pressing need for us to do so other than our need for new experience and our need to know.

Younger children are, of course, notorious for their apparently insatiable curiosity. Like puppies and kittens, they are into everything, looking here, sniffing there, touching this, and investigating that—just because it's there. Ordinarily, with maturation this generalized, indiscriminate curiosity becomes more localized and specific. Sometimes with maturation, curiosity seems to vanish entirely. Developmental psychologists point out that by the time they reach adolescence, some people display very little curiosity about anything. Others are curious about only a few particular subjects or situations in which they have acquired a strong interest. Still others continue to be motivated by a healthy, active, intellectual curiosity about a wide variety of things.

Differences among individuals in this respect can probably be attributed to differential reinforcement. If a child is encouraged to try to find things out for himself and is praised or otherwise rewarded for his attempts to satisfy his curiosity, the chances are that he will continue to engage in exploratory behavior. Moreover, his open-minded, questioning attitude toward new situations is likely to be strengthened. But, if he is discouraged from asking too many questions, is told that curiosity killed some cat, is made to feel that he is stupid because of the kinds of questions he asks, is either scolded or simply ignored for interrupting the flow of a teacher's explanation with inquiries that he perceives as unrelated to his discourse, his curiosity is likely to be extinguished through nonreinforcement or stifled through punishment (Day and Berlyne 1971).

Conditions Conducive to Curiosity

Like creativity, to which it is closely related, curiosity is unlikely to flourish in a repressive atmosphere or in one where a premium is placed on such behaviors as following directions, doing what he is told, mastering a predetermined body of knowledge, and giving the correct answers. Since there is more to life than creativity and more to learning than curiosity, behaviors such as these undeniably have their place in the classroom. But, at the moment, we are considering only curiosity as one factor in intrinsic motivation. I am not suggesting that there is anything wrong with expecting students to do as they are told or to master certain bodies of subject matter. But I am suggesting that such conditions as anxiety about grades, fear of displeasing the teacher, and the feeling of being under pressure to achieve are hardly conducive to spontaneous, uninhibited, intrinsically motivated exploratory behavior.

Curiosity is more likely to develop in an emotionally comfortable, nonthreatening, relaxed kind of atmosphere in which the individual student feels secure and free to investigate the kinds of things he wants to investigate. Thus, a classroom atmosphere conducive to intrinsic motivation is one in which the student feels free to make mistakes as he ventures into new areas on his own, knowing that he will not be ridiculed or rejected for making the effort.

For reasons such as these, a relatively open, unstructured, permissive, student-centered classroom making use of inquiry or discovery methods of learning and emphasizing student initiative and responsibility is commonly regarded as more effective than a traditional teacher- or subject-centered classroom for the purpose under discussion. The terms *inquiry* and *discovery* refer to a variety of learning activities that are characterized by a minimum of teacher guidance, intervention, direction, explanation, or supervision, and a maximum reliance on the student's experiences, observations, questions, explorations, experiments, intuition, hunches, and inductive reasoning (Morine 1975).

Since this is a book about motivation rather than methods of teaching, we shall not go into a discussion of the pros and cons of discovery learning or a detailed description of how it works. But we should note that two of the main claims for discovery learning is that it encourages curiosity and makes schoolwork interesting. As I am sure you will recognize, several of the ideas expressed earlier in this chapter (with respect to John Dewey's views on problem-solving, for example, and student-centered strategies for making schoolwork interesting) go hand in hand with the concepts of discovery learning and curiosity.

Curiosity Arousal

Our curiosity is aroused (or, strictly speaking, *we* are aroused) when we encounter stimuli that are ambiguous, incongruous, unexpected, or otherwise unusual. Such stimuli bring about feelings of surprise, doubt, wonder, perplexity, uncertainty, or some other form of internal tension. Frequently, such stimuli give rise to a kind of conflict. For example, hearing a strange sound, being attracted by an unfamiliar sight, or being exposed to a new idea, we are not sure about the nature, meaning, or significance of the stimulus or about how to respond. Consequently, we launch an investigation to acquire the additional information that we need to resolve the conflict, alleviate the tension, or reduce the arousal.

A good example of curiosity arousal and conflict involves what has been called *cognitive dissonance.* Cognitive dissonance refers to a conflict between a new idea and our accumulated store of old ideas. When the new idea or experience does not fit in with our existing knowledge or beliefs, the lack of harmony bothers us. The idea that George Washington was something less than perfect, to take a very simple example, might not be in accord with what we had previously learned about him and had come to accept as true. The tension produced by this discordant note might stimulate us to try to find out a bit more about the Father of our Country.

The extent and persistence of our exploratory behavior depends on the strength of the tension. While so-called idle curiosity about relatively insignificant matters produces only a slight degree of arousal and casual investigation, strong curiosity about a situation that we regard as highly important is likely to produce more intense arousal and sustained exploration. Ordinarily, curiosity about a particular stimulus persists until the conflict is solved, until boredom sets in, or until the object of our curiosity is supplanted by more potent simuli.

Attention

Curiosity can be thought of in terms of certain stimuli attracting or holding our attention. At any given moment, our sensory receptors are exposed to more sights, sounds, tactile, and other stimuli than our neural systems can possibly assimilate. Consequently, we do not and cannot respond to all of them. In a supermarket, for example, the shelves are lined with thousands of items that we literally see but do not notice. Similarly, we hear a variety of sounds, but to most of them we pay no attention. That is, we do not react to them. They have little if any effect on our behavior.

The same is true in a classroom. Teachers often complain that their students do not pay attention. Actually, students are *always* paying attention to *something.* The problem is that they do not always focus their attention on what the teacher is saying or doing. The reason that they do not is that there are other things that they find more attractive or consider more worthy of their notice. Much as one particular brand of toothpaste, for example, is competing with the thousands of other supermarket items to capture your attention, so must a teacher compete with an infinite number of stimuli, memories, images, etc., for the attention of his students.

Because of the vast array of stimuli to which we are or have been exposed and the limited capacity of our neural system to transmit the corresponding impressions to our brains, we have apparently been endowed with a psychoneurological mechanism that somehow screens the messages that reach the brain. Weaker stimuli are blocked out while stronger ones reach the cerebral cortex, where they are recorded, interpreted, and translated into some sort of behavior. We cannot always consciously or deliberately control the stimulations that do or do not get through this neurological gate. Sometimes, through conscious deliberate effort and determination, we can force ourselves to concentrate on particular stimuli, such as the words of a teacher or those in a book, even though they are not especially interesting. But there are other kinds of stimuli—such as loud, sudden noises, bright, flashing lights, intense heat or cold, and physical pain—that we simply cannot exclude from our awareness.

Factors Affecting Attention

Berlyne has identified three kinds of factors that are most likely to attract our attention: psychophysical, ecological, and collative. *Psychophysical* factors include such qualities as the size, color, pitch, and intensity of stimuli. For example, a brightly colored object against a dull background, or an unexpected increase in the intensity of a sound is all but certain to attract our attention, if only for a short while. *Ecological* factors are those which are primarily biological in nature and have emotional overtones. For example, anything perceived as a threat or anything that arouses us sexually is likely to hold our attention. So is something that makes us very angry or is perceived as somehow outrageous.

Collative factors are so called because they involve the collation or comparison of information from different sources. Essentially cognitive in nature, they include such qualities as novelty, ambiguity, complexity, and incongruity that were mentioned in connection with curiosity arousal. Collative factors, in short, include an element of uncertainty or unexpectedness that gives rise to such internal tensions as doubt, surprise, cognitive dissonance, or intellectual conflict. Berlyne regards collative properties as potentially most productive in the development of curiosity and the promotion of exploratory behavior in the classroom because they, more so than psychophysical or ecological factors, can be regulated by the teacher (Berlyne 1971).

Interest, Curiosity, and Attention

Thus far, we have been discussing three closely interrelated concepts: interest, curiosity, and attention. The key element in each of these, or in all three taken together, seems to be self-involvement. We are interested in, curious about, and attentive to situations that we perceive as somehow related to our particular needs, goals, problems, or welfare. Part of a teacher's job with respect to intrinsic motivation, therefore, is to help students to perceive the relationship between the material that he would like them to learn and the qualities that they themselves want to develop. Among these qualities are such outcomes as self-fulfillment, personal satisfaction, financial and social success, etc.

But there is another dimension to the teacher's role in this respect: to arouse interest, curiosity, and attention in areas where the payoff or relevance is neither immediate nor apparent. Here, we are talking about a kind of intellectual curiosity or a set of academic interests that the teacher considers worthwhile in and of themselves, for their own sake.

As has been suggested, one way to stimulate intellectual curiosity and attract students' attention is to create doubts in their minds about some of their existing beliefs or values. As a teacher, you might help your students to recognize that their viewpoints on two or more subjects are inconsistent (if such is the case), or that their opinions on some particular topic are quite different from the opinions held by others.

To hold the students' interests, you need not try to entertain them or emphasize the practical value of your material. You might be able to stimulate interest simply by encouraging your students to ask questions. You might want them to know that you value good questions more than you do the memorization of correct answers. You yourself might want to raise more questions than you answer, and instead of giving answers to students' questions, you might encourage or even require them to try to find their own answers.

In many subject areas, a teacher can inform his students that experts in a given field often do not agree with one another. The teacher can help them to understand that there are some problems to which no one has *the* solution. He can then use these situations as a point of departure for what might turn out to be a very interesting discussion. Or he might thus be able to bring about the kind of internal tension that seems to be so closely related to curiosity.

Having available a wide variety of instructional materials including audio/visual aids; arranging field trips and bringing outside speakers into the classroom; varying your own classroom procedures so that you do not fall into a monotonous methodological rut; structuring activities that will give rise to genuine problems that the students will want to try to solve; trying to make classroom activities intrinsically enjoyable; giving each student a chance to experience success in some activity that he finds challenging and worthwhile—all of these are potentially useful means of intrinsic motivation. But, in the final analysis, the most critical factor is that of helping the student to perceive how your subject matter will help him to become the kind of person that he is capable of becoming and wants to become.

RECOMMENDED READING

Avila, Donald L., and Purkey, William W. "Intrinsic and Extrinsic Motivation—A Regrettable Distinction." In Avila, Donald L., *et al.*, Eds.,

The Helping Relationship Sourcebook. Boston: Allyn and Bacon, 1971. In this article, the authors, two well-known humanists, maintain that extrinsic and intrinsic motivation are not mutually exclusive. They show how behavioral and humanistic principles can and should be integrated into an effective motivational program.

Bledsoe, J. C. "Comparison of Interests of Urban Disadvantaged Boys and Girls." *Psychological Reports, 36*: 932–934, 1975. Results of a study comparing the responses of disadvantaged and middle-class children in grades 4–7 to the "What I Like to Do" interest inventory. Also compares sex differences within both socioeconomic classes and relates them to differences between the classes.

Combs, Arthur W., *et al. The Professional Education of Teachers.* Boston: Allyn and Bacon, 1974. 2nd ed. Subtitled "A Humanistic Approach to Teacher Preparation," this book describes the kind of teachers needed to implement educational programs based on intrinsic motivation and personal discovery. Recommends that teacher-education curricula and methodologies be based on these principles.

Day, H. I., and Berlyne, D. E. "Intrinsic Motivation." In Lesser, G. S., Ed., *Psychology and Educational Practice.* Glenview, Ill.: Scott, Foresman, 1971. Explains the nature and theory of intrinsic motivation and reviews much of the research on the problem. A good source of information about various aspects of curiosity.

Deci, Edward L. *Intrinsic Motivation.* New York: Plenum Press, 1975. A rather thorough discussion of intrinsically motivated behavior from a philosophical as well as a psychological perspective. The author evaluates the theories and research findings of several scholars in the area and brings out the implications of the concept with which the entire book deals.

Dewey, John. *Interest and Effort in Education.* Carbondale, Ill.: Southern Illinois University Press, 1975. One of Dewey's classics, originally published in 1913, reprinted with a valuable preface by James E. Wheeler. Historically one of the most important books ever written on the subject and still very much up-to-date. An easy introduction to Dewey's philosophy of education and his recommendations for its implementation.

Hurlock, Elizabeth R. *Developmental Psychology.* New York: McGraw-Hill, 1975. 4th ed. This popular and attractive textbook is recommended because of the wealth of information that it contains about the interests of individuals at various stages of development from infancy to old age. The listings in the index under the heading "Interests" are very helpful.

Morine, Harold, and Morine, Greta. *Discovery: A Challenge to Teachers.* Englewood Cliffs, N.J.: Prentice-Hall, 1973. A very practical book that explains and illustrates how discovery methods can be used in the classroom.

Rogers, Carl R. *Freedom to Learn.* Columbus, Ohio: Charles E. Merrill, 1969. In this book, Rogers gathers his thoughts on education. He maintains that students at every level can be trusted to learn and will enjoy learning if they are encouraged to participate responsibly in the selection of their goals and in the means of reaching them.

Schmuck, Richard A., and Schmuck, Patricia A. *A Humanistic Psychology of Education.* Palo Alto, Cal.: National Press, 1974. A nonconventional textbook that brings out some practical applications of humanistic psychology to classroom problems. Emphasizes intrinsic motivation, individual growth, and social interaction rather than the mastery of subject matter.

Silberman, Melvin L., *et al. The Psychology of Open Teaching and Learning.* Boston: Little, Brown, 1972. Subtitled "An Inquiry Approach," this book of readings includes several articles pertinent to intrinsic motivation, student-centered education, discovery methods of teaching and learning, and other topics related to the concept of student freedom and responsibility.

Torrance, E. Paul. "Motivation and Creativity." In Torrance, E. Paul, and White, W. F., Eds., *Issues and Advances in Educational Psychology.* Itasca, Ill.: F. E. Peacock, 1975. 2nd ed. In this short article, the author, one of the country's foremost authorities on the subject, explains and defends the proposition that if we keep alive and guide students' creative processes "we shall have all of the motivation we need."

CHAPTER 8: PREVIEW QUESTIONS

(After you have finished reading Chapter 8, you should be able to answer the following.)

1. Why or how does the effectiveness of praise and reproof depend upon the personal qualities of the individuals giving and receiving the approval or disapproval?

2. What are some research findings on the value of feedback? What are some recommended means or principles of keeping students informed of their progress?

3. What are some objections to the use of grades as an incentive? Which of these objections do you think have the most validity?

4. What are some of the arguments that have been advanced in defense of grading?

5. What is your overall position on the grading issue?

6. What is the relationship between grading and testing? Does one necessarily imply the other? What are the two main purposes of grades? How might these two purposes conflict?

7. What is the difference among norm-referenced, criterion-referenced, and individualized systems of grading? Which do you prefer and why?

8. What is the theory behind contingency management as a means of motivation? What are some objections to motivation through contingency management? What do you think or how do you feel about these objections?

9. What is the Premack principle? Give a couple of examples to show how it works.

10. What is your opinion of the use of tangible (token) reinforcers?

11. What are contingency contracts? How do they work? What are your views on their utility or desirability?

12. What are some findings of research studies on the relative effectiveness of individual versus group competition?

13. What are some possible undesirable side effects of competition on the losers? The winners?

14. Under what conditions is competition likely to be most effective? Most undesirable or objectionable?

15. What are some recommendations for using competition in the classroom while minimizing undesired side effects on students' personality development and subsequent achievement or motivation?

16. What are some arguments on research findings in favor of cooperation as opposed to competition for purposes of classroom motivation?

17. What are the net conclusions of research studies on the relative effectiveness of cooperation and competition?

CHAPTER EIGHT

Extrinsic Motivation .

Chapter 7 centers on intrinsic motivation. This one deals with motivation of the extrinsic variety. Actually, the line between motives from within and those from without cannot always be clearly drawn. For example, a person might be interested in playing pingpong not only because of the pleasure or personal satisfaction that he derives from the activity itself but also because of the prize or recognition that he hopes to win. Similarly, a student might enjoy English literature, recognize its value, and want to learn it for its own sake but still be interested in receiving a good grade. It is with such incentives as grades, social approval, and more tangible rewards—or reinforcers—that this chaper is concerned.

APPROVAL AND DISAPPROVAL

As we have seen, one of the basic tenets of behavioral psychology is that we act as we do to gain some sort of reward or to avoid punishment. Reward and punishment correspond, respectively, to the concepts of success and failure that were discussed in Chapter 5. Success and failure, in turn, correspond, respectively, to the attainment or nonattainment of goals. One of our most coveted goals—corresponding to one of our basic human needs—is the approval of others. In behavioral terms, anything that contributes to the satisfaction of that need can be thought of as a social reinforcer. Few, if any, reinforcers are more powerful than approval.

Effects of Praise and Scolding

Among the most commonly used incentives, not only in education but in other areas as well, are praise and reproof. The preponderance of evidence indicates that praising a person for good work is likely to be more effective than scolding him for poor work. But there is also reason to believe that in many instances scolding is more effective than ignoring the person and in some cases reproof might actually be more productive than praise.

In one of the classic experiments of educational psychology, Hurlock (1925) set out to ascertain the relative effectiveness of praise and reproof. She began by dividing her subjects, approximately 100 fourth and fifth graders, into four groups. Those in the first group were consistently praised for the quality of their work in arithmetic. Members of the second group were scolded for their carelessness, mistakes, and failure to improve. Those in the third group were ignored—each day, these boys and girls heard some of their classmates praised and others scolded but they themselves remained unnoticed. The fourth group, which acted as a control, was placed in a separate room where no one was praised or reproved.

At first, both the praised and the reproved groups were apparently more highly motivated than the ignored or the control groups. But, after the second day of the experiment, the scolded group declined markedly in achievement and the praised group continued to improve steadily. The scolded group, however, surpassed the ignored group throughout the experiment, while the control group did the poorest of all. Apparently receiving unfavorable attention is more productive than receiving none at all, and simply being in the presence of others who are praised or scolded, even though one is neither scolded nor praised himself, has certain advantages.

Source Variable

Although several other studies have corroborated Hurlock's findings in general, not all of them have yielded the same clear-cut evidence in favor of praise. Schmidt, for one, found no significant difference between the motivational effects of praise and scolding per se. He noted, rather, that the source of the reaction is a critical factor. Praise (or reproof) from one person does not have the same effect as praise (or reproof) from another (Schmidt 1941).

As you may have noticed, a compliment, a word of encouragement, or a pat from one person does not necessarily carry the same weight as the same word or gesture coming from another person. Maybe the reason is that you like the one person better than the other, that you value one person's opinion over the other's, that you want to identify with one person and not the other, or consider one person to be more discriminating than the other. Some teachers or employers, for example, are so parsimonious with praise that the slightest sign of approval coming from them is valuable because it is so unusual. Others are so free and easy with their compliments that the words of praise they utter become practically meaningless.

Recipient Variables

The relative effects of praise and blame depend not only on the personality of the individual giving but also on that of the individual receiving them. This is particularly important with respect to the recipient's degree of introversion or extroversion, as was brought out in a study by Thompson and Hunnicutt.

In this experiment, 124 fifth-grade students were classified as extroverts or introverts on the basis of their scores on a personality test. Then, they were given the simple task of drawing a line through each of the 7s in a randomly arranged list of numbers from 0 through 9. Six such tests were given. In one section, the extroverts were praised and the introverts blamed after each test.

The praise and blame consisted of the teacher's marking the papers G for good or P for poor. In the second section, the procedure was reversed with, the extroverts being blamed and the introverts being praised. In two other sections, the procedure was alternated so that approximately the same number of students were found in each of the four experimental groups: praised extroverts, praised introverts, blamed extroverts, and blamed introverts. In a fifth section, which was used as a control, neither praise nor blame was given.

Thompson and Hunnicutt found that either praise or blame was more effective than no reaction at all in improving the performance of introverts and extroverts. Apparently when introverts and extroverts are grouped together, as they are likely to be in a typical classroom, the two kinds of incentives are equally effective. But, after repeated trials, they found that the achievement of praised introverts was significantly higher than that of blamed introverts or praised extroverts. On the other hand, the blamed extroverts surpassed the praised extroverts and the blamed introverts to an even greater degree (Thompson and Hunnicutt 1944).

This study suggests that both praise and blame can be used effectively if the personalities of the students are taken into account; that one is not always or necessarily better than the other in general; that praising introverts is likely to be more beneficial than scolding them; but that extroverts might be more strongly motivated by criticism than approval. Kennedy and Willcutt (1964) found that not only extroverts but also underachievers and very bright students as well are likely to profit from a bit of goading now and then. The general recommendation, however, is that when reproof is used the teacher should not dwell on the shortcomings of the student's past performance but should stress the possibilities of improvement in the future.

Feedback

A number of experiments have shown that the practice of keeping students informed about the quality of their work has beneficial effects on their motivation and subsequent achievement. For example, in a study by F. J. Brown, elementary school children were divided into two parallel groups. Those in the experimental group were given a daily report on their progress and were encouraged to keep track of their scores on a graph. Those in the control group received no such feedback. Brown used a rotation group procedure so that every student worked for a time under both experimental and control conditions. He found that those in the experimental group consistently made greater gains and received higher scores than those who were not kept informed (Brown 1932).

At the college level, Angell (1949) found that freshmen chemistry students who were informed of the correct answers immediately after finishing quizzes did significantly better on their final examination than comparable students who did not receive their quiz results until the next class meeting. Studies by Selankovich (1968), Chansky (1964), and others have shown that relatively frequent quizzes that provide steady feedback are not only favored by college students but are related to their scholastic growth and achievement.

There is reason to believe that when students are not given reinforcement or corrective feedback the quality of their work might very well deteriorate. Ewell and Grinley have found that students who were not kept informed of their progress did not profit from further practice at all, whereas those who were kept informed showed steady improvement over a long period of time. But later, when feedback was withheld from those who had previously been kept informed, the quality of their performance underwent a sharp and sudden decline (Ewell and Grinley 1938).

As Anderson and Faust (1973) point out, knowledge of results serves two purposes: it provides the student with reinforcement when his work is satisfactory and with corrective feedback when it is not. They cite studies that suggest that it is more important to inform a student when he is wrong than it is to tell him when he is right. Corrective feedback is likely to be more effective when it informs the student about what the correct response should be instead of simply letting him know that he is wrong. To rely mainly on corrective feedback and to ignore or minimize the reinforcing factor of complimenting him for work well done would be a mistake however.

Continuously bringing a student's errors or lack of improvement to his attention might serve only to discourage him. When his work is unsatisfactory, therefore, point out why it is unsatisfactory and give him an idea of how it can be improved. Whenever possible, let him discover and correct his own mistakes himself. Let him know that you have confidence in his ability to do better in the future and that you are looking forward to his doing so. And do try to assign him tasks that you are reasonably sure he will be able to complete successfully so that he will be able to earn reinforcing feedback.

Teacher Comments

No doubt you've had tests or other papers returned to you with nothing on them but a letter grade. But remember how much better you felt on those occasions when the teacher took the time and trouble to write at least a brief encouraging comment on your paper? Page conducted an experiment to ascertain the effects of such comments.

In this experiment, seventy-four participating secondary school teachers gave their students (more than 2000 students in all) the tests that they ordinarily would have given in their particular subject areas and graded them in the usual manner: A, B, C, D, or F. Then the papers were randomly assigned to one of three groups: no comment, free comment, or specified comment.

Papers in the no-comment group were marked with nothing but the grade. On papers in the free-comment group, the teacher wrote whatever comment he or she considered to be appropriate for the individual student. Papers in the specified-comment group all received the same comment, depending on the student's grade. For example, on all the A tests in this group, the teachers wrote, "Excellent! Keep it up." On the C papers they wrote, "Perhaps try to do still better?" and on the F papers, "Let's raise this grade!" Both the free and specified comments were supposed to be encouraging.

Page then compared the grades of the same students on the second test with their grades on the first. He found that those who received the free comments gained the most; those who received no comments gained the least; and even those who received the "canned" comments tended to do better on the second test than on the first (Page 1958).

GRADING PRACTICES AND PROBLEMS

The desire to receive good grades or to avoid low report-card marks is hardly the loftiest goal to which a human being can aspire. Ideally, the use of grades as incentives leaves a great deal to be desired. But realistically, they have been found to work, particularly in situations where intrinsic motivation is not particularly high.

We need not dwell on the obvious point that a great many students—from elementary through the graduate school level—would not even think of studying if it were not for the prospect of a test and the consequent grade in a course. In some cases, the mark is not only their major incentive. It seems to be their only one! This is not the way it should be but the way it is.

Some Objections to Grading

John Holt (1974), Ernest Melby (1977), and Sidney Simon (1977), among many others, have advanced a number of arguments to the effect that the conventional grading practices that have for so long characterized our schools actually do more harm than good in the long run and, consequently, ought to be abolished. Among the more common of these arguments are the following.

1. Grading students causes them to study in the wrong way for the wrong reasons. Instead of learning for the sake of learning, their main concern becomes to please the teacher and get a good mark. Thus, learning, which should be an enjoyable experience, worthwhile in and of itself, becomes a chore, an unpleasant task, a means to an end rather than an end in itself.

2. As grades rather than learning become their main, if not their only, concern students are likely to adopt an end-justifies-the-means approach, which underlies such practices as cheating, cramming, bluffing, and the pursuit of brownie points.

3. The grading system creates an adversary relationship between students and teachers. Instead of working together

toward common goals, the system pits teachers and students against one another. Thus, while teachers are busily engaged in checking up on students and perhaps threatening them with low grades if they do not produce, students come to regard the classroom experience as a kind of game in which they feel challenged to beat the system by getting the highest possible grades with the least possible expenditure of time and effort.

4. Grading tends to stifle creativity, initiative, self-expression, individuality, and independent critical thinking, while it fosters the student's preoccupation with giving the teacher what he wants. Thus, the student becomes overly dependent upon the teacher for approval and correspondingly less self-reliant and self-motivated.

5. Grading promotes an unnecessary, unwholesome attitude of rivalry among students as they compete with one another for the coveted high grades. In these competitive situations, it is usually the same students who win while others consistently lose. This creates a situation in which the winners learn to be motivated primarily by a vain desire for self-glorification and the losers tend to become discouraged, demoralized, and to develop a feeling of personal inferiority. Students should learn to cooperate rather than to compete, and each student should be encouraged to do his best without being compared with others.

6. Grading produces needless pressures and anxieties, not only among the poorer students who dread the Ds and Fs that they expect to receive but also among the more able students who worry about losing their straight-A record, dropping below a 3.75, or having their names removed from the honor roll. All students, it is alleged, would do better in a more relaxed atmosphere where they would be free to learn instead of having to worry about grades.

In Defense of Grading

I'm sure that you could add to this list of objections and expand on the points that have been mentioned. But let's go on to consider the other side of the coin: some arguments in defense of grading.

1. The potential dangers and undesirable side effects of grading have been grossly exaggerated. While the kinds of consequences mentioned above are possible, they ordinarily do not

(and certainly need not) occur to any great extent. Like anything else, grading systems are not perfect. They could stand a great deal of improvement. In some cases, the importance of grades has undoubtedly been overemphasized. Occasionally, the grading system has had unfortunate effects. But these are not sufficient reasons to abandon the system entirely.

2. The notion that most students would study and learn without the extrinsic motivation implicit in grading is an unrealistic, romantic illusion, the product of wishful thinking. Whatever the theoretical objections to grades might be, from a practical standpoint they do serve as effective incentives.

3. Although there has been agitation for years to do away with grades, and a few schools have been conducted without them on an experimental basis, so far no one has been able to come up with a viable alternative to grading that has met with widespread success or general acceptance.

4. Students want, need, expect, and have a right to know how well they are doing, what their strong points are, and in what areas they need improvement. Parents, school administrators, prospective employers, college admissions officers, and others also want this information. Part of a teacher's job is to supply it.

5. To instruct large numbers of unselected students, it is necessary to group them somehow. The best way of doing this is on the basis of their past achievement and present educational needs. To individualize instruction, it is necessary to ascertain what the student has already learned. Thus, some system of grading is necessary to distinguish those who have learned from those who have not.

6. If the school is to maintain a respectable set of scholastic standards and provide a high-quality educational program, there has to be some way of determining whether, to what extent, and by whom those standards are being met.

For some other arguments in defense of grades, see the articles by Ebel (1977) and Feldmesser (1977) cited in the bibliography.

Pass/Fail Systems

As an alternative to the conventional grading system, many colleges offer the Pass/Fail (or Credit/No Credit) option in at least some courses. As Ahmann and Glock (1975) point out, the main justification for the Pass/Fail plan is that it gives students a chance to elect certain courses that they otherwise might not take for fear of failure. Other justifications are that this system reduces pressure and anxiety, allows the student to control his own study time, emphasizes learning rather than grade-getting and contributes to greater interest in and healthier attitudes toward the subject. In essence, the Pass/Fail system relies heavily on intrinsic rather than extrinsic motivation.

After reviewing a few studies of the Pass/Fail (P/F) system, Gage and Berliner (1975) conclude that student motivation is not as high under that system as it is when conventional grading procedures are employed. Their findings corroborate the views of many instructors who have taught classes under both plans. By their own admission, a sizable proportion of students spend less time and effort on P/F courses than they do on those where they have a chance to earn an A or are faced with the possibility of getting a D or an F. While some claim that they learn more under the relaxed P/F conditions, we have only their opinion that such is the case.

The elementary and high school counterpart of Pass/Fail is the Satisfactory/Unsatisfactory (S/U) system of grading. The arguments for and against both systems are similar. Under the S/U plan, one student who does extremely well in a subject and another who barely gets by are both given the same mark. This system has been criticized not only because the terms *satisfactory* and *unsatisfactory* are usually poorly defined but also because the system allegedly removes a potentially useful incentive. "Why," a student might ask himself, "should I knock myself out when I can get the same grade with just a little effort and when there is no special reward for outstanding performance?"

Critics of grading contend that students have been conditioned to think too much in terms of grades and that it's time we began to shift the emphasis toward learning and self-fulfillment. Perhaps some day we will.

Importance of Grades

Whether or not grades are absolutely essential to or desirable for the educational process remains a debatable issue. But so long as grades remain a part of the educational system, to disparage them, or to tell students (as some teachers do) that they are meaningless or insignificant is as wrong as it is to overemphasize them. However the teacher might feel about grades personally, and whatever dangers there might be in attaching exaggerated value to report-card marks, those marks are usually a matter of great concern to the students. Perhaps ideally they should not be, but realistically they are likely to have what for him are some very important implications.

The grades that a student receives could have a significant bearing on his educational and vocational future as well as on his personal life and self-concept here and now. They could make the difference between his being rewarded or punished by his parents. They could determine his promotion or nonpromotion, his graduation or failure to graduate with his class, his acceptance or rejection for admission to the college or to the career of his choice. They could make the difference in his receiving a scholarship or financial aid for further education. They could determine his eligibility to participate in athletics or to hold some school office. Even more important, perhaps, are the effects that his grades might have on his feelings about himself.

As a teacher, therefore, please do not take lightly the matter of assigning grades and marking report cards. Do not be a party to the propagation of the trite half-truth that grades really do not matter so long as the student learns something. And don't think of your role in this respect as one of casually giving students whatever grade you happen to feel like giving them. Grades are important to your students and to their parents, and therefore should be important to you as a teacher.

Role of Tests

Even though grades and tests usually go hand in hand, they are by no means inseparable. One does not necessarily imply the other. A teacher can assign grades without ever giving a test, and students can be tested without the teacher's using the results for report-card marking purposes. Test results are probably the most common source of students' grades, but in certain subject areas and grade levels, criteria such as the student's classroom recitations, participation and homework assignments, projects, term papers, book reports, oral presentations, demonstrated competence in some skill, etc. might be far more valid.

Even if grading procedures were abolished, tests would continue to serve a variety of important instructional purposes. For example, tests can be used to diagnose students' difficulties and to indicate the particular areas where more work is necessary. They can be used as a check on the effectiveness of the teacher's methodology. They can help a teacher to determine whether the objectives of a particular unit have been achieved and whether the students are prepared to go on to the next unit. They can be used as pretests to find out what the student already knows about a subject before a new unit of work is introduced. They can be used for counseling purposes, as a basis for placement or grouping of students, and in at least a few other ways. And, of course, they do have something to do with motivation.

Although the evidence is by no means conclusive, there is reason to believe that students who are given weekly quizzes achieve more and, by inference, are more highly motivated than those who are tested less frequently. To keep their students on their toes and to encourage daily preparation, some teachers favor the use of surprise (sometimes known as *pop*) quizzes. However, students often maintain that they do not and cannot study as carefully for these as they do for tests that are announced in advance. When surprise tests are used, a student is placed in a position where he must, in effect, gamble. Every night, he must decide whether he will take a chance on not being tested the next day or be cautious and assume that he will. The result is often a kind of contest with students and teachers trying to outguess one another. Much more effective, it seems, would be an announcement that on a certain day a test covering specified material will be given. Still, the relative advantages and effectiveness of announced versus surprise tests has yet to be proved.

Some teachers find daily quizzes to be advantageous, and perhaps in some subject areas they are. But one study found them to be less valuable than no quizzes at all. Apparently, the use of tests for motivational purposes can reach a point of diminishing returns. It is impossible to set down a hard-and-fast rule as to the most effective number or frequency of tests. However, regularly scheduled quizzes do seem to provide students with short-range goals and the opportunity for frequent feedback, or reinforcement.

Purpose of Grades

One of the two main purposes of grades is, of course, motivational: to reward students for good work, to encourage them to do better work, and, possibly, to punish them for poor work. The other, and possibly more important purpose, is to inform the student, his parents, and school administrators about the quality of his work. Later, this information might also be transmitted to college admissions officers, prospective employers, and others who want to know and have a right to know how much Johnny has learned. Sometimes, these two purposes conflict.

Johnny, for example, might be trying very hard to learn spelling, but his test scores are by far the lowest in the class. So that you don't discourage him you, as his teacher, might give him a higher grade than he actually deserves. Your motives in doing so might be quite commendable. But, by telling his parents via the report card that he is doing C, or average or satisfactory, work in spelling, you might actually be *misinforming* them and Johnny. Still, because of his good attitudes, effort, etc., you might hesitate to give him the D or E that his work warrants.

Depending on the format of the reporting system used in your particular school, whether or not you have personal conferences with the parents, and other factors, there are various ways in which you might resolve this kind of conflict and fulfill the two main purposes of grades. We'll return to this problem, but first let's examine the three basic systems of grading: norm-referenced, criterion-referenced, and individualized.

Norm-Referenced Grading

Norm-referenced grading is perhaps most familiar to you in the form of taking the class average into account or grading on the curve. When this system is used, the individual's grade depends not only on how well he does but even more on how his achievement compares with that of others in the class. His grade is relative to a norm, that norm being the achievement of the class as a whole.

Some teachers, particularly at the college level, use this method of grading in connection with a quota system. For example, they decide in advance that the top 10 percent of the class will receive As; the next 20 percent, Bs; the middle 40 percent, Cs; the next 20 percent, Ds; and the lowest 10 percent, Fs. Under this system, it is possible for a student who has averaged, say, 92 percent on tests to end up with an F in the course simply because most of the class scored above 92 percent. Similarly, a student who answers 35 percent of the questions on a test correctly could conceivably be the highest scorer in the class and receive an A. In another class, when compared with another group of students, that same score of 35 percent might well have earned an F.

Even when such a rigid quota system is not used, norm-referenced grades do not indicate how much the student has learned or how well he is able to perform. A mark of C, for example, signifies that his work is average, but unless we have a clear idea of how much the average student has learned, we really do not know what the C means.

Criterion-Referenced Grading

Criterion-referenced grading refers to the system in which an individual's grade depends upon the extent to which he has achieved the stated objectives of the course regardless of what any one else in his class does. Rather than being compared with other students, his work is compared with an absolute, predetermined standard (the criterion).

Criterion-referenced grading is most commonly used in connection with explicit performance objectives and some form of mastery learning (Block 1975). It implies arbitrary standards that everyone is expected to achieve to pass or to receive a certain letter grade. If the objectives are clearly stated and publicized, this system yields information that is considerably more meaningful than that of a norm-referenced system. For example, instead of simply indicating that a student's work is above/below average in a certain subject area, this method might reveal that he has correctly spelled 75 percent of the words on a given list, or satisfactorily answered five out of ten questions on a science test, or that he has solved 100 percent of his math problems.

Under this system, when test scores are translated into letter grades, the correspondence is purely arbitrary. For example, 90 percent might be the minimum for an A in one class; 85 or 95 percent might be the minimum in another, depending upon the nature and importance of the subject. But the standards do not vary with the class average. Thus, it is possible that, with a criterion-referenced approach, when letter grades are used, each and every member of the class could receive an A or a C or an F.

Individualized Grading

A third approach is to grade each student on an individual basis, with little or no reference to class norms or predetermined criteria. Under this system, the teacher takes into account such factors as the student's abilities, the effort set forth, and the progress being made. The teacher might also consider the student's attitudes, dependability, spirit of cooperation, and other personality characteristics. Perhaps to a very limited extent factors such as these should be considered in deciding the student's grade. But there is a point at which these considerations become irrelevant. When this individualized system is used, the student's grade might well come to depend not so much on what he has learned but on how the teacher happens to feel about him; not so much on objective evidence but on the teacher's personal subjective impressions of him.

While the theory behind individualization is highly commendable, this system of grading has at least two serious drawbacks. It might distort the meaning of the student's grades in his academic subjects so as to render them practically useless. It raises the possibility of favoritism.

Presumably a good mark in, say, science signifies that the student knows his science reasonably well. If the student does not know much science but the teacher gives him a high grade in that subject because he is cooperative, tries hard, or impresses her with his good manners, the mark is not only meaningless, but she is actually deceiving his parents and anyone else who looks at the grade. Most report cards have a separate place for evaluating the student's citizenship, study habits, or efforts. His science mark should indicate how much he has learned about science.

A teacher should never, of course, give a student a lower mark than he has earned simply because she dislikes him. By the same token, she should not give him a higher grade than his work warrants because she happens to like him, feels sorry for him, or wants to cheer him up or raise his self-concept. But neither should she ignore the motivational factor. She should not adhere rigidly to any predetermined system if doing so will discourage the student, lower his self-concept, cause him to feel that he is too dumb to learn, or have other adverse effects on his subsequent attitudes or performance.

Alternative Procedures

Thus far, no one has devised a grading system that is perfectly satisfactory to all concerned, and I doubt that anyone ever will. Norm-referenced, criterion-referenced, and individual-referenced systems all have their adherents. But many teachers have devised procedures of their own for their particular classes that incorporate elements of each. Some, for example, begin with predetermined standards that they expect everyone to achieve but take into account the class average and individual factors in determining the student's grade. While some teachers assign top priority to the motivational aspect of grading and others regard the informational function as taking precedence, most probably try to fulfill both purposes simultaneously.

A variety of grading and reporting procedures have been used, with varying degrees of success, to give parents a clear understanding of their children's scholastic achievement and growth without their having to rely solely on such discouraging terms as unsatisfactory, failure, below average, D-, or poor. Among these are parent/teacher conferences, letters to parents, diagnostic checklists indicating the student's particular strengths and weaknesses, and the use of such descriptive phrases as

Works up to Capacity.

Needs Improvement.

Is Making Steady Progress.

Does Not Follow Directions.

Shows Little or No Curiosity.

Volunteers for Assignments.

Works Well Independently.

Cooperates with Other Students.

Displays Cheerful Attitudes.

Other grading and reporting procedures involve some form of a dual marking system. For example, a mark of C/A might indicate that the student has done C work (usually meaning average) for his class but that he warrants an A for effort. In another situation, a mark of S/4 would indicate that the student's work is satisfactory for a person of his ability level, but the 4 signifies that on a four-category basis his scores on a test of scholastic aptitude place him in the lowest quartile.

Still another alternative is to use social, tangible, or activity reinforcers in addition to, or instead of, grades for motivational purposes. This brings us to the subject of contingency management.

CONTINGENCY MANAGEMENT

Perhaps it would be well to begin this section with a brief review of some of the points that were discussed in earlier chapters, particularly in Chapter 4.

While humanistic educators and psychologists are inclined to emphasize interest or intrinsic motivation, behaviorists rely much more heavily on incentives. Incentives correspond to the principle of reinforcement, which is basic to the entire process of behavior modification. One of the key ideas of behavior modification is that behavior is shaped by its consequences. From a behavioral standpoint, the most effective way (and possibly the only effective way) to arouse and sustain students' interests and to motivate them toward scholastic achievement is to reward their desired behavior or to offer them some sort of incentive.

One of the most important functions of a teacher, therefore, is to provide suitable reinforcement. One difficulty with this function is finding reinforcers that work. Some students perceive social approval or good grades as reinforcing. Others do not. Consequently, more attractive reinforcers must be used. The ideal form of reinforcement is that which comes from within the student, the internal feeling of satisfaction or enjoyment that is derived from the activity itself. Thus, the concept of reinforcement is not limited to extrinsic motivation or to rewards doled out by the teacher. It also pertains to intrinsically motivated behavior for which the student reinforces himself.

If your students are (or can readily be made) intrinsically motivated, fine. If they respond to verbal approval or feel that they are adequately rewarded by good grades, perhaps those two kinds of incentives are all that you will need. But if, despite your best efforts, you have difficulty in making your work interesting, or if your students do not seem to care much about either grades or your words of approval, you might want to consider the use of activity reinforcers.

The Premack Principle

According to the Premack principle, which was mentioned in Chapter 4, any enjoyable activity (such as watching television) can be used to reinforce a less enjoyable activity (such as studying) if the former is made contingent upon the latter (Premack 1959). Without having heard its name, a great many parents in effect use the Premack principle when they say to their children,

"After you have finished doing your homework, you may watch television."

or

"When you clean your room, you can go out and play."

or

"If you wash the car this afternoon, you may use it tonight."

Note, first of all, the emphasis on the positive in these examples. They are not stated in terms of "If you don't, you can't," but in terms of "If you do, you may." The negative implications are present, but it is the desirable positive consequence that is made explicit. Note, secondly, that the pleasant consequences *depend on* the young person's first doing something that he is likely to find less than pleasant or not personally satisfying. Note, finally, that if this principle is to be effective it must be clearly understood by the young person that if and *only if* he does this will he be able to do that (see Figure 15).

Homme (1970) refers to this principle as Grandma's Law in a kind of tribute to generations of grandmothers who have laid down the dictum, "First you eat all of your vegetables, then you can have some ice cream." Becker (1975) states the principle more broadly in these terms: "You do what I want you to do before you get to do what you want to do." A still more forceful way of phrasing it is: "There is no way that you will be able to do what you'd like to do except by first doing what I'd like you to do." This might sound terribly authoritarian and perhaps it is. But it is also a tremendously effective way of getting things done.

A wide variety of activity reinforcers, geared to the tastes and personal preferences of individual students, along with more tangible reinforcers such as food or money are available for use in connection with the much-discussed token economy.

Token Economies

The term *token economy* refers to the practice of giving students plastic chips or, sometimes, points on a chart or little slips of paper for prescribed behavior or achievement. A specified number of these tokens can be exchanged for candy, toys, comic books, a special privilege such as a field trip or free time, or some other type of backup reinforcer. The underlying principle is essentially

CONDITIONS	CONSEQUENCES
If and *only if* you do	Then and *only then* will you receive or be permitted to do
A	B
X	Y

FIGURE 15. A Contingency-Management Model.

that used by parents who offer their children money as an incentive, or as a reward, for good grades.

Token reinforcement is very closely associated with, but is by no means essential to, behavior modification. Literally hundreds of studies, however, testify to the effectiveness of tokens in situations where more conventional forms of reinforcement were unsuccessful (Blackham and Silberman 1975). The token economy has been used not only with normal children in regular classrooms but, perhaps even more successfully, with retarded, delinquent, and emotionally disturbed individuals of all ages in clinics, psychiatric hospitals, rehabilitation centers, and prisons (Craighead 1976).

In classroom situations, token reinforcers have been found to be far more effective with younger than older children. While a six-year-old might be motivated to work hard to win, say, a wad of bubble gum or a trip to the zoo, it is less likely that a sixteen-year-old would be inclined to do so. But, even the older student might find something like a transistor radio or extra gym time more appealing than the customary good grade as a reward for desired behavior. One of the practical problems with the use of token economy, particularly at the higher grade levels, is that of finding suitable backup reinforcers that the students will find attractive and that the school or teacher can afford (Stainback 1973).

Contingency Contracts

Token reinforcers are commonly used in connection with student/teacher contracts. Sometimes these contracts, which may be written or oral, are prepared by the teacher unilaterally and simply given to the students. In other cases, they are bilateral; the terms are negotiated by the teacher and the students somewhat as labor and management negotiate the terms of their contracts in business and industry. In either case, the contract stipulates the specific rewards for specified behavior or levels of achievement.

These agreements are sometimes referred to as contingency contracts because the reward is contingent upon (it depends upon) the student's acting in the desired way. The reward could be a better grade; it could be a specified privilege or activity; it could be a certain number of points or tokens. Whatever the nature of the reward, the contract specifies what the student must do to receive it.

For example, according to the terms of a particular contract, any student who scores at least 80 percent on a mathematics test receives ten tokens. To earn fifteen tokens, one would have to score at least 90 percent; to receive twenty tokens, 100 percent. A contract might stipulate that anyone whose grade improves by, say, 10 percent from one test to another, receives x tokens. Tokens might also be awarded for doing one's homework satisfactorily, exerting what the teacher judges to be a reasonable effort, or even for just sitting quietly and paying attention for a certain amount of time. A contract might also include provisions for losing points as a consequence of undesired behavior, such as not doing one's homework. But, ordinarily the emphasis is on rewards for desired behavior rather than punishment for failure or deviant behavior.

Just as token can be used without formal contracts, so can contracts be used without tokens. For example, a contract can be used in connection with conventional grading procedures. ("If you do this, that, and the other thing satisfactorily, you will receive an A. If you do this and that but not the other thing, your grade will be a B. To earn a C, you need do only this *or* that. If all you do is the other thing, you will receive a D.")

In negotiating a bilateral contract, whether grades, or tokens, or both are used, students and teachers do a bit of give-and-take bargaining as they define this, that, and the other thing in terms of the amount and quality of work required for a particular reward.

Student-Selected Incentives

Negotiating contracts gives students a voice in determining not only what they will be expected to accomplish but also in what they will get as a reward when and if they do accomplish their goal. In at least one elementary school classroom, the teacher informed his students that, if they fulfilled certain conditions with respect to scholastic achievement and decorum for the entire week, they would be given a prize. Then he asked each student to suggest the kind of prize each would like to receive. Among the suggestions were the following:

A candy bar.

Write a note to my mother telling her how good I was.

Let me sit next to Michael T.

Have a party with ice cream and cake but only the good children can come.

I'd like to make believe I'm the teacher.

More time for gym and recess.

I would like to wash the blackboards.

How about a triple Dairy Queen?

Some of the suggestions had to be rejected for financial or other reasons. Some were modified or made more explicit. Most were written on individual slips of paper and placed in a box. On Friday afternoon, all of the students who had been good all week were eligible to draw one of the slips. The slip indicated his or her reward for that week. To add to the interest of the weekly drawings, it was decided that students would be permitted to trade their prizes with one another if a mutually agreeable exchange could be worked out. Thus, a student who had his heart set on a note to his mother, for example, but drew something else could either arrange a trade or wait until the next week when he would have another chance at drawing the prize he really wanted.

Even if this type of lottery does not appeal to you as a teacher and even if you do not use tokens or contracts, you might still wish to consider the strategy of asking your students for their suggestions as to the kinds of activities or other reinforcers that they would find attractive.

Objections to Contingency Management

One of the most commonly voiced objections to contingency management, particularly as it involves the use of tangible or activity reinforcers, is that it constitutes a form of bribery. The use of that word in this context, however, is misleading and unwarranted. Ordinarily the term *bribery* carries with it the connotation of secretly paying someone for doing something that is of questionable legality. But there is nothing illegal or immoral about learning arithmetic, for example, and the tokens (candy bars or trips to the museum) are not awarded surreptitiously.

Nevertheless, there are those who object on principle to the very idea of paying students to do what they should be doing freely. Teachers and parents would "have it made" if children and young people did what was expected of them without a payoff. But this is perhaps as unrealistic an expectation in the home or classroom as it is in the professions or the world of business and industry. Most teachers, I suspect, teach not only for the intrinsic love of teaching, but because of the extrinsic tangible reinforcers that they receive in the form of their paychecks. Similarly, the parents of most students work at their jobs, whatever those jobs might be, not because of intrinsic motivation but because of the weekly financial payoff. Perhaps it is neither reasonable nor realistic to expect students to differ in this regard from their teachers or parents.

Another common objection to contingency management is that it involves programming people to behave as others want them to behave. The very thought of conditioning human beings or manipulating their behavior is distasteful to some critics of behavior modification and frightening to others. Such procedures have been perceived as detracting from the person's freedom, individuality, human dignity, and right to self-fulfillment while placing an unconscionable amount of power in the hands of the contingency manager. The argument here is not that contingency management is ineffective but that it is *too* effective. Objections to its use have been raised, therefore, on ethical grounds.

This is not the place for an extended discussion of the complex, controversial moral issues surrounding the use—and the possible misuse or abuse—of behavior modification techniques. Let us simply recognize that contingency management is a tool or an instrument. In the hands of "bad" people, it can be (and has been) put to bad uses. But the same instrument, used by "good" people can be (and has been) put to good uses. If you are particularly interested in the ethical dimensions of this problem, you might want to read the Carl Rogers/B. F. Skinner debate which is recommended in Chapter 6, Skinner (1971, 1976), Holt (1972), Rogers (1977a), or the short but excellent discussion by Williams and Anandam, recommended at the end of this chapter.

Turning Play into Work

Greene and Lepper (1974) have advanced another kind of objection to contingency management. They have found that under certain conditions the use of incentives such as tokens has the undesirable effect of transforming play into work. For purposes of their discussion, they use the distinction made by Mark Twain: "Work consists of whatever a body is obliged to do. . . . Play consists of whatever a body is *not* obliged to do." This, you will recognize, corresponds roughly to the distinction between extrinsic and intrinsic motivation that we have noted in earlier chapters.

What are the certain conditions under which the use of incentives is likely to have an adverse effect? Greene and Lepper believe that when a child is engaged in an activity that he finds interesting and enjoyable and is then offered a reward for engaging in that activity, his perceptions of that activity undergo a change. What had been intrinsically motivated now becomes extrinsically motivated. The activity (whether it be playing a game or reading, for example) that was originally perceived as an end in itself now becomes a *means* to some external end (the reward). Thus, they claim that the use of external reinforcers can actually undermine the student's intrinsic motivation.

They recognize that if a student has no interest in the activity to begin with, there is no intrinsic motivation for him to lose. They also recognize that when he lacks the basic skills that are necessary for him to discover the intrinsic satisfaction of such complex activities as reading, the use of extrinsic rewards can help him to acquire those skills. They are not, therefore, by any means unalterably opposed to the use of incentives. But they do recommend that extrinsic rewards be used sparingly and only when necessary.

Greene and Lepper maintain that teachers or parents should not *assume* that such rewards are necessary unless they have first given intrinsic motivation a fair trial. They also recommend that when they are used, extrinsic rewards should be phased out as soon as possible so that the student will not become overly dependent upon them. One way of phasing them out is to present verbal approval along with the tangible reward so that the two become closely associated. As the tangible reward is gradually withheld or withdrawn, the verbal reinforcer continues. Eventually, the verbal reinforcer can also be eliminated and the student might be able to proceed under his own direction.

COMPETITION AND COOPERATION

The desire to succeed, or the need to achieve, frequently implies competition. Perhaps it should not and need not, but it frequently does. Success, as we have seen, is often a relative matter. Thus, our concepts of ourselves and our perceptions of the degrees of success or failure that we have achieved commonly involve the comparison of our own performance or acquisitions with those of others. Similarly, as other people judge us, we are likely to be evaluated in terms of having more than or less than someone else or of being better than or worse than our peers or associates.

Competition is one of the oldest motivational strategies in the history of education. The ancient Greeks and Romans used it. So did the ancient Chinese and Israelites. The fact that competition has been used for thousands of years does not mean, of course, that it should therefore be used for the next thousand years, or even for the next two weeks. But the longevity and universality of this tactic suggests that it must have something in its favor. In recent years rivalry as a motivational device has been rather strongly criticized in certain educational and psychological circles, while the recommendation has been made that it be deemphasized, if not eliminated, and supplanted by cooperation. Let's focus on competition first and then consider cooperation.

Forms of Competition

To begin with, we might make a distinction between individual and group competition.

Individual competition, as the name suggests, refers to an individual's striving to surpass other individuals. Thus, a student might try to earn the highest test score in his class or at least to exceed the class average, to earn a position on the honor roll or dean's list, to win some sort of certificate or trophy indicating that his work was, if not the very best, among the best of those with whom the comparison was made. The honor, the recognition, the A, the scholarship, or whatever, is for the individual alone. This form of rivalry is likely to be most characteristic of schools that place a premium on high grades, especially when the class average is used in determining those grades. In those schools where the students are already highly motivated toward scholastic standards, individual competition is often highly effective.

Group competition usually involves the dividing of a class into teams and encouraging them to try to outdo one another. In my own elementary school days, for example, the boys and girls were often required to compete with one another. The girls also always won, of course, but we males, as I recall, pretended that we could not have cared less. Still it did motivate us as well as them to study a little harder than we otherwise would have done. Once in a while, our fifth grade (boys and girls together) would compete with What's Her Name's fifth-grade class across the hall. Even as an eleven-year-old, I remember wondering why our teachers didn't arrange such matches more often. They struck me then as being rather effective and I still think they have good potential. Not only did we study at least a bit harder to uphold the honor of our room, but competing with the other room brought about some useful cooperation and healthy peer-group pressures within our own room. Besides, it was fun!

Research Findings

Way back in the 1920s, when educational psychology was barely approaching the adolescent stage of its development as a science, a great deal of research was done on the relative effects of individual versus group competition. One general conclusion to be drawn from this research is that students are likely to work harder for individual rewards than for group rewards and to learn more when competing than when not competing. Not all of the evidence supports this conclusion unequivocally, as we shall see. But a few highly regarded and frequently cited studies do.

J. B. Maller conducted a study in which more than 800 students from grades five through eight were alternately placed in three different situations. In the first, they were given no special motivation at all. In the second, they were encouraged to try to win a prize for their group. In the third, each student was encouraged to try to win a prize for himself. The assigned task involved arithmetical computation. Maller found that the students did their best work while competing as individuals; their second best while working for the group reward; and their poorest work in the noncompetitive situation. He also found that when they were given a choice of working for individual or group rewards, most preferred to work for themselves (Maller 1938).

In a similar study, V. M. Sims divided his subjects into three comparable groups: an individual-motivation group, a group-motivation group, and a control group. In the individual-motivation situation, students worked in pairs. Each kept his own records as well as those of his partner (or rival), with whom he was expected to compete. In the second situation, group competition was used. In the third, there was no competition at all. As was the case in Maller's study, Sims found that the individual competitors made the greatest gains, the group competitors came in second, and the noncompetitors gained the least (Sims 1928).

In a study conducted by Elizabeth Hurlock, approximately 150 elementary school students were matched and divided into two parallel groups on the basis of age, sex, and ability. Those in the experimental group were further divided into subgroups, the members of which were encouraged to compete with one another in arithmetic. The scores of each group were written on the blackboard and the names of members of the winning team were read aloud. The control group was not encouraged to compete at all. Hurlock found that after one week, the duration of the study, members of the experimental groups had earned considerably higher scores than those in the noncompetitive control group. She also found that, in general, the younger and slower students made greater gains when motivated by competition than did the older or brighter students (Hurlock 1935).

A number of other studies have supported the effectiveness of competition not only as a motivational device but as a means to greater achievement. E. P. Torrance, for example, found that competition has a positive effect on creativity. In one of his many studies of creative thinking, Torrance asked a group of children to think of as many ways as they could to improve certain common toys so that they would be more fun to play with. He noted what he called a fairly consistent tendency for children who performed this task under competitive conditions to come up with a greater variety of recommendations, reflecting a higher degree of originality, than those who worked in a noncompetitive situation (Torrance 1965). After reviewing a great many of the early studies of the problem, Vaughn and Diserens conclude that competition does indeed tend to increase learning efficiency. This conclusion has never been convincingly refuted (Vaughn and Diserens 1938).

Side Effects of Competition

For the past three or four decades, the question has not been "Does competition work?" but "Should competition be encouraged?" Despite the fact that competition has been shown to be rather effective in a great many different kinds of learning situations, many educational psychologists have expressed concern about the possible adverse side effects of this motivational technique. Objections have been raised that competition not only might be detrimental to the individual's overall personality development, but that it also actually weakens the learning process and distorts the whole idea of what education is supposed to be all about (Wax and Grenis 1975).

Losers

In every form of competitive activity, one or a few people win. The majority do not. Somebody's winning depends upon someone else's losing. While winning might provide a boost to the ego of the elite, consistent failure to win can have a demoralizing effect on the rank and file. Quite commonly, the same few individuals are the winners time after time while others are consistently among the also rans. Thus, competition tends to reinforce those who are least in need of reinforcement and reinforcement is withheld from those who really need it and could profit by it.

Consistent losers, it is argued, are not motivated by competition. They are threatened by it. For students who are forced to compete in situations in which they feel that they have no chance to win, competition becomes an aversive stimulus. About all that they are likely to derive from the experience is a deepened sense of frustration, a lowered feeling of personal worth, perhaps a feeling of guilt, and a depreciated self-concept. When the competition becomes intense and personal, the losers might even develop feelings of bitterness, jealousy, and hostility toward their "opponents."

Believing that they will inevitably fail to win, the losers are likely to lose interest in the activity itself, stop trying, or simply go through the motions indifferently. Besides withdrawing psychologically from the field of competition, the consistent losers are also apt to be looking for other areas in which they can excel or in which they feel that they have a good chance to win recognition. As Alfred Adler warned us in Chapter 3, the form of the activity that they choose as a means of compensation might be some sort of mischief that falls into the category of disruptive behavior.

Winners

As for the consistent winners, it has been claimed that competition contributes to their feelings of vanity, selfishness, and an attitude of "Me first and to hell with everyone else!" Competition does sometimes seem to bring out the worst in people, particularly when the importance of winning is overemphasized and when failure on the part of some people is a prerequisite for the success of others.

Even if it does not result in the winners' gloating, the main idea behind the competition is often to motivate a person toward self-glorification. It would seem, then, that there ought to be a better way to reinforce students than by making them feel that they are somehow better than others. Instead of having the more competent students trying to surpass one another for their own personal benefit, it has been suggested that it would be better to encourage them to help one another.

Competition, as we have seen, is likely to be effective only with those who feel that they have a good chance of winning. But even among these, competition is likely to contribute to needless pressures, anxieties, and frustrations as, for example, when Susie worries about dropping down from a 4.0 to a 3.9 average or when

Boris feels threatened by Igor who is challenging him for Top Honors.

Uses and Abuses of Competition

The adverse side effects of competition that have just been mentioned are not, of course, inevitable. They are only possibilities. But, in the opinion of some educational psychologists and others, these possibilities are strong enough to warrant deemphasis, if not abandonment, of competition as a means of motivation. We might note that there is very little if any hard scientific evidence based on careful research to substantiate the probability of such side effects occurring. Objections to competition are based more on the opinion of clinical psychologists than on the findings of experimental psychologists or seasoned teachers.

Clinical, education, and other psychologists are in general agreement that, when such adverse consequences occur, they are not necessarily directly attributable to competition per se but to misuses or abuses of a potentially useful procedure. Interpretations of research findings, along with the testimony of clinicians and teachers, have yielded a number of suggestions about how competition can be used constructively and how these possible adverse side effects can be held to a minimum. Among these recommendations are the following.

1. Be sure that the participants are evenly enough matched so that each one has a reasonably good chance of winning. We would not, I hope, expect an 85-pound girl to compete on a football field with a 200-pound boy. Neither should we require slow learners to compete in, say, mathematics with our average students, or our average students with those who have been endowed with an exceptionally high aptitude in that area.

2. Avoid a dog-eat-dog approach where the competition is so intense that the individual's feeling of personal worth or self-concept is at stake. Try to keep the competition on a fun basis and do not overemphasize the importance of winning. Even in sports, contrary to what some coaches might claim, winning is not the only consideration.

3. Have the individual's grade depend at least in part on

noncompetitive activities—projects, papers, reports, participation, etc.—that challenge each student to do the best work of which he is capable without comparisons to what others have done.

4. Keep the students' test scores and report-card grades confidential. The practice of posting grades on a bulletin board or reading them off in front of the rest of the class has little, if anything, to recommend it. What a student got on a test is none of his classmates' business. How would you feel if your name were publicly announced as being at the bottom of the list?

5. Try to give every student an opportunity to experience a degree of success. Those who do not excel in arithmetic, for example, might be rewarded for neatness, effort, punctuality, special interests, or in some other areas in which they have done well.

6. Balance individual competition with other motivational techniques. Try to develop an interest on the part of the students in the subject itself and work toward intrinsic motivation. Make use of self-competition and group competition involving cooperation among the group members. To try to do away with competition entirely would be a mistake if not an impossibility. But to rely on it exclusively, or even primarily, might be just as bad a mistake.

7. Use competition as a learning device. Through appropriate kinds of competitive activities, students can learn such old-fashioned virtues as good sportsmanship, fair play, how to be a gracious winner, and how to accept defeat without going to pieces. Competition can also be used to help the individual student to test himself, learn more about himself, discover his own strengths and weaknesses, make career plans, etc.

8. Encourage self-competition. Instead of comparing students with one another, have each student compare his present level of achievement with his own past performance. Perhaps, with the help of a simple chart or graph, each student can record his own progress, reinforce his own improvement, and try to do better this week than last. Self-competition would seem to be particularly well suited to individualized instructional programs. This procedure requires a consistent system of feedback to keep the student informed of how well he is doing and what he can or should do to surpass his previous record.

Cooperation

One of the main arguments used in support of competition as a motivational device is that we are living in a competitive society, that competition is part of the American way of life, and that, to prepare young people for life in the real world, the school should help students to learn how to compete. There is, of course, a certain amount of validity in that position. But it has also been argued that what our country (and world) needs is not more competition but more in the way of cooperation. Thus, instead of—or in addition to—teaching students to vie with one another, the school might focus on helping them to learn to study, work, and live together. Cooperation through various forms of group learning activities, it has been said, is no less effective than competition for motivational purposes, and has the added advantage of yielding more desirable kinds of side effects.

Cooperative learning takes a variety of forms, including small-group projects, discussions, symposia, the use of committees, student/teacher planning, peer tutoring, and other kinds of activities, the purpose of which is to encourage students to help one another. Such group activities, it has been claimed, not only are useful in stimulating interest and making learning enjoyable, but also contribute to the improvement of human relationships within the class. Cooperation is also assumed to help to satisfy the student's needs for acceptance and belonging and to help him to develop such traits as reliability and concern for the welfare of others (Stanford and Roark 1974).

Research on Cooperation

Earlier in this chapter, we noted the findings of a few classic research studies that lent strong support to competition as a motivational instrument. Other studies, however, have pointed to the advantages of cooperative effort.

In one of the most widely cited studies of this type, Deutsch divided a number of students into ten groups of five members each. Half of the groups were informed that members would each receive the same grade, which would depend on how well the members worked together. In the other five groups, each student was to be graded separately on a competitive basis and his performance was to be compared with that of the others in his particular group. The assigned tasks were to find solutions to puzzles and problems in the area of social relations.

Deutsch found no difference in the total amount of learning that took place under the two kinds of situations. Students in both groups not only achieved equally but seemed to be equally determined to do as well as possible (Deutsch 1960). Thus, depending upon one's own personal prejudices with respect to the relative merits of competition and cooperation, it could be said that (with respect to scholastic achievement) competing students did no better than cooperating students or that cooperators did no better than competitors.

With respect to personal and social side effects, however, Deutsch found some important differences. He noted, for example, more signs of anxiety and insecurity in the competitive groups and more of a willingness to share ideas in the cooperative group. Members of the cooperative groups made more friendly remarks to one another and fewer aggressive remarks. When asked to rate the performance of other members of their groups, the cooperators responded more favorably than the competitors. Deutsch's study was done at the college level. Similar studies with similar results have been also done at the high school and elementary school levels.

Stendler and her associates, for example, conducted a study in which a group of second graders were assigned the task of painting murals, first with the understanding that if everyone did his part and the murals were satisfactory, each child would receive a prize, and then with the understanding that only the best painters in the group would be rewarded. Presumably impartial judges found no difference in the quality of the two murals. Apparently, the effects of cooperation and competition in this situation were negligible. But, among the cooperating students, they found more in the way of friendly conversation, mutual assistance, and the sharing of materials, while the competitors were characterized by more signs of selfishness, obstruction, and unfriendly conversation (Stendler 1951).

Net Conclusions

The net conclusion to be drawn from these and a host of other studies on the relative effectiveness of cooperation and competition is that both can serve a useful purpose (D. W. Johnson 1975). To consider the two in either/or terms would be an unnecessary mistake. The consensus of experimental evidence seems to be that there is no good reason for a teacher to rely solely on either one of these strategies to the neglect of the other. While individual competition seems to have a slight advantage over group competition with respect to motivation toward scholastic achievement, the advantage is by no means great, universal, or consistent. Cooperation does, however, seem to contribute to more desirable side effects in the area of personality development, mental health, and social relations.

Assuming that learning to get along with others is an important objective of the total educational program, a teacher can certainly use cooperative group methods without endangering the quality of students' scholastic achievement. But, also assuming that learning to work independently and to stand on one's own two feet is an important outcome of schooling, the teacher can confidently use competition in moderation without worrying too much about harmful consequences.

It is unlikely that a teacher can completely eliminate competition from his classroom even if he wants to. Despite his efforts to the contrary, students will be inclined to compare their work (or grades) with their classmates' and there is no compelling reason why they should not do so. Still, there are areas in which cooperation can be just as effective and a great deal more enjoyable (D. W Johnson 1974, 1975, 1976).

RECOMMENDED READING

Allen, B. V. "Paying Students to Learn." *Personal and Guidance Journal,* 53:774–778, 1975. Discusses the generally favorable results of an experimental program conducted over a nine-year period in which ten minority-group high school and college students were given financial incentives for academic achievement.

Block, James H. *Mastery Learning in Classroom Instruction.* New York: Macmillan, 1975. A short but comprehensive booklet explaining how students can be motivated and otherwise helped to achieve mastery of prescribed instructional objectives on an individualized basis.

Cullen, F. T., Jr. *et al.* "Effects of the Use of Grades as an Incentive." *Journal of Educational Research, 68*: 277–279, 1975. Discusses the results of an experiment at the high school level, which shows the positive effect that grades have on assignment completion. In this study, loss of points for not completing assignments was found to be a more effective incentive than the awarding of points for completing them.

Feldmesser, Robert A. "The Positive Function of Grades." In Hamacheck, D. E., Ed., *Human Dynamics in Psychology and Education.* Boston: Allyn and Bacon, 1977. 3rd ed. Recognizes the possibility of grades being misused but brings out the benefits of the traditional marking system.

Graubard, Paul, and Rosenberg, Harry. *Classrooms That Work.* New York: E. P. Dutton, 1974. Describes a number of classroom situations in which behavior modification strategies are employed effectively.

Holt, John. "Marking and Grading." In Gall, Meredith, and Ward, Beatrice, Eds., *Critical Issues in Educational Psychology.* Boston: Little, Brown, 1974. Argues that testing and grading should be abolished because they actually impede learning. Offers several guidelines that teachers should use when they are required to grade students.

Johnson, David W., and Johnson, Roger T. *Learning Together and Alone.* Englewood Cliffs, N.J.: Prentice-Hall, 1975. Shows the uses and limitations, the advantages and disadvantages, of competitive, cooperative, and individualized classroom strategies. Suggests how each can be used most effectively with respect to cognitive and affective objectives.

Lepper, Mark R., and Greene, David. "When Two Rewards Are Worse Than One: Effects of Extrinsic Rewards on Intrinsic Motivation." *Phi Delta Kappan, 56*: 565–566, 1975. This is another version of the article "Intrinsic Motivation: How To Turn Play into Work," by Greene and Lepper, *Psychology Today*, Sept. 1974. The authors' main points are summarized in the present chapter of this book.

Nagel, Thomas S., and Richman, Paul T. *Competency-Based Instruction.* Columbus, Ohio: Charles E. Merrill, 1972. Subtitled "A Strategy to Eliminate Failure," this is a short branching programmed text that illustrates as it explains the widely discussed concept of competency-based instruction. Part of a series that includes the books by Stainback and Williams mentioned below.

Stainback, William C., *et al. Establishing a Token Economy in the Classroom.* Columbus, Ohio: Charles E. Merrill, 1973. Argues for the use of token reinforcers as effective incentives and explains in some detail how token economy programs can be implemented.

Wax, Joseph, and Grenis, Michael. "Conflicting Views on Competition." *Phi Delta Kappan,* 57: 197–200, 1975. Two separate articles. In the first, Wax criticizes competition; in the second, Grenis defends it. Each also responds to the other's article.

Williams, Robert L., and Anandam, Kamala. *Cooperative Classroom Management.* Columbus, Ohio: Charles E. Merrill, 1973. Emphasizes the use of positive reinforcement through student/teacher contracts. The first chapter presents a balanced discussions of the ethical issues involved in behavior modification.

CHAPTER 9: PREVIEW QUESTIONS

(After you have finished reading Chapter 9, you should be able to answer the following.)

1. Which of the twelve external factors mentioned in this chapter as contributing to student misbehavior do you regard as especially significant? Which do you consider relatively unimportant? Give the reasons for your choice.

2. Which of the twelve internal factors do you think are particularly noteworthy? Which, if any, do you think are comparatively insignificant? Why?

3. How critical do you think personal factors are as compared with internal or external factors? Explain your answer.

4. Which of the twelve main recommendations made in this chapter for preventing misbehavior do you think are likely to be relatively ineffective? Why?

5. Which of the suggestions made in this chapter for correcting misbehavior do you think are likely to be most effective? Why? Which do you think are least likely to work? Why?

6. Give three or four examples of ways in which teachers might inadvertently reinforce undesired classroom behavior.

7. What are some conditions under which certain forms of misbehavior should perhaps best be ignored?

8. What is meant by the saturation principle? What are some conditions under which it can be used effectively? Under what conditions do you think it should not be used?

9. What is meant by negative reinforcement? Give a couple of examples of cases in which you think it can or should be used. If you think it should never be used, explain why.

10. In your opinion, what is and what is not the purpose of punishment?

11. What are some conditions under which you think punishment is most likely to be effective? If you think punishment is never effective or should never be used, explain why.

12. What are some criteria to be used in evaluating particular forms or methods of punishment with regard to their possible side effects? Which of these do you regard as most critical? Why?

13. Explain and give a few original examples of the principle of logical consequences.

14. How are *time out* and *response cost* alike? How do they differ from one another?

15. What are some forms of punishment that experts regard as generally objectionable? Which of these do you regard as the most objectionable? Why? If there are any of these that you do not find objectionable, explain your position.

16. What are some forms of punishment that experts accept, approve, or recommend? Which of these do you regard as most acceptable? Why? If there are any of these that you do not approve, explain your position.

CHAPTER NINE

Motivation and Classroom Management

This chapter is largely a summary of practical suggestions for motivating students—or helping students to motivate themselves—toward orderly classroom behavior. In other words, it deals with the problems of discipline, classroom management, and disorderly, or disruptive, student behavior. The next chapter summarizes recommendations with respect to motivation toward scholastic achievement. These last two chapters are, of course, very closely interrelated. While orderly behavior, or good discipline, does not in and of itself guarantee that scholastic learning will follow, it is doubtful that much learning can or will take place without it. Moreover, if students are highly motivated toward scholastic achievement, chances are that discipline problems will be minimal.

In terms that we have been using throughout this book, especially in the two preceding chapters, discipline involves both extrinsic and intrinsic motivation, both incentives from without and feelings or desires from within. It pertains not only to things that teachers do to students, but also (and perhaps more importantly) to things that student do to, by, and for themselves. Ideally, discipline does not imply a power struggle, conflict, or adversary relationship between teachers and students but, rather, a cooperative venture in which both parties work together toward their common purposes. However, one of the realities of teaching (to put the matter as mildly as possible) is that students are not always as cooperative as their teachers would like them to be. Nor are teachers always as cooperative as their students would like *them* to be.

WHY STUDENTS MISBEHAVE

If a teacher is to deal intelligently with the problems of classroom management, he should have some understanding of why students misbehave. In earlier chapters, we noted some of the more commonly held theories on the matter. Freudians, you will recall, are inclined to attribute misbehavior to innate aggressive tendencies arising from the id and from unconscious, repressed feelings or desires of which the individual himself is unaware. Adlerians are more likely to attribute it to the individual's striving for superiority, as a form of compensation for a feeling of inferiority. Humanists, by and large, perceive misbehavior as an attempt to satisfy some personal, social, or emotional need. Behaviorists claim that people misbehave because, in effect, they have been rewarded for misbehaving.

For our present purposes, we can identify a number of more specific factors that are popularly thought of as contributing to deviant classroom behavior. These factors fall into three main categories: external, internal, and personal. *External factors* are those that pertain primarily to situations originating outside the school and over which the teacher has little or no control. *Internal factors* pertain to school and classroom conditions over which teachers do have control, and to the personality and behavior of the teacher herself. *Personal factors* are those originating within the individual student.

External Factors

Among the major external factors that are frequently mentioned as contributing to classroom misbehavior are the following:

1. Lack of discipline in the home; parents who reject or overprotect their children, who do not know or do not care what they do, who are unable or unwilling to regulate their behavior.

2. Peer-group influences, including imitation of undesirable models, attempts to gain the acceptance and approval of one's peers, and to impress them with one's virility, maturity, independence, sophistication, etc.

3. Prevailing socioeconomic conditions. Here, we refer not only to the effects of poverty (inadequate housing, poor nutrition, broken families, alienation, etc.) but also to those of affluence and the production of "spoiled brats" who have been brought up to believe that they have a right to whatever they want, whenever they want it.

4. Easy access to drugs and alcohol.

5. Laws and court decisions that protect the rights of students who misbehave while restricting the authority of teachers and school administrators to punish offenders.

6. A general disrespect for the concept of authority in the home, community, state and federal government, church, and elsewhere that filters down to the schools.

7. Excessive violence, brutality, sadism, and pornography in films, television programs, comic books, and magazines.

8. The gross materialism, hedonism, and selfishness of adult society.

9. Corruption in government, industry, labor organizations, and in other high places.

10. Uncertainty about the future with respect to such bleak prospects as unemployment, pollution, the deterioration of our cities, increases in crime statistics, etc.

11. The women's liberation concept which has been used to explain a sharp increase over the past few years in misbehavior, delinquency, and felonies on the part of females.

12. Inadequate recreational facilities in the community, nothing to do in one's spare time, no place to use up excess energy.

Please note that these are factors over which neither the teacher nor the school administration has very much, if any, control. Insofar as factors such as these contribute to classroom misbehavior, it hardly seems fair to blame teachers for it or to expect them to reduce it significantly.

Internal Factors

While a teacher might not be able to do anything about the kinds of external factors that have just been mentioned, he or she *can* do something about other factors that contribute to misbehavior on the part of students. Among the more commonly mentioned internal factors are these:

1. Student boredom with work that is uninteresting, nonchallenging, or not perceived as useful.
2. Crowded classrooms; less opportunity for students to receive individual attention; more opportunity for them to get away with misbehavior and remain undetected.
3. Teachers who try to be pals with their students, who act like one of the crowd and are therefore treated accordingly.
4. Teachers who are rude or sarcastic, who embarrass students, who dare them to just try to get away with misbehavior, who punish students more severely than their misbehavior warrants, or who are inconsistent and vacillating in their classroom management policies.
5. *Permissive* psychological theories and educational philosophies that emphasize freedom, individuality, self-expression, democracy in the classroom, and encourage students to do their own thing.
6. *Repressive* psychological theories and educational philosophies that lead to the imposition of needless rules and regulations dealing with relatively insignificant matters.
7. Failure on the part of the school administration to support teachers in their confrontations with defiant or unruly students.
8. Inadequate guidance and counseling facilities; the lack of personnel to help students with their personal, social, and emotional problems and with conflicts with parents or teachers, and to head off misbehavior before it has a chance to get out of hand.
9. Teachers who are incompetent, poorly prepared, disorganized, irresponsible, or who do not really care enough about their students to discipline them when necessary.
10. Lack of special attention to the particular needs of slow learners (who sometimes misbehave because of their inability to understand the material being taught) and bright students (who sometimes are tempted to misbehave when they find the work too easy).
11. Lack of clear-cut rules about specific behaviors that are required or prohibited.

12. Failure on the part of teachers to recognize and reward desired behavior while trying to eliminate undesired behavior.

Personal Factors

A third set of factors contributing to discipline problems originates within the student himself. As we have seen, many psychologists believe that students who habitually misbehave do so because of some unresolved personal, social, or emotional problem. They point out that a student's needs for attention, recognition, approval, and belonging are just as real, and almost as compelling, as needs for food and drink. Just as a person who has been deprived of food over a long period will resort to almost anything to satisfy that need, a person with unmet social or emotional needs might resort to any activity that seems to promise satisfaction of that need. The teacher or parent who dismisses a student's misbehavior with the explanation that he is trying only to get attention is implying that this need is something trivial or insignificant. But it is not.

Children—and for that matter adolescents and adults—often do not know how to satisfy this need in a socially accepted manner so they attempt to satisfy it in a socially unacceptable manner. Acts of misbehavior such as lying, bullying, fighting, showing off, clowning around, interrupting, and going out of one's way to appear different from the majority of one's classmates are probably all bids for attention.

Teachers sometimes ask the misbehaving student why he engages in such activities. A very articulate, introspective, precocious student might respond somewhat as follows.

Well, you see, the main reason why I started that fire in the wastebasket was to satisfy my need for recognition. Nobody pays much attention to me at home or at school, and like everyone else I want to be noticed. I felt that starting the fire would make other people aware of my existence. Of course, I did not expect approval for that act. But at least I've gotten your attention. For a person who craves attention as much as I do, unfavorable recognition is better than no recognition at all.

Far more likely, when asked why he misbehaved, the student

will respond, in all sincerity, with, "I don't know." But his teacher should know without having to ask.

In addition to the need for attention, every student has a need for power or self-assertion, a need to feel that he is free and strong, and independent and important. To bolster one's self-concept, a person needs a certain amount of freedom from restrictions that are imposed by others. To develop one's individuality and feeling of personal worth, a person must feel free to express himself, to make his own decisions, and to determine his own behavior. The student who is disorderly, disobedient, uncooperative, habitually truant or tardy, who talks when he is expected to be listening, or who pushes ahead when he should be waiting his turn might be attempting to satisfy this kind of need (Dreikurs 1968, 1971).

In trying to understand the reasons for misbehavior, we should also keep in mind the Freudian concept of unconscious motivation. It is quite possible that certain forms of misbehavior, particularly those of an aggressive nature, can be explained as the student's attempt to release repressed hostilities. For example, vandalism and fighting as well as defiance of a teacher or school administrator are often regarded as cases of displacement. Other forms of misbehavior such as cheating and lying might well be, at least in part, instances of projection or rationalization.

Before hastening to the conclusion that a disruptive student is necessarily bad or willful, we should at least consider the possibility that his misbehavior arises from instinctive impulses that he has never learned to control, perhaps through no fault of his own. This, of course, does not imply that we should overlook his misbehavior or absolve him from responsibility for it. But it does suggest that we should look beneath the surface of defiant behavior before deciding how to try to change it (Redl 1977).

PREVENTING MISBEHAVIOR

The ideal means of classroom management is to try to prevent misbehavior from occurring in the first place so that you will not have to deal with it afterwards. Unfortunately, there is no nice, neat, foolproof formula for the prevention of deviant behavior. There are, however, a number of general principles and practical suggestions that you might wish to consider in this regard.

The recommendations that follow are not new or revolutionary. Some of them are based on or supported by carefully conducted research. Some have been derived from one or more of the psychological theories that we have discussed in earlier chapters. All of them, however, reflect procedures that have been used successfully by countless teachers in their particular classrooms. These recommendations can help you to reduce the frequency and alleviate the seriousness of misbehavior in your classroom. But, please recognize that, no matter what you as a teacher do or try to do to prevent it, some misbehavior is almost certain to occur. As has been suggested, the reason why teachers cannot eliminate misbehavior completely is that they are unable to control the many external causes or contributing factors that have been discussed. The following suggestions deal with internal and personal factors over which the teachers do have at least some control.

Adopt a favorable but realistic attitude toward your students. Do not assume that they are a group of little devils whose main preoccupation is to torment you. However, do not begin with the romantic assumption that they are all darling little angels either. They are neither angels nor devils but flesh and blood human beings, like yourself, with a capacity for both good and bad behavior. Show your students that you like them and want to help them, but do not be naive or too easygoing. Give them the benefit of the doubt and regard them as innocent until proven guilty. Be prepared for trouble, but don't assume that it will necessarily occur. The overly suspicious teacher who doesn't trust his students and goes out of his way looking for trouble is likely to find it. Recognize, in short, that the vast majority of your students (and very likely all of them) are not bad apples but, like yourself again, sometimes less than perfect. Regard them, then, not as objects to be controlled, but as friends to be helped.

Do not assume, as some teachers do, that the students' main

preoccupation in life is to put something over on you and that your main mission is to make sure that they do not succeed in doing so. Above all, do not challenge your students to misbehave or carry the proverbial chip on your shoulder. Remember, too, that a certain amount of whispering, giggling, scuffling, talking aloud, seat-leaving, inattentiveness, and other minor annoyances are to be expected of the student as a normal part of his or her growing-up process. While you should not go out of your way to encourage such behavior, neither should you attempt to outlaw it. Persistent behavior of this type might have to be repressed, but ordinarily you should not make a big issue of it.

Establish your position of authority.   Be as warm and friendly and pleasant as possible, but make it clear to your students that you are and intend to remain in charge of the classroom situation. It is neither necessary nor desirable that you pound your desk, wear a stern countenance, make threatening noises, or play the role of the unbending autocrat. But do convey the message that you expect your students to do their assigned work and abide by classroom rules and regulations. It might not be necessary for you to tell them this in so many words. Perhaps you can get the message across even more effectively by the subtleties of your behavior, mannerisms, and overall personality.

In establishing your position of authority, the first few days or weeks are critical. But it might take longer than that. This is why the stock advice of old pros to beginning teachers very often is, "Don't smile until Christmas." Please do not take this bit of conventional wisdom literally or even very seriously. But do recognize that it is easier and usually more effective to start off the school year a little too strict and then gradually ease up than it is to begin too leniently or permissively and then try to crack down.

It should be pointed out that not everyone would agree with this recommendation. For example, Thomas Gordon, founder of Parent Effectiveness Training and Teacher Effectiveness Training programs, might take a very dim view of this authoritarian approach. One of Gordon's main tenets is that teachers and parents should abandon the use of power absolutely and unequivocally. He concedes that in certain situations physical power might be necessary to restrain a child from injuring himself but he firmly opposes verbal or psychological displays of power such as pulling rank or showing who's boss. Such flaunting of authority, he believes, weakens if it does not actually destroy human relationships, causes psychological damage to the child, and undermines the rational kind of problem-solving approach to conflict-resolution that is at the heart of his programs (Gordon 1975).

Rudolf Dreikurs, the prominent Adlerian psychologist, is another who might well take issue with this recommendation. Among his key ideas are that parents and teachers should not allow themselves to be drawn into power struggles with their children or students. While the authority figures in such situations might win most of the battles, he believes that in the long run they are more likely to lose the war. Homes as well as schools, he contends, should be conducted in a democratic society such as ours along democratic lines as well (Dreikurs 1968). Like Gordon, Dreikurs does not entirely reject the concept of authority, but both suggest that teachers and parents soft-pedal their power, not make a big show of it, use it judiciously, and temper it with some of the more humane kinds of strategies that will be recommended later in this chapter.

Nevertheless, with all due respect to democracy and humaneness in the home and classroom, I am inclined to agree with Robert Ebel when he points out that most young people need control and know that they need it. Most of them, he maintains, actually prefer "firm, consistent authoritative guidance to indecisive, uncertain vacillations in requirements, and unpredictable parent or teacher reactions" (Ebel 1977a). I also agreee with Don Dinkmeyer's recommendation that you try to develop a relationship of mutual respect by combining kindness with firmness (Dinkmeyer 1976). My present recommendation about establishing your position of authority has to do with the firmness aspect. Several other recommendations I shall offer center on the kindness aspect.

Inform your students of the rules governing classroom behavior. If you expect your students to adhere to regulations, they must have a clear understanding of what those regulations are. Vague admonitions to the effect that they should behave themselves or be good are not enough. They need clear-cut statements specifying what they must and what they may not do (Becker 1975a).

In formulating your rules, try to have as few of them as possible. Try to limit your regulations and prohibitions to such matters as you consider necessary for the attainment of educational goals or the welfare of your students. Avoid establishing rules that are based on nothing more than your own personal whims or preferences. If you have any reason to doubt the need for a certain regulation, that regulation is probably unnecessary. Both you and your students will probably be better off without it. The fewer rules you have, the easier the enforcement process is likely to be.

Whenever possible, state your rules positively. Specifying what students are expected to *do* (e.g., sit quietly) is likely to be more effective than presenting them with a long list of *thou shalt nots.* Don't forget to explain the reasons for your rules if they are not immediately obvious. Students have a right to ask why they must do this and why they may not do that. "Because I said so" is not a reasonable answer. Make it as clear as possible to your students that each requirement or regulation has been established for a sound purpose and is intended for *their* benefit, not yours.

You might also allow your students to help to formulate the rules governing their class. If they feel that they have had a voice in drawing up the regulations, they will be more likely to appreciate the need for them, observe them, and cooperate in enforcing them. As William Glasser, the founder of Reality Therapy, maintains, to have students behave responsibly they should (1) know the rules; (2) within reason, accept and agree with the rules; (3) help to make the rules; and (4) understand the consequences that they will have to face if they break the rules (Glasser 1965, 1969).

Be fair, consistent, honest, and genuine. Do not attempt to play the role of a cool, casual, easygoing, highly permissive type or that of a stern rule-with-an-iron-hand authoritarian. Do not play any role at all but let your normal, natural personality come through. Do not pretend to be something that you are not. Admit your mistakes when you make them and your lack of knowledge in situations where you simply do not know the answer.

Keep your promises and don't play favorites or show partiality toward individuals whom you happen to like more than others. Be consistent in enforcing classroom regulations so that your students will know where they stand and where you stand. You will, of course, want your students' respect. But it will not come automatically. You will have to earn it. Being as fair, honest, consistent, and genuine a person as possible is probably the most effective way of doing so.

You might do well to think of your role as a classroom manager in terms of what Carl Rogers calls a "helping relationship." Among the main characteristics of such a relationship, he believes, is that the person to be helped (the student) perceive the helper (the teacher) as trustworthy, dependable, open, sensitive, accepting, straightforward, and psychologically mature (Rogers 1971). From a Rogerian standpoint, what you *do* is not as important as the kind of person you *are*. Assuming that you are the kind of person that Rogers describes, or that you are trying to become such a person, let your own personality come through.

Show your students that you care about them. It is not nearly so important that your students love *you*, as it is that you love *them*—not in some mushy, sentimental way but with a genuine concern for their welfare, based on an understanding and appreciation of what they are and what they are capable of becoming. A teacher who consciously tries to win the affection of her students is likely to run the risk of confusing their whims and wishes with their needs. So don't cater to your students' wishes to be popular with them. If your students can be made to see that your main purpose as a teacher is to help them (assuming, of course, that such is indeed the case), they will very likely come to respect you. They might also come to love you, but first they must feel that you really care about them.

Use your sense of humor. A good laugh—though never at a student's expense—can often prevent some minor incident from developing into one of major proportion. Don't try to be a standup comedian or think that your function as a teacher is to keep your students entertained with clever witticisms. But do recognize that a good-natured humorous response can sometimes alleviate tensions that might be building up in the classroom. An element of humor can also demonstrate to the class that you, the teacher, are secure, at ease, in control of yourself, and therefore capable of controlling the class.

Have your day's work carefully planned. There is a great deal to be said in favor of flexibility, spontaneity, and informality with respect to teaching, but you are well advised to come into your classroom with a fairly detailed, structured lesson plan. You, as well as your students, should have a clear idea of who should be doing what, and when, where, how, and why. You might not always be able to carry out your plan and there are times when you will want to depart from it. But you should at least have a plan in mind, if not on paper, for keeping each of your students busily engaged at every moment in some activity that they know they are expected to accomplish.

This, of course, does not mean that all your students must necessarily be doing the same thing at the same time on a rigidly fixed schedule. But it does imply that your program should be organized so that students can proceed from one lesson or activity to another with a minimum of commotion. Try to establish in advance definite procedures for such routine transitional activities as entering and leaving the classroom, distributing books and materials, collecting students' work, etc.

While some routine is both necessary and desirable if not literally essential to effective classroom management, too much of it can contribute to boredom and restlessness, which in turn sets the stage for misbehavior. In planning your day's work, therefore, try to vary your procedures by using a variety of different kinds of instructional strategies and materials.

Try to avoid unnecessary conditions for misbehavior. Students are more likely to misbehave when they are not being observed by the teacher. This does not mean that you should keep an eagle eye on them at all times or convey the impression that you do not trust them. But such activities as turning your back to the class for several minutes while writing on the chalkboard is the kind of condition that you should try to avoid. Whenever possible, try to have your board work completed before the class begins.

Move about the classroom frequently. Ordinarily, the closer you are to a particular student, the less likely he is to misbehave. Here again, the suggestion is not that you should act like a policeman walking a beat. But it might be well to casually stroll over toward the seat of a student who is beginning to act up. While physical proximity can have the effect of reducing students' temptations to misbehave, it has the more important effect of giving each student a feeling of being part of the total classroom situation.

Give serious thought to the seating arrangement. Early in the school year, students might be seated alphabetically to facilitate your learning their names. After a few days, you might want to let them select their own seats and see how things work out. Later you might want to change the seating arrangement in order to separate troublesome twosomes, to place those with hearing or visual defects closer to the front of the room, or for other reasons that may arise.

As you get to know your class better, you will undoubtedly discover for yourself other conditions, or antecedents, of misbehavior. It might well be, for example, that your students are particularly restless just before lunch, just after recess, or when you are working with individuals or small groups. Although conditions such as these can hardly be avoided, you can identify them and plan your strategy accordingly. The point of this suggestion is that your students will have enough opportunities to misbehave in the normal course of events without your giving them more.

Help your students to satisfy their personal, social, and emotional need in a constructive manner. Try to maintain a classroom atmosphere in which every student feels wanted, accepted, and emotionally secure. Try to structure the situation so that every one has a chance to experience a feeling of achievement and success. Go out of your way, if need be, to help students to fill their needs for attention, recognition, approval, etc., so that they will not resort to disruptive behavior in order to do so. Make a conscious effort to reduce, if you cannot completely eliminate, feelings of tension, frustration, anxiety, inferiority, and hostility in your classroom, and to help the individual student form a favorable self-concept and feelings of self-respect, self-confidence, and personal worth (Bernard 1970, Kaplan 1971).

Know your students as individuals and treat them as such. Simply knowing the interests, needs, abilities or disabilities, problems, backgrounds, etc., of each student will not, of course, in and of itself prevent them from misbehaving. But such knowledge on your part can certainly help to head off trouble that might be developing. Insofar as misbehavior is related to boredom or poor scholastic achievement, providing as much individualized assistance as possible might in the long run prove to be one of the most effective of all these preventive measures. Even if this extra help does not bring about a great improvement in the quality of the student's work, it can at least show him that you are genuinely interested in trying to help.

Make an effort to call as many as possible of your students by name as often as possible. If nothing else, this will show them that you are aware of them as individuals. This is particularly important in those critical first days of the term when your students are sizing you up much as you are trying to get to know them. As the school year progresses, do not expect them all to behave in the same way. Also, avoid making comparisons. However well little Geoffrey's brother might have done in your class last year, this is this year and you are no longer teaching Geoffrey's older brother. You are teaching Geoffrey, who wants to be recognized and treated as such.

Encourage constructive group interaction. In addition to knowing as much as possible about the individuals in your class, try to find out about the group roles that each plays and the patterns of social interaction among these individuals. Sociometric isolates, rejectees, and stars are often potential sources of disruptive behavior. So are members of any cliques that might exist. As a minimum, you should know who these people are. You might be able to put such information to good use in helping individuals with their personal, social, and emotional problems and in using group relations for better classroom management.

Make a special effort to identify the classroom leaders and try to make allies of those students whom the others admire, imitate, and are ready to follow. If these can be made to cooperate with you and set a good example for the rest of the class, many of your discipline problems will disappear or never materialize. Without showing any favoritism or giving them preferential treatment, you might try to have these leaders understand the special responsibility that they have and help them to channel their leadership potentialities along constructive lines.

Also, make use of group learning activities and group rewards.

Encouraging students to work together in small groups on projects that are in line with their interests and abilities is one means of helping the individual to identify with the welfare of others. Such activities can also help to meet the social needs that a student might otherwise attempt to satisfy by means of unacceptable behavior. The practice of punishing the entire group for the misbehavior of one or a few students is difficult to justify, usually unfair, and ordinarily not recommended. But you can still make use of group pressure in a more positive way by offering some sort of special reward to the class as a whole on the condition that each and every member of the class behave in a prescribed manner.

Try, too, to develop pride in your classroom. Students will tend to have a greater sense of responsibility and concern for classroom decorum if they can be stimulated to think in terms of *our* group. Younger children particularly will be pleased if visitors or administrators find *our* room attractive and *our* class well-behaved. Even older students will appreciate feeling that they are a part of a group that others admire.

Have your students evaluate their own behavior. Various means can be employed to give students an opportunity to examine and criticize their own behavior as individuals or as a group and to suggest means of improving in the future. Some elementary school teachers, for example, reward the group for a day's good behavior by placing a star on a chart especially prepared for this purpose, allowing the students themselves to decide whether or not they have earned the star for that day. Taking a few minutes at the end of the school day to discuss the matter, these teachers often find that the standards of the students are more demanding than their own. While older students would hardly be impressed by the daily star incentive, they should be able to participate in self-evaluatory discussions even more profitably than younger ones.

Just as your students should have a voice in determining the rules and regulations governing procedures in their class, so should they be entrusted with some of the responsibility for the enforcement of those regulations. If such opportunities and responsibilities are presented as something more substantial than mere token gestures, there is a good chance—no guarantee, of course—that their participation and self-evaluation will be highly beneficial to all concerned (Williams and Anandam 1973).

And so forth.   There are a number of other suggestions that could be offered to help you to motivate your students toward desired behavior and to prevent undesired behavior. Do not get into the habit of yelling at your students. Do not lose your temper. Do not make threats that you will be unwilling or unable to carry out. Compliment or otherwise reward your students for their good conduct instead of or in addition to scolding or otherwise punishing them for their misconduct. Work closely with the school counselor and administrators. Seek advice from other teachers. Cooperate with parents and keep them informed. *And so forth.*

CORRECTING MISBEHAVIOR

Even if you follow all the suggestions that have just been offered, and take a number of other preventive measures that you might learn about from other sources, some of your students will probably still misbehave. When they do, their behavior will have to be corrected. Actually, there is no sharp line that can be drawn separating preventive from corrective strategies. Quite frequently, the two overlap: correcting misbehavior today is a means of preventing it tomorrow. But, for purposes of discussion, the two can be dealt with separately. What then can you do, what should you do when students misbehave despite your very best efforts at prevention? Some form of punishment might be necessary. But let's not be in too big a hurry about punishment. There are other responses you can make that might be just as or even more effective.

Begin by having a friendly, informal talk with the misbehaving student.   In a constructive, nonthreatening manner, help him to understand why his behavior is unacceptable, how it can be improved, and why he should try to improve it. You need not, and usually should not, lecture. Instead, let him do most of the talking.

Try to draw him out so that he will reach the conclusion that you want him to reach: namely, that the classroom rules he has violated are primarily for his own good and that it is to his advantage to observe them.

In the course of the conversation, try to get him to tell his side of the story and listen carefully as he does so. In this way, you might learn some things about that student that will help you to understand his behavior more clearly. You might also acquire some clues that will be useful to you in your future relationships with him or other students.

Help the student to clarify his own perceptions and understand his own motives in misbehaving. In expressing your disapproval, distinguish between the person and his behavior. Try to make it clear that although you love and respect and accept him as a fellow human being certain of his behaviors cannot be permitted to continue.

In some cases, these friendly little chats will be all that is needed to correct the undesired behavior; in other situations, they might be quite unproductive. But they are never a waste of time. A scolding or some more intense expression of your disapproval along with punishment might eventually become necessary. But do try this positive, constructive approach as your first tactic.

Try the "no lose" method of problem solving. Thomas Gordon, the originator of this method of resolving teacher/student and parent/child conflicts, refers to it as Method III. This he does to distinguish it from Method I, authoritarianism, in which the teacher always wins and the students lose, and from Method II, permissiveness, in which the students win and the teacher loses. With Method III, the conflict is resolved in such a way that neither party loses.

In using this strategy, Gordon recommends that you begin by telling your students that you would like to try a *new* method of problem solving whereby the differences between your wishes and theirs can be resolved in a manner that will be acceptable to both. Because of the novelty element, perhaps, and the prospects of their getting what they want, they are likely to agree to cooperate. Then six steps are followed:

1. Define the conflict. For example: "I want you to pay attention to what I'm saying. You want to talk among yourselves."

2. Do some brainstorming with the students and try to elicit as many possible solutions as you can. Give them an opportunity to set forth their ideas on how the conflict can be resolved to their *and* your satisfaction. (Here you might even want to challenge them to use their minds!)

3. Discuss and evaluate the solutions that have been proposed.

4. Select the one solution that you and they agree is most likely to work.

5. Decide how the plan will be implemented.

6. After a trial period, evaluate the plan to see whether it has worked to your and their satisfaction. If it has worked, fine. If it has not, return to the appropriate prior step and try again.

Gordon's Parent Effectiveness and Teacher Effectiveness Training programs (P.E.T. and T.E.T.) offer a number of detailed suggestions for using this system (Gordon 1975).

Negotiate behavior contracts with your students. Back in Chapter 8, as you may recall, we discussed contingency contracts. These are essentially agreements, either verbal or written, specifying what each party (teacher and student) will do and how the other will reciprocate. Such contracts are very much in keeping with the principles of operant conditioning and behavior modification and are highly recommended by behaviorists as effective means of cooperative classroom management (Williams and Anandam 1973).

But the idea of *negotiated* contracts (as opposed to unilateral if-then conditions imposed by the teacher) is attractive to a great many nonbehaviorists as well. Thomas Gordon, for example, is very much a humanist in the Carl Rogers tradition. Most behaviorists, I suspect, would disagree with some of his methods and assumptions about human nature. Still his no-lose method of problem solving comes very close to resulting in contingency contracts.

Although they may be philosophically quite far apart from one another on various other issues, Dreikurs (1971), De Cecco and Richards (1975), William Glasser (1969), Gordon (1975), and Williams and Anandam (1973) are in accord with a host of other educators and psychologists on the potential effectiveness of give-and-take negotiations between students and teachers. Contracts, of course, are no panacea. Even the best of them will be violated.

Part of your job will be to see to it that the terms and conditions are observed and to deal with violations when they occur. Still there is a good chance that the time and effort that you and your students spend on negotiations will indeed pay off.

Reinforce desired behavior. Along with preventive measures, positive reinforcement of desired behavior is most highly recommended as a kind of ideal in the area of classroom management. Instead of expending a great deal of energy trying to devise and implement effective means of punishing students for misbehavior, use your imagination, ingenuity, and rational problem-solving skills in finding new and better ways to reward them for good behavior. Of course, you cannot and should not be constantly praising students—much less be giving them tokens or other tangible rewards—for doing what they are expected to do. But you can and should recognize and indicate your approval of their good behavior (Farson 1977).

Most students ordinarily will not need a steady flow of positive reinforcement from an external source to keep them on the right track. They will probably be reinforced from within, experiencing a feeling of inner satisfaction that they are behaving as they should. However, you might make a special effort to recognize, compliment, or otherwise reinforce the usually disruptive student when he is quiet, the seat-leaver when he is in his seat and working, the usually aggressive student when he is not behaving aggressively, and the student who is ordinarily uncooperative at those rare moments when he is cooperative, and so on.

Be sure that you do not unintentionally reinforce misbehavior. Attention, you will recall, is often a powerful reinforcer. A nice, quiet, friendly talk with a student of the type that was recommended earlier might be quite reinforcing. Thus, it can have the undesired effect of strengthening the very kind of misbehavior that you are trying to reduce. Even unfavorable attention, in the form of singling out the individual and scolding, warning, or threatening him, can be positively reinforcing. The student might well perceive unfavorable attention as preferable to none at all.

By all means, talk to the student privately and try to reason with him as a first resort. Then, if necessary, warn him or reprimand him. But if he seems to be enjoying the attention that these measures bring him and there is no accompanying improvement in his behavior, try something else.

Other commonly used disciplinary measures, such as requiring a student to stand in the corner or depriving him of the opportunity to participate in some activity that you think he enjoys, might actually be rewarding to the student. Temporary relief from what he perceives as the drudgery or monotony of classroom activities might be just what he wants. Maybe, for a reason that you do not know, he really detests the activity (gym or art, for example) from which he has been excluded. Perhaps by punishing him in some other way you are actually rewarding him with peer-group approval which he receives concomitantly.

To avoid the inadvertent reinforcement of undesired behavior, it is necessary that you know the misbehaving student as an individual and that you attempt to foresee as clearly as possible all the possible consequences of the strategies that you might want to employ. A certain amount of trial and error behavior on your part might be necessary to identify responses that will and will not be reinforcing. But the principle under discussion is well worth keeping in mind.

If the particular form of misbehavior is not very disruptive or dangerous, try ignoring it. Theoretically, the most effective way to eliminate misbehavior is to make sure that it is not reinforced at all. Technically, this is the surest and very likely the only way that misbehavior can be permanently extinguished. For example, if the student's motive in sticking out his tongue is to gain your attention and if you do not respond by noticing, chances are that he will eventually cease to behave in that fashion without being told to do so.

If the child's behavior is annoying but if he is not hurting himself or others, if it is not interfering with the work of the rest of the class, and if you are reasonably certain that it is not being reinforced in some other way, such as by peer-group approval, your best bet might be simply to ignore it (Krumboltz 1972). There are, of course, situations where the misbehavior cannot be simply ignored, in which case you will have to use some other form of corrective action.

In situations where it is feasible, use the saturation principle. This strategy consists of allowing, or requiring, the student to continue performing the undesired behavior until he tires of it. For example, you might tell a student who persists in, say, humming in class to come to the front of the room and "do his thing" until you give him permission to stop. He will, of course, be receiving attention, but presumably a great deal more of it and in a manner different from what he had anticipated. If you don't want to waste the time of the other students by having them sit and listen to the Hummer, you might choose to have him remain in the room during recess or after the others are dismissed for the day, and have him hum for your benefit alone.

As is the case with ignoring, there are circumstances under which the saturation principle can be used effectively and others where it would be disastrous. To stop a young child from starting fires in the classroom, for example, it would hardly make sense to require him to repeat that behavior until he tires of it. Neither would it be a good idea to require a student who uttered an obscenity or struck a classmate to persist in that kind of behavior. Nor should you use saturation as a means of humiliating a student or holding him up to ridicule. But, when and if the principle can be applied in a spirit of fun and good will, it can be quite effective (Krumboltz 1972).

Consider the use of negative reinforcement. As you will recall from our discussion in Chapter 4, negative reinforcement is not the same as punishment. Both imply unpleasant (or aversive) consequences. But punishment involves the *imposition* of pain or deprivation as a consequence of *deviant* behavior whereas negative reinforcement involves their *withdrawal* as a consequence of *desired* behavior. Thus punishment is used to induce a person to avoid misbehavior and negative reinforcement is employed to bring about desired behavior.

One way to use negative reinforcement in a classroom is to place the misbehaving student in a stiuation that he can bring to an end whenever he wishes by acting in the desired way. For example, you might require a disruptive student to stand in the corner until he is ready to settle down and get to work. The key words here are *until he is ready.* Assuming that standing in a corner is an aversive situation, you give the student the opportunity to terminate it whenever he decides to fulfill the prescribed conditions.

Negative reinforcement is a means of inducing a person to act in a desired way so that he can avoid or terminate or escape from so-called aversive stimuli. Among the more commonly used aversive stimuli are scolding, nagging, ridicule, sarcasm, detention, and loss of some privilege or opportunity. Theoretically, through this form of aversive control, the student will come to act in the desired way to avoid the unpleasant consequences of not doing so. His motivation, in other words, is to avoid the *threat* or the probability of some form of pain or deprivation.

The main objection to negative reinforcement, like the main objection to punishment, is that the student will learn to avoid the aversive situation, not by acting in the desired manner but by behaving in a way that is just as objectionable as the first, and maybe even more so. For example, to terminate your scoldings, the student might develop more subtle ways of misbehaving that will escape your detection.

Negative reinforcement is likely to be effective when there is one and, ideally, only one way of terminating the aversive situation and when the student has a clear understanding of what he must do to terminate it. Negative reinforcement is by no means the most highly recommended corrective measure that you can employ. But, as with punishment, it does work and is one of the strategies that you should have available in your repertoire of possible responses.

Be sure that you understand the purpose of punishment and the conditions under which it is likely to be effective. So here your are, trying to manage your classroom. You've tried all the preventive measures that you've ever heard of and some of your students still misbehave. You've tried talking with them and reasoning with them, but to no avail. You've used positive and negative reinforcement. You've tried the saturation principle. But none of these things seem to work. Now, you believe, some form of punishment is necessary. But which form? Before you try to answer that question for yourself, there are a couple of other questions that you should ask yourself first: "Why should I punish the child?" "What do I hope to accomplish?" "Will punishment work any better than the other corrective and preventive measures that I have tried?"

First of all, please remember that the purpose of punishment is not to release your own hostilities toward the offending student, to get even with him, to demonstrate your superiority, or to make you feel better. The purpose of punishment, rather, is to teach the child to avoid certain specified undesired or inappropriate forms of behavior. For this purpose, some type of punishment involving pain or deprivation or both *might* be effective under certain conditions. Among them are the following: (1) when the misbehavior is so frequent or intense that it simply cannot be allowed to continue without jeopardizing the welfare of the misbehaving student himself or that of his classmates; (2) when the child knows that he did wrong, when he realizes that he violated a rule and did so deliberately, or when he is too young to reason with and cannot understand the importance of or reasons for your regulations and prohibitions; (3) when the child perceives you, the person administering the punishment, as a friend who has a genuine interest in helping him to learn better ways of behaving; (4) when the punishment is administered swiftly and consistently, usually as soon after the misbehavior as possible; (5) when it is followed by positive reinforcement for the desired behavior or the termination of the undesired behavior.

Analyze and evaluate various punitive measures with particular reference to their possible undesired side effects. Having decided that young Curt needs punishment or that he is likely to profit from it, the next questions have to do with the particular form or means of punishment. What should you do? Keep him after school? Spank him? Make him write 'I must not throw spitballs' 10,000 times? Send him to the office? Cut off his supply of token reinforcers? Hang him up by the thumbs?

In deciding on a form of punishment that is likely to be effective with young Curt, there are certain criteria that you should use, certain questions you should ask yourself. Among them are the following:

> Which form of punishment is most likely to terminate the undesired behavior immediately and permanently?

- What effects are this form of punishment likely to have on the attitudes and morale of the rest of the class? Will they perceive this form of punishment as unfair, unreasonable, unnecessarily harsh? Might it lead to sympathy for Curt and antagonism on their part toward you?

- Is this form of punishment likely to act as a deterrent to other students?

- Is this form of punishment legal in your state or school district? Is it in accordance with established policies in your particular building? Is it generally acceptable to your school administrators? Will they back you up if you should need their support?

- Might this form of punishment be, as previously suggested, unintentionally reinforcing to young Curt? Might he actually gain peer group approval or some other kind of reward for being punished in this way?

- What effects are this form of punishment likely to have on Curt's overall personality development, socialization, attitudes toward school and toward himself? Might it lead to a feeling of hostility on his part, or a desire for revenge, or an unnecessary lowering of his self-concept or self-respect?

- Might this form of punishment actually worsen rather than improve Curt's behavior?

- Is it suited to his particular personality?

- Might it have some of the undesirable side effects that we noted in Chapter 4? Might it, in effect, teach him to lie or to try to conceal his misbehavior in an attempt to avoid being punished?

- Is the form of punishment logically related to, or a logical consequence of, the particular misbehavior that it is intended to correct?

Classroom management experts—be they self-proclaimed or nationally recognized—do not always agree on which particular forms of punishment meet or violate the above criteria. Certain punitive measures are, however, generally frowned upon and others are generally approved. Still others are quite controversial.

Avoid generally objectionable means of punishment. In the final analysis, it will be up to you to decide whether—and if so, how—to punish. In making your decision, note that among the generally disapproved forms of punishment are the following: (1) using sarcastic, humiliating remarks of a personal nature, such as derogatory references to the individual's physical appearance, intellectual abilities, ancestry, racial or ethnic background; (2) excluding the offender from the classroom without supervision; (3) forcing him to apologize, to play the role of a hypocrite, or to tell a lie and say he is sorry when, in fact, he is not; (4) sending the child to a lower grade temporarily; (5) using "cruel and unusual" forms of punishment that are physically very painful or psychologically very embarrassing to the culprit; (6) punishing the entire group for the misconduct of one or a few students; (7) depriving the person of something to which he has a right (such as lavatory privileges) or which he really needs for purposes of his overall education.

Perhaps the most controversial of all punitive measures is the use of physical punishment. Although the United States Supreme Court has ruled that corporal punishment is not in and of itself unconstitutional, in some states, school districts, and particular school buildings spanking and paddling are either prohibited or restricted to use under carefully specified conditions. If you are interested in this matter, you should find out what the policies are in the state, district, and building where you are or will be employed.

Even where it is allowed, a great many psychologists (perhaps a majority) have strong doubts as to whether it should ever be used. Clarizio, for example, argues against it and takes issue with what he labels four "myths": (1) that physical punishment is good for students in that it helps to develop moral character, personal responsibility, and self-discipline; (2) that occasional paddling contributes to the child's socialization by suppressing undesired behavior; (3) that physical punishment is the "only thing some kids understand"; and (4) that parents and even many students favor its use (Clarizio 1977).

Ebel, on the other hand, maintains that physical punishment does work, that its possibly harmful side effects have been exaggerated, and that it is not necessarily worse than reproof, loss of privilege, or other forms of psychological punishment. He believes, in short, that "carefully considered, carefully supervised, occasional use of moderate physical punishment should not be ruled out as a possible method of classroom management" (Ebel 1977a).

When punishment is necessary, select methods that are generally acceptable.   Among the forms of punishment that are generally acceptable to those who have researched and written extensively on the subject are these: (1) scolding the child, preferably in private first and then, if necessary, in public, but without personal, derogatory remarks; (2) temporary exclusion from the classroom or from classroom activities, but in a place where the person can be observed and supervised; (3) detention for a specific purpose, such as to make up work that was not done when it should have been; (4) sending the student to the school's disciplinary officer or counselor in accordance with school policies on these matters; (5) notifying the offender's parents; (6) requiring restitution or reparation in the case of stealing or vandalism; (7) withholding or withdrawing something that is indeed a privilege and not a right or a necessity.

The two basic forms of punishment, you will recall, involve some sort of pain (application of aversive stimuli) or deprivation (withholding of positive reinforcers.) Of the two, the latter is all but universally preferred.

Deprivation itself takes two main forms: time out and response cost. These are the punitive techniques that are most commonly used in behavior modification programs. *Response cost* refers to the withdrawal of previously acquired reinforcers. Essentially, this involves the levying of a fine. You can, for example, deduct points or take back tokens as a consequence of the student's misbehavior. *Time out* entails the removal of an opportunity for the student to earn points or tokens or other privileges. For example, you might isolate the child temporarily so that for a specified period of time he is cut off from any chance of acquiring positive reinforcement (Becker 1975a).

Whichever of these "acceptable" forms of punishment you decide to use, please remember that punishment is likely to be most effective and most acceptable when it is accompanied by a provision, contingent upon desired behavior, for the student to earn positive reinforcement.

Arrange unpleasant consequences that are logically related to the particular form of misbehavior.   This is kind of a euphemistic way of stating that the punishment should fit the crime. There should be, in other words, a reasonable connection, a kind of cause-and-effect relationship between what the student does and what he experiences as a consequence. Ideally, the relationship should be so clear that the student will readily understand it and accept the consequences, even if he doesn't particularly like them, simply because they are so logical, so reasonable, so fair (Dinkmeyer 1976).

Before continuing with our discussion of *logical* consequences, let's briefly consider the concept of *natural* consequences. As a consequence of overeating or excessive drinking, a person might get sick in the normal course of events and without any human intervention—his indigestion or his hangover might be regarded as nature's own way of punishing him. Similarly, if a child touches a burning match, he naturally experiences pain; if he runs on ice or down a slippery corridor, he might fall and hurt himself. But note that *he hurts himself.* He experiences pain, but the pain is not inflicted on him by anyone else. The pain occurs naturally as a consequence of his own behavior. These consequences are frequently very effective in weakening the behavior that brought them about. If the consequences are not harmful to the individual, a good policy might be to let nature take its course and allow them to occur.

As a classroom manager, you cannot simply rely on the principle of natural consequences. Very likely, you will have to intervene and arrange consequences that are logically though not naturally related to the misbehavior. Let's take a few examples to illustrate this principle.

Timothy marks up the walls in the lavatory—a logical consequence might be to require him to clean the walls. Willie neglects to do his homework. Requiring *him* to wash the lavatory walls as a form of punishment would hardly be logical. But keeping him after school to make up the work that he neglected to do might be regarded as far more logical.

Michelle steals some money from Rickie—a logical consequence would be to require her to repay Rickie, perhaps with interest. Linda destroys school property—a logical consequence would be to require her (or her parents) to repair the damage. Jonathan refuses to remain in his seat—a logical consequence might be to require him to remain out of his seat, standing in a corner perhaps, for an extended period of time. You might even offer him a choice: "Either sit down now or remain standing for the rest of the afternoon." Once he makes his choice, he should be expected to accept the consequences (Dreikurs 1968, 1971).

In some cases, it might be difficult to concoct unpleasant consequences that are logically related to the particular acts of misbehavior that you want to correct. In such cases, you might have to be rather arbitrary. But even here there is no need for you to be illogical. Without necessarily threatening the student, give him a clear understanding of what the consequences will be if he persists in that manner of misbehaving.

RECOMMENDED READING

Becker, Wesley, *et al. Teaching 1: Classroom Management.* Chicago: Science Research Associates, 1975. A partially programmed textbook designed for self-paced individualized study. Includes many practical suggestions for the use of behavior modification strategies with respect to discipline.

Brown, Catherine C. "It Changed My Life." *Psychology Today,* Nov. 1976. A field report comparing a number of popular parent-training programs: Thomas Gordon's Parent Effectiveness Training; William Glasser's Parent Involvement Program; the Responsive Parent Training Program based on principles of behavior modification; and programs based on the teachings and methods of Alfred Adler and Rudolf Dreikurs.

Clarizio, Harvey F. *Toward Positive Classroom Discipline.* New York: John Wiley, 1976. 2nd ed. Based on research in classroom settings and on teachers' personal experiences, this how-to book is concerned largely with the use of behavioral means to achieve humanistic objectives in the areas of classroom management.

DeCecco, John P., and Richards, Arlene K. "Civil War in the High School." *Psychology Today,* Nov. 1975. The authors maintain that neither permissiveness nor a tough law-and-order approach can end what they perceive as anarchy in many of our high schools. Instead, they recommend serious democratic negotiations between students and school authorities.

Dinkmeyer, Don, and Dinkmeyer, Don, Jr. "Logical Consequences: A Key to the Reduction of Disciplinary Problems." *Phi Delta Kappan, 57:*

664–666, 1976. Makes a useful distinction between punishment and logical consequences; recommends the latter and shows how it can be used effectively.

Dreikurs, Rudolf, and Cassel, Pearl. *Discipline without Tears.* New York: Hawthorn Books, 1972. Rev. ed. A short book that reflects the influence of Alfred Adler and develops the concept of logical consequences. Dreikurs' views are developed at greater length in his *Maintaining Sanity in the Classroom,* which was recommended in Chapter 3.

Grossman, Herbert. *Nine Rotten Lousy Kids.* New York: Holt, Rinehart and Winston, 1972. The story of a unique, radical experimental school for delinquent boys, this book reads like a lively novel. It shows what a small group of dedicated teachers and psychologists did to help them.

Hall, R. Vance, *et al.* "The Effective Use of Punishment to Modify Behavior in the Classroom." In Clarizio, Harvey F., *et al., Contemporary Issues in Educational Psychology.* Boston: Allyn and Bacon, 1974. 2nd ed. Includes concise summaries of four simple experiments, the results of which are generally favorable to systematic punishment procedures.

Hamacheck, Don E. "Removing the Stigma from Obedience Behavior." *Phi Delta Kappan, 57:* 443–447, 1976. Emphasizes the need for healthy, rational obedience (which the author carefully distinguishes from irrational, destructive obedience) and offers five helpful suggestions for developing it in young people.

Madsen, Charles H., Jr., and Madsen, Clifford K. *Teaching/Discipline: A Positive Approach for Educational Development.* Boston: Allyn and Bacon, 1974. 2nd ed. Includes an analysis of several typical situations in which the principles of contingency management are applied to problems of dealing with student misbehavior.

Neill, A. S. *Summerhill.* New York: Hart Publishing Co., 1970. Written by the founder and headmaster of the famous school in England well-known for what its critics regards as its extreme permissiveness. Neill describes and defends life at Summerhill and the philosophy of student freedom on which it is based. For further information on the subject, see Hart, H. H., Ed. *Summerhill: For and Against.* New York: Hart Publishing Co., 1970.

Redl, Fritz. "Disruptive Behavior in the Classroom." *School Review, 83:* 569–594, 1975. The author expresses his dislike of the term *disruptive behavior,* but discusses and interprets various causes of it and suggests a number of ways of dealing with it in particular situations.

CHAPTER 10: PREVIEW QUESTIONS

(After you have finished reading Chapter 10, you should be able to answer the following.)

1. Think of a person whom you consider to be very highly motivated scholastically. Which of the reasons why some students study discussed in this chapter are most applicable to the person whom you have in mind? Which apply least? Explain your answer.

2. Analyze your own motives toward scholastic achievement. When and if you study, why do you do so? What are your goals in studying? What kinds of incentives are operative?

3. In a classroom situation, do you regard motivation as something that originates within the student or as something that a teacher does, or both? Explain.

4. What is your opinion of the *Learn it or else. . .* approach to classroom motivation? What are some consequences of not studying that many students typically want to avoid? How or to what extent, if at all, do you think teachers should use fear or threats to motivate students?

5. What is your opinion of the proposition that students should be required or expected to learn only material that is relevant to their present needs or will be practically useful to them in the future?

6. Explain why you do or do not agree with the idea that teachers should try to make all schoolwork as pleasant, interesting, and enjoyable as possible.

7. What is meant by an emotionally comfortable classroom? How is such an atmosphere related to the development of curiosity, creativity, and independent thinking?

8. What are your views on the idea that high scholastic achievers be singled out for special public recognition?

9. What are some steps that teachers can take to help slower students to build up their self-confidence, self-esteem, and levels of aspiration?

10. To what extent or under what conditions do you think that students should be allowed (or required) to formulate the objectives for their class and evaluate the manner in which the class is conducted?

11. What is meant by reinforcing students programatically? What are your views on the general concept of programming students?

12. How can group activities or group rewards be used for purposes of motivating individual students? What do you regard as the main advantages and disadvantages of group (as opposed to individual) motivation?

13. How is the careful formulation of clear objectives likely to be a factor in effective motivation?

14. Which of the particular recommendations made in this chapter do you regard as relatively unimportant, ambiguous, potentially ineffective, or of doubtful validity? Give the reasons for your answer. If you think that none of the recommendations fall into these categories, explain your position.

15. Which of the recommendations made in this chapter impress you as being most useful, important, or particularly worth following? Explain your choice.

CHAPTER TEN

Motivation Toward Scholastic Achievement

As is the case with classroom management, there is no one best way of motivating students toward scholastic achievement. Rather, the effectiveness of a particular kind of strategy depends on at least three variables: the teacher, the student, and the material to be learned.

As we noted in Chapter 1, a procedure that works very well for one teacher might not work nearly as well for another. A technique that works with one student (or one kind of student) might not work at all with another. A strategy that is highly effective in one subject area might be quite ineffective in another. For reasons such as these, no one can tell you in advance precisely what to do two years from today to motivate Karen to learn high-school biology or Stanley to study his third-grade mathematics. You really have no alternative, therefore, other than to experiment with a variety of possible strategies and try to find out for yourself which will work best for you, with your particular students, in your particular subject area.

In the preceding chapters, we have considered a number of concepts, general principles, and specific suggestions that you can use in planning and implementing your own motivational program. Several of these are parts of the model offered as Figure 1 in Chapter 1. It is reproduced as Figure 16. In this final chapter, we shall briefly summarize some of the more important of these ideas and recommendations as they relate to scholastic achievement.

THE "WHY" ASPECT: UNDERSTANDING

At the very beginning of this book, we observed that one of the two main reasons why we study psychology is to understand why people (including ourselves) behave as they (we) do. According to our model, the first step in a classroom motivation program is to try to understand certain things about our students—their needs, goals, aspirations, etc.—so that we can use, capitalize, or build on them.

Thus, as a first step toward helping students who are *not* motivated toward scholastic achievement, we might do well to consider the motives of those who *are.*

Every student, as we have seen, is motivated—but not necessarily toward scholastic learning. Every person has goals that he or she wants to attain. But, the goals that your students wish to pursue here and now might not be the goals that you would like to have them pursue in your classroom. Similarly, every person has needs that he wants to satisfy. But the manner in which your students attempt to satisfy their needs might have little if any relationship to the material that you are trying to teach. Still, a great many students apparently *are* motivated to learn and do try to learn. The question is *Why?* An understanding of the motives of students who do study should offer some clues that we can use in trying to motivate those who do not. Let's review some of these motives.

Fear

One reason why some students study is simply to avoid the unpleasant consequences of not studying. They fear failure or low

TRY TO UNDERSTAND AND CAPITALIZE ON YOUR STUDENTS'

needs	drives	potentialities
interests	urges	anxieties
goals	values	beliefs
aspirations	attitudes	perceptions
unconscious		developmental
motives		characteristics
	etc.	

AND USE A VARIETY OF STRATEGIES AS

modeling	grades	competition
positive reinforcement	tests	cooperation
negative reinforcement	programming	punishment
performance objectives	contracts	verbal approval
curiosity/stimulation	assignments	verbal disapproval
contingency management	games	questions
discovery methods	simulations	explanations
	etc.	

THAT WILL ENABLE YOUR STUDENTS TO

experience a feeling of success
receive tangible or symbolic rewards
be granted certain privileges
acquire or maintain a feeling of personal worth
develop a more favorable self-concept

win your praise	overcome their fears
earn parental approval	satisfy their needs
gain peer-group recognition	reduce their drives
feel good about themselves	resolve their conflicts
enjoy themselves	grow in self-confidence
etc.	

AND HELP TO BRING ABOUT

orderly classroom behavior
and
scholastic achievement

FIGURE 16. A Model for Classroom Motivation. This model can be used to help you to organize some of the concepts that were discussed in earlier chapters and to guide you in planning your own motivation program.

grades. They fear that they will not be promoted, that they will have to repeat the course, or that they will not graduate with their class. They fear making mistakes or not pleasing the teacher. They fear a scolding or ridicule for not giving the teacher what she wants. They fear a lowering of their self-concepts or a loss of self-esteem if they do not measure up to her expectations. They fear that, unless they produce, they might not be admitted to a particular college or that they will be denied an opportunity to pursue a particular career. Younger children might even fear a spanking for low grades. Older students might fear the loss of a scholarship or some special privilege that is contingent upon their scholastic success.

For centuries, teachers have not only used but actually cultivated such fears to get students to study. From a theoretical standpoint, this "Learn it or else. . ." strategy has, of course, been strongly condemned (Holt 1964; Glasser 1969). From a practical standpoint, however, it must be admitted that this approach sometimes works in situations where other strategies do not. Ideally, it should not (but realistically it does) explain why some students are highly motivated.

Approval

Many students are also motivated toward scholastic achievement by their need for approval. This motive is likely to be especially strong in younger children who want and need the affection and approval of their parents and teachers. Frequently, they find that doing well in school is their most effective means of satisfying these needs.

Take little Tommy, for example. Tommy is by no means a brilliant student but he does well in all of his subjects, including spelling. It so happens that he does not particularly enjoy spelling, but he tries very hard to learn spelling simply because he feels that he is expected to do so. His parents and teachers (for some reason that he might not even understand or accept) seem to think that it is important that he learn how to spell. So he learns how to spell. Because he either loves them or values their approval very highly, he doesn't want to disappoint them. It's not that he has been threatened if he fails to learn spelling. Rather, he feels that he will please them and *earn* their approval if he does.

It is important to note that approval, not learning how to spell, is Tommy's primary goal. Spelling, in his case, is a means to an end. It is not spelling in and of itself that he finds reinforcing. Rather, he is reinforced by the approval that he receives as a consequence of spelling.

Now, take the case of young Bradley. As with Tommy, Bradley also has a strong need for approval. But he doesn't get much of it for scholastic success. His parents hardly glance at his report card. They pay little or no attention to the work he brings home. They indicate, perhaps by a mere shrug of their shoulders, that they do not regard schoolwork as particularly important or scholastic success as worthy of any special attention. Neither does he receive any praise, encouragement, or reinforcement from his teacher, his friends, or anyone else. It is unlikely that Bradley will persist for very long in trying to satisfy *his* need for approval by striving for scholastic success. More likely, he will try to find some other way of winning the approval of his parents or concentrate his efforts on gaining the approval of his friends.

Esteem

Some students, such as Debbie, are scholastically motivated mainly by their need for esteem. Debbie has been doing excellent work in her chemistry class even though she actually detests chemistry. She has no interest in that subject and is sure that she will never use it. She does not work for the sake of parental approval because she is already satisfied in that respect. She knows that her parents love her and will continue to reinforce her in various ways regardless of what she does or fails to do in chemistry. But Debbie is very much concerned with getting a good grade in chemistry.

Debbie needs good grades to bolster her ego, strengthen her self-concept, and develop her feeling of personal worth. She wants to feel that she can do anything that anyone else can do. She wants to feel that she is at least as bright as her classmates and maybe brighter than most. She not only wants to be recognized and admired, but also perhaps even envied a bit. She wants to prove to herself as well as to others that she is capable not only of succeeding in her schoolwork, but also of surpassing other students.

In Adlerian terms, Debbie might be trying to compensate for some feeling of inferiority. But she is neither driven by any compulsion to excel nor is she obsessed with good grades. By any acceptable standards, she is a normal, healthy individual but somewhat higher in achievement motivation than other girls of her age.

Nancy also has a need for recognition, self-esteem, and a feeling of superiority. But, for her, scholastic success is not a promising means of satisfying these needs. Finding her schoolwork too difficult, she has become discouraged. Recognizing that she cannot compete or even keep up with the Debbies in her class, she has given up trying. To protect her ego, she tries to convince herself and others that schoolwork is not worth bothering with, that she could master it if she really wanted to, that there are other things that she considers more important, etc. So while Debbie is trying to satisfy her need for esteem by excelling in chemistry, Nancy is seeking other means of satisfying that same need (Covington 1975).

Utility and Relevance

Some students are scholastically motivated primarily by what they perceive as the practical value or applicability of the material or skills that they are expected to learn. For example, without having to be sold on the idea, Miguel wants to learn how to read because he recognizes the value of that accomplishment as a source of information and enjoyment as well as prestige. Jennifer is intent upon learning mathematics because she wants to become an accountant. Daisy studies psychology industriously because she believes it will help her to understand herself and to influence the behavior of her children when she has some.

Other students see particular subjects—or education in general—as stepping stones to social or economic success, as necessary tools for more advanced learning, as directly related to the kinds of things that they would like to do in later life, or as somehow immediately applicable to their existing problems, concerns, interests, or needs. They believe that somehow they will be able to *apply* the things that they have learned and that learning will, therefore, do them some practical good (Kolesnik 1970).

Enjoyment

Finally, we have those rather rare students who study and learn simply because they like to study and want to learn. For these individuals, scholastic achievement is not primarily a means to an end; it is an end in itself. For them, learning is its own reward. They find it to be a pleasant, enjoyable, personally satisfying experience in and of itself. Their reinforcement comes from within. Unlike the others whom we have mentioned, who are said to be extrinsically motivated or outer-directed, the students currently under discussion are intrinsically motivated or inner-directed (Deci 1975; Schlosser 1976).

Larry, for example, enjoys studying much as some of his friends enjoy eating, playing games, or being entertained. He likes some subjects better than others, but derives a great deal of satisfaction from adding to his store of knowledge in just about any area. Larry is a very secure person. He does not study to avoid any of the dreadful kinds of things that other students fear. He is reasonably well satisfied with respect to his needs for approval and esteem, so he does not study to please or impress others or to earn high grades. Nor is he particularly concerned with putting his knowledge to any practical use. His main purposes in studying are to satisfy his curiosity, broaden his mind, deepen his understanding, enrich his life intellectually and aesthetically, and fulfill himself as a human being (Rogers 1969; Read and Simon 1975).

Combinations of Motives

Larry, of course, is a stereotype. So are Debbie, Tommy, and the other characters to whom we have referred. None of them acts as he or she does for any one purpose alone. Actually, the fear-reduction, approval, esteem, utility, and enjoyment motives are sometimes so closely interrelated as to be practically inseparable.

As we noted in Chapter 6, much of our behavior is multi-motivated, which means that it is directed toward the simultaneous satisfaction of more than one need. Thus, with real human beings who are highly motivated toward scholastic achievement, all five of these motives might be operative in varying degrees. It is doubtful, for example, that Larry or anyone else is completely free of fear or has all the approval and esteem that he wants. In all probability, some expectation of utility and some degree of enjoyment usually accompany one another. These five kinds of motives can, nevertheless, be separated for purposes of discussion and they do suggest some kinds of strategies that you might be able to use in motivating your unmotivated students.

THE "HOW" ASPECT: STRATEGIES

While one purpose of psychology is to help us to understand human behavior, another is to help us to guide or direct or influence or improve it. According to the model shown in Figure 16, for this second purpose we are advised to use a variety of strategies or tools or techniques or methods of teaching. By way of conclusion, let's review some of the strategies and, hopefully, helpful hints for scholastic achievement motivation that were offered in earlier chapters.

Begin with a clear set of objectives. If you want to motivate a person to reach a certain destination, you and they should have a clear idea of the destination that you would like them to reach. Similarly, if you want your students to respond in a particular manner, you and they must know precisely what it is that you want them to do. In subject areas where there is specific content to be learned or skills to be mastered, state your objectives in concrete behavioral terms (Kibler 1974). Make use of so-called performance objectives and inform your students of what these objectives are. Be sure that they know in advance not only what it is that they will be expected to learn, but also—and perhaps more important—what they will be expected to *do* (on a test, for example) to show that they have learned it (Herman 1977).

In subject areas that are less structured, where you would like to be more flexible and spontaneous, and where there is not a specific body of content to be mastered, precisely specified desired outcomes might be neither possible nor desirable (Kneller 1977; Ebel 1977b). But, even in such situations, you as well as your students should have as clear an idea as possible of what you are trying to accomplish and what you want your students to know, feel, believe, value, or be able to do as a consequence of the instruction that they receive (Skinner 1968).

Combine intrinsic and extrinsic motivational strategies. These, you will recall, correspond to interests and incentives, respectively. Neither of these is in and of itself either always or necessarily better than the other. Both have their uses as well as their limitations. Extrinsic motivation usually produces more immediate observable results and intrinsic motivation is likely to be more beneficial for purposes of lasting, long-range outcomes. Give top priority to making the class as interesting as possible, but be realistic enough to recognize that in some situations incentives might be far more productive (Becker 1975).

There is no good reason why you should rely on either interest or incentives exclusively. You probably could not do so if you wanted to. Intrinsic and extrinsic strategies are neither incompatible nor mutually exclusive. In some particular situations, an emphasis on one or the other might prove to be more effective, but in most cases both can and should be used together (Avila and Purkey 1971).

Invite your students to participate in the planning and evaluation of their curriculum. The key word here is *their*. Try to get them to feel that it is indeed *their* curriculum and not yours or the school's or the administration's. Students, like anyone else, ordinarily have a greater interest in and sense of responsibility for activities that they help to plan. So, give them an opportunity to help to decide what they will learn and how they will learn it (Silberman 1972).

In some subject areas, as we have just seen, a predetermined set of specific performance objectives is recommended. But, in other classes, activities centering on the students' existing interests, problems, and needs will be more beneficial. Just exactly how much voice students should have in planning their curriculum depends, of course, on a number of variables, not the least important of which is their own level of maturity. However, the recommended policy is that they be given as much responsibility in this regard as you believe they are capable of handling (Rogers 1969).

Have your students evaluate the class from time to time by using a questionnaire or an open discussion. If they do not seem to be interested in what you are teaching or they are not setting forth as much effort as you would like, ask them why. Invite them to make suggestions as to how the class could be made more interesting or useful to them. You will not always be able to implement their suggestions, but you can at least be open to them.

Show your students how they can use the material that you want them to learn. Relate the material to things that they already know and care about. Help them to perceive how they can apply this material to situations outside the school or to more advanced forms of learning in which they are interested. Instead of or in addition to just talking about the relevance or utility of the material, give them opportunities to *make* such applications. Offer them a variety of examples of ways in which the material can be transferred into their everyday lives. Better yet, ask them for such examples so that they will discover its applicability themselves.

In cases where the subject is not obviously useful or immediately applicable, explain what good you think the subject will do them. Use your persuasive powers to sell them on the value of your material. Show them how it can make them fuller human beings and add to their enjoyment of life or how it can at least indirectly help them to become what they are capable of becoming and really want to become. Here again, instead of merely telling them how important your subject matter is, open up the matter for discussion and ask them why *they* think that they are expected or required to learn it. They might convince themselves and one another that the material is indeed worthy of their attention.

Display some enthusiasm about the subject that you are teaching. Convey the idea that you yourself consider your material to be interesting, exciting, and important. Enthusiasm is often contagious. Even when it isn't, it can help to attract and hold your students' attention and give them the idea that maybe—just maybe—what you are teaching really is worth their learning. Do not try to fake enthusiasm that you do not genuinely feel. Even younger students can recognize and tend to be repelled by duplicity. But do express, as dramatically as your own personality will allow, your interest in and perhaps love for your subject.

Build on your students' existing interests.   Do not allow yourself to be carried away by the principle of interest, and do not restrict your curriculum to matters pertaining to current fads or ephemeral fancies. But do at least try to find out what your students' present interests are. Find out as much as you can about their hobbies, vocational plans, favorite forms of recreation, personal goals, etc., and then capitalize on those interests. Use them as a foundation on which to develop new, broader interests. Relate your material to things in which they have already expressed an interest so that they will feel that they are learning the kinds of things that they really want and need to learn (Dewey 1975).

Student participation in curriculum planning is, of course, one way in which you can use your students' interests to help them to learn material that you would like them to learn. Student/teacher contracts, which we have previously discussed, is another. But, even apart from these strategies and even in a very conventional, teacher-centered kind of classroom, students' existing interests, problems, and needs are frequently an excellent point of departure for the construction of an instructional program.

Help your students to develop self-confidence.   Some of them will not need much help in this regard. But with others, their lack of motivation toward scholastic achievement might very well be attributable to feelings of personal inadequacy or the belief that the work that you expect is too difficult for them. The object in such cases is to get the individual to believe in himself, to have faith and trust in his own abilities (Purkey 1977).

A student's degree of self-confidence depends, in great measure, often on what he perceives as his teacher's expectations of him and on his previous record of success and failure (Rosenthal 1977). So, show your students that you have confidence in them. Indicate that you expect a high level of achievement from them and that you believe that they are capable of reaching that level. (The assumption here, of course, is that your standards or expectations are not unrealistic.)

Many of the recommendations in this section, you will recognize, are closely interrelated and overlap. A few of the recommendations that follow are in effect extensions of the very important principle presently under discussion.

Help your students to raise their levels of aspiration. One's level of aspiration, you will recall, refers to one's personal achievement goals, to the quality and quantity of work that one expects to accomplish. A realistic level of aspiration is high enough to be challenging but not so high as to be out of reach. Perhaps the best way to raise a person's level of aspiration is to ensure that he succeeds with relatively simple tasks, thus building up his confidence in his ability to succeed at a slightly higher level the next time around. While it is ordinarily better to have students aim a bit too high rather than too low, try to help them to raise their sights gradually and realistically in order to avoid unnecessary feelings of frustration.

Give each student an opportunity to experience success. I know of no better way of developing self-confidence or raising a person's level of aspiration. Use your imagination and go out of your way, if necessary, to arrange your classroom situation so that everyone can get at least a taste of the sweet feeling of having done something well. Without being too obvious about it, call on your slower students to answer the easier questions. Give assignments that you are confident that your students will—not *should be* but *will*—be able to handle. Individualize your instructional program so that, regardless of their particular talents or abilities, each member of the class will have a chance to satisfy his need for a feeling of competence, achievement, or self-satisfaction (Klausmeier 1971; Gronlund 1974).

Recognize and compliment or otherwise reward your students for such qualities as dependability, punctuality, neatness, industry, etc. when their scholastic achievement leaves something to be desired. As a kind of last resort, praise them for excellence with which they have carried out some assigned classroom responsibility, even if it is only feeding the goldfish, passing out books, or erasing the blackboard. But do find something that each can do well and whet their appetites for reinforcement by giving them a sample of the kind of reward (or good feeling) that they can gain by at least making an honest effort to learn.

Be generous, but not lavish, with praise.   One implication of the previous recommendation is that you afford every student an opportunity to *earn* verbal approval. But do not give it unless it is deserved. Praise that is obviously unwarranted is likely to be worse than meaningless in that your students will perceive it as phony and not worth much in situations where it is deserved.

You will have to experiment to find out for yourself how much praise is the right amount for each student and how often and under which conditions to give it. In some cases, a little too much might be better than not quite enough. With other students, you might get better results if you leave them a bit hungry for approval instead of satiating them with it (Fish 1975; Farson 1977).

Don't forget that for some students expressions of disapproval (if they are deserved and not too frequent) will be more productive than praise and that scolding a student might be more effective than ignoring him. It's impossible to be much more specific in this respect. But a good principle to follow is this: Don't think of praise as something that you simply give away. Think of it, rather, as an investment that is likely to pay handsome dividends (Hackett 1975).

Make use of both competition and cooperation.   Neither one of these two kinds of strategies is categorically more effective than the other in general, but in particular situations both can serve useful purposes. As we noted in Chapter 8, although competition seems to have a slight advantage over cooperation with respect to scholastic achievement, it seems to contribute more to undesirable side effects in the areas of human relations, mental health, and personality development. You need not, of course, pledge your undying allegiance to either. If possible, give your students some experience with both. But use competition only when your students are fairly well matched, when each has a reasonably good chance of winning, and when the losers are not likely to suffer undue humiliation (D. W. Johnson 1975, 1976).

Use fear and the threat of failure sparingly. Do not, on the one hand, deliberately create or intensify anxieties in your students or, on the other, attempt to eliminate them entirely. While strong anxiety can have a detrimental effect on learning as well as on personality development, mild anxiety often stimulates effort and has a beneficial effect. By all means, place your major emphasis on positive reinforcement and the concept of success. But keep the possibility of failure open. Without dwelling on the subject or terrifying your students, give them a gentle reminder of that possibility when their performance seems to warrant your doing so.

Explain your system of grading when you use marks as an incentive. As we noted in Chapter 8, objections continue to be raised against the very idea of using grades as incentives. There can be no doubt that for many students good grades or the avoidance of bad ones serve as tremendously powerful reinforcers. But the practice of students working primarily *for* grades can also have adverse side effects on their personalities as well as on the quality of their learning (Melby 1977).

There is no one best system of grading students any more than there is any one best method of motivating or teaching them. Within the framework of the policies of the school in which you are teaching, it will be up to you to decide on the criteria that you will use with your particular students in your particular class: test results, papers, projects, recitation, participation, homework, or whatever. Having made your decision, let your students know the factors on which their grades will depend and the manner in which those grades will be calculated. Do not dwell on the subject but do give them a clear idea of what they will be expected to do to get an A or an S, and so on.

Try to evaluate the students' work—their actual achievement, performance, test papers, etc.—as objectively as possible without letting your personal feelings toward individuals intrude. Do consider the likely effects of a particular mark on the student's self-concept, level of aspiration, attitudes, and future achievement.

To help to hold down unnecessary and possibly unhealthy competitiveness, avoid the use of quota systems in assigning grades. To encourage your students to keep up with their assignments, consider basing their grades in part on surprise quizzes or daily recitations. Do not give undeserved low grades in scholastic achievement as a means of punishing a student for misbehavior. Do not overmotivate your students to the extent that they will resort to cheating to obtain the coveted good marks.

There are a number of other do's and don'ts regarding grading practices and procedures in Chapter 8. Perhaps you would do well to review that section.

Challenge each student to do the best work that he is capable of doing without comparing him to other students. Encourage him to compete with himself, to try to surpass his own previous performance without your making reference to what others have done. Suggest that each student keep his own individual progress chart on which he can systematically record his improvement. Challenge the student to prove to himself that he can do better next time than he did this time. Get him to make a commitment to try to improve. Let him know that you think he *can* improve. Reinforce whatever progress he makes, as well as his commitment, effort, and good intentions when his progress is nil. Treat each student as an individual. Help each to develop and use *his* potentialities, however great or small they may be, to the fullest extent possible. In some situations, however, comparisons might be inevitable. But try to keep them to a minimum (Nagel 1972).

Provide informational feedback. Keep your students informed of their progress. Students are often unable to evaluate their own work. Even apart from grading, part of your job, therefore, is to let them know how they are doing and what they need in order to do better. Usually, the sooner the feedback is received, the more useful it is (Skinner 1968). So, return test papers as promptly as you can. Bring the student's particular errors or shortcomings to his attention and whenever possible have him correct his mistakes himself. Offer constructive criticism of the student's work and specific suggestions for improvement. In cases where the student's work is very good, communicate this bit of information to him as soon as you can so he will not only *feel* good but also *know* that he is on the right track and can proceed accordingly (Becker 1975b).

Try to increase your students' degree of achievement motivation. Adapt for use in your own classroom the kinds of systematic training procedures discussed in Chapter 5. Explain to your students what achievement motivation is and how it works. Discuss the personal characteristics and behavior of people with high and low degrees of achievement motivation. Point out the differences between success-oriented and failure-oriented individuals. Help them to understand the risk-taking factor and the possibility of conflicts between achievement and affiliation needs (Atkinson 1974).

Use specially prepared achievement-motivation training materials if they are available in your school. Devise your own if they are not. Guide your students toward an awareness of their existing goals, needs, or motives. Help them to understand that they are not mere pawns in some mysterious game of life, but originators of their own behavior, that what they become is largely up to them (de Charms 1971). Indicate your willingness to help them to achieve their goals. But also stress the fact that in the final analysis the responsibility for what they achieve or fail to achieve is primarily theirs (Glasser 1969).

Consider the use of contracts with your students. A negotiated agreement spelling out what your students will accomplish and what they will receive as a consequence is one way of individualizing instruction as well as motivation. Contracts are also useful in that they offer the student some leeway in setting his particular goals and give him a chance to suggest activity or other reinforcers for which he would be willing to work. Do not expect contracts to solve all your problems. But see if they can help with some of them.

Give your high achievers public recognition. Do not identify low achievers by name or make public comparisons that might embarrass your slower students. But do publicize the accomplishments of your superior students. Mention them by name. Display their work. Congratulate them in front of the rest of the class. Give them some sort of prize or honor them in some other way. Why should the top athletes be the only ones whose talents are publicly recognized and applauded? However, know the individuals with whom you are working. Some of your brighter students might actually be embarrassed by this type of recognition or dislike being identified as brains, but most of them will probably appreciate and profit by such recognition.

Strive for variety in your classroom. Do not allow yourself to fall into a fixed pattern of procedures (otherwise known as a *rut*). Routine serves some very useful purposes, but don't become a slave to it. Balance routine with flexibility and spontaneity. To attract and maintain your students' attention, occasionally do something that they are not expecting. To reduce boredom and alleviate monotony, use a variety of instructional methods and materials as well as a variety of reinforcers. Try, in short, not to be so rigid or predictable that your students' invariable response will be, "Oh, no, not that again!" (Berlyne 1971).

Make your class enjoyable but don't turn it into a circus. The school is not primarily an entertainment center and your main purpose is not to amuse your students. But enjoyable, entertaining, amusing activities can be used to help to make learning a pleasant experience. As a means of providing variety and making learning fun, use games, puzzles, brain-teasers, simulations, role-playing, projects involving group interaction and cooperation, audiovisual aids, field trips, guest speakers, and your own sense of humor. The possibilities in this regard are limited only by your own imagination. Don't go overboard on the idea of trying to make the students' total educational experience fun. But do recognize that the more they enjoy that experience, the better it is likely to be for you and them (Silberman 1972).

Maintain a classroom atmosphere that is physically and emotionally comfortable. With respect to their physical comfort, do not expect your students—especially at the elementary level—to sit still too long. Make sure that they are seated where they can see and hear, but give them a chance to get up and move around and do something other than look and listen. And don't overlook the possible importance of such factors as lighting, ventilation, and room temperature. The point here is that some of your very best efforts might be to no avail if your students are physically uncomfortable.

With respect to their emotional comfort, try to avoid practices and procedures that are likely to contribute to or intensify feelings of tension, anxiety, frustration, hostility, guilt, or alienation. Instead, make every effort to maintain a set of classroom conditions in which each student has a reasonably good chance to develop a favorable self-concept and feeling of personal worth and to satisfy his or her needs for acceptance, affiliation, approval, and esteem. Keep in mind Maslow's principle that, unless their physiological, safety, love, and esteem needs have been reasonably well satisfied, it is doubtful that any of your efforts to motivate them toward learning for its own sake will be very productive (Maslow 1970).

Reinforce your students programmatically. When your material is relatively difficult or complex, present it to your students in small, easy, logically organized steps. Begin with the simplest, most basic concepts in that lesson and, building on these systematically, gradually move on to material that is slightly more advanced. If possible, have your students respond after each of these steps—for example by answering a question—to show that they have indeed learned that portion of the lesson (Becker 1975b).

Unless you are using programmed materials, you will usually not be able to have all your students respond after each step in sequence. So, to help keep them attentive and prepared to answer, call on students at random as often as you can. If your presentations and questions are properly structured, every student should be able to respond correctly at almost every step and, thus, receive immediate reinforcement (Skinner 1968).

One advantage of a programmed strategy is that students need not wait until they have achieved mastery of an entire lesson or unit of work before being reinforced. Rather, they can be reinforced frequently as they advance, slowly perhaps but surely, toward mastery. Little mistakes can be corrected before they have a chance to grow into big ones.

In addition to grades and verbal approval, consider the use of some form of token system with attractive objects or activities as backup reinforcers. Work out effective schedules of reinforcement, through trial and error if necessary, to help you to decide how frequently and in what manner to reinforce a particular student. As part of your program, gradually withdraw external reinforcers when you have reason to believe that a student is beginning to experience self-reinforcement. Enlist the cooperation of parents so that their motivational strategies will complement yours (Enzer 1975).

Make use of group activities and group reinforcers.   Avoid the practice of punishing the entire class for the shortcomings of one or a few students. But arrange situations where rewards for the class as a whole are contingent upon each member's achieving at a certain level. This is one way of helping students to develop a spirit of cooperation and of using peer-group approval as a reinforcer. An alternative is to have teams or subgroups cooperate among themselves in competition with other teams for some group reward. When this procedure is used, vary the composition of the teams to prevent the formation of divisive factions in your class. Encourage team members to help one another and do not permit them to blame any one of their number when their team fails to win (Schmuck 1975).

Cultivate curiosity and creativity.   Take advantage of the students' propensities for exploration and self-expression. Give them ample opportunities to investigate their environments and find out for themselves the kinds of things that they want to learn. Encourage and reward originality. Show them that you value a good question as much as or more than a good answer. Go out of your way, if necessary, to elicit questions, comments, personal reactions to your material, including possible objections, expressions of doubt, and demands of proof in controversial or ambiguous areas. Do not scold your students for asking foolish questions. Do not ridicule them for expressing opinions that are different from your own. Encourage them to try out their original ideas and to attempt new kinds of activities. Assure them of your continued support if their efforts prove to be unsuccessful (Torrance 1965, 1975).

Organize at least part of your curriculum around real-life problems. Try to relate what you and your students are doing *in* school to significant on-going activities *outside* the school. Bring to their attention some of the social, moral, economic, political, scientific, or other kinds of problems with which adults in their own families and neighborhoods are concerned. Better yet, have your students take the initiative in introducing problems that they feel affect them personally. Do not pretend that you or they will be able to come up with final solutions to momentous world, national, or community problems. But show them how the material or skills that you are teaching *can* contribute to the solution of such problems.

Launch discussions, assign projects, or involve the students in classroom activities out of which practical problems will emerge that they will genuinely want or need to solve to continue that activity. Help them, but also resist the temptation to give them the solution or to extricate them from their difficulties. Let them know, rather, that you believe them capable of solving these problems themselves and that you expect them to do so.

Stimulate your students to think for themselves. Challenge them to reach their own conclusions and make their own decisions. Raise problems or issues on which the "experts" in your subject area disagree. Present conflicting viewpoints on such controversial matters and give your students a chance to formulate and try out their own ideas. Conduct classroom discussions in which they have an opportunity to express their views, and compare them with the views of others. Show them, when such is the case, that their opinions are inconsistent, contradictory, or not supported by available evidence. Help them to perceive implications of their positions and foresee consequences of their views that they may have overlooked. Try, in short, to produce a state of doubt or uncertainty in their minds so that they will want to remove the tension and think the matter through more carefully on their own.

RECOMMENDED READING

Becker, Wesley C., *et al. Teaching 2: Cognitive Learning and Instruction.* Chicago: Science Research Associates, 1975. Similar to *Teaching 1: Classroom Management,* which was recommended for reading in connection with Chapter 9. This volume presents an operant-conditioning model for the teaching of concepts and problem solving behavior.

Deutsch, Martin, and Deutsch, Cynthia P. "Intelligence, Heredity and Environment: The Critical Appraisal of an Outmoded Controversy." In *Annual Editions: Readings in Education 76/77.* Guilford, Connecticut: Dushkin, 1976. Attempts at motivating students toward scholastic achievement presume that they have the necessary intelligence for learning. This short but carefully documented article summarizes research findings and apparently conflicting viewpoints on the questions of what intelligence is and how it is acquired.

Ebel, Robert L. "What Are Schools For?" *Phi Delta Kappan, 54:* 3–7, 1972. Your philosphy of educational motivation and the strategies that you choose to try will depend to a great extent on your answer to the question raised in the title of this article. You might not agree entirely with Ebel's answer, but it will still probably stimulate you to do some serious thinking about the question.

Glatthorn, Allan A. *Alternatives in Education.* New York: Dodd Mead, 1975. Points out the need for and describes several kinds of alternatives to conventional educational programs. A good review of the most important developments in the movement toward alternative schools and programs.

Good, Thomas L., *et al. Teachers Make a Difference.* New York: Holt, Rinehart, and Winston, 1975. Although it does not focus directly on motivation per se, this book is recommended because of its fine coverage of teacher effectiveness, testing, acccountability, criticisms of schools, goals of education, and other related subjects.

Hamacheck, Don E. *Behavior Dynamics in Teaching, Learning, and Growth.* Boston: Allyn and Bacon, 1975. Especially pertinent are Chapter 1, "Major Views about the Psychology of Human Behavior"; Chapter 11, "Motivational Processes and Human Learning"; Chapter 12, "Self-Concept Variables and Achievement Outcomes"; and Chapter 15, "Understandings and Strategies for Achieving Positive Classroom Management."

Hammill, Donald D., and Bartel, Nettie R. *Teaching Children with Learning and Behavior Problems.* Boston: Allyn and Bacon, 1975. This resource book for preschool, elementary, and special education teachers is recommended because of its practical value in motivating and otherwise helping children with special problems in such basic areas as reading, writing, spelling, and arithmetic.

Holt, John. *How Children Learn.* New York: Pitman, 1967. Although he has published several books since, this one and his *How Children Fail* (1964) are Holt's most useful contributions. Holt strongly condemns traditional teacher-directed motivational procedures, particularly reliance on fear and threats. He offers several positive suggestions tending toward student freedom, activity, and individual responsibility as substitutes.

Macht, Joel. *Teacher/Teachim: The Toughest Game in Town.* New York: John Wiley, 1975. A light, highly readable book that discusses how teachers influence students, often without realizing that they are doing so. It emphasizes teacher/student relationships that help students to experience greater success in the classroom

Nolan, Ronald G., and Craft, Lynda H. "15 Approaches to Motivate the Reluctant Reader." *Journal of Reading, 19:* 387–391, 1976. Briefly discusses fifteen strategies that were found to be successful in a remedial reading program for students between the ages of seven and sixteen.

Orem, R. C. *Montessori: Her Methods and the Movement.* New York: G. P. Putnam, 1974. Using a question-and-answer format, this is a clear introduction to the Montessori method, its techniques, and the philosophy on which they are based.

Talmage, Harriet, Ed. *Systems of Individualized Instruction.* Berkeley, Cal.: McCutchan, 1975. A publication of the National Society for the Study of Education, this book includes a description of three tested systems for the individualization of instruction: Individually Guided Education, Planning for Learning in Accordance with Needs, and Adaptive Environments for Learning.

White, William F. "The Teacher's Personality Is the Primary Motive in the Classroom." In Torrance, E. Paul, and White, William F., Eds. *Issues and Advances in Educational Psychology.* 2d ed. Itasca, Ill.: F. E. Peacock, 1975. In this short article, White explains and supports his belief that nothing is more important in motivating students than the teacher's own personal and emotional characterstics.

Bibliography

Abidin, R.R., Jr. "What's Wrong with Behavior Modification?" *Journal of School Psychology,* 9:38–42, 1971.

Ackerman, P.D. "The Effects of Honor-Grading on Students' Test Scores." *American Educational Research Journal,* 8:321–333, 1971.

Adkins, A. "Testing: Alternative to Grading." *Educational Leadership,* Jan., 1975.

Adler, A. "The Child: Neither Good nor Evil." *Journal of Individual Psychology,* 30:191–193, 1974.

————. *The Practice and Theory of Individual Psychology.* Totowa, N.J.: Littlefield, Adams, 1968.

————. *The Problem Child.* New York: Capricorn, 1963.

————. *The Science of Living.* Garden City, N.Y.: Anchor Books, 1969.

————. *Social Interest: A Challenge to Mankind.* New York: Capricorn, 1964.

————. *Superiority and Social Interest.* 3d ed. New York: Viking, 1973.

————. *Understanding Human Nature: A Key to Self Knowledge.* Greenwich, Conn.: Fawcett, 1954.

Ahmann, J.S. and Glock, M.D. *Evaluating Pupil Growth.* 5th ed. Boston: Allyn and Bacon, 1975.

Allen, B.V. "Paying Students to Learn." *Personnel and Guidance Journal,* 53:774–778, 1975.

Allport, G.W. *Becoming: Basic Considerations for a Psychology of Personality.* New Haven: Yale University Press, 1955.

Alper, T.G. "Achievement Motivation in College Women." *American Psychologist,* 29: 194–203, 1974.

Alschuler, A.S. *Motivating Achievement in High School Students.* Englewood Cliffs, N.J.: Educational Technology Publications, 1972.

Ames, L.B. *et al. Stop School Failure,* New York: Harper and Row, 1972.

Anderson, H.E. *et al.* "Generalized Effects of Praise and Reproof." *Journal of Educational Psychology,* 57: 169–173, 1966.

Anderson, R.C. and Faust, G.W. *Educational Psychology.* New York: Dodd Mead, 1973.

Angell, G.W. "The Effects of Immediate Knowledge of Quiz Results on Final Examination Scores in Freshman Chemistry." *Journal of Educational Research,* 42: 391–394, 1949.

Ansbacher, H.L. "Alfred Adler and Humanistic Psychology." *Journal of Humanistic Psychology,* 11: 53–63, 1971.

———. "Alfred Adler: Individual Psychology." *Psychology Today,* Jan., 1970.

——— and Ansbacher, R.R., eds. *The Individual Psychology of Alfred Adler.* New York: Harper Torchbooks, 1964.

Asbury, C.A. "Selected Factors Influencing Over- and Under-Achievement in Young School-Age Children." *Review of Educational Research,* 44: 409–428, 1974.

Atkinson, J.W. "Motivational Determinants of Risk-Taking Behavior," *Psychological Review,* 64: 359–372, 1957.

——— and Feather, N.T., eds. *A Theory of Achievement Motivation.* New York: John Wiley, 1966.

——— and Raynor, J.O. eds. *Motivation and Achievement.* New York: V.H. Winston, 1974.

Ausubel, D.P. *Educational Psychology.* New York: Holt, Rinehart and Winston, 1968.

Avila, D.L. and Purkey, W.W. "Intrinsic and Extrinsic Motivation—A Regrettable Distinction." In Avila, D.L. *et al. The Helping Relationship Sourcebook.* Boston: Allyn and Bacon, 1971.

Badaracco, M.R. "Psychoanalysis and Society: Which Leads, Which Follows?" *American Journal of Psychoanalysis,* 34: 229–236, 1974.

Baer, D.M. "Let's Take Another Look at Punishment." *Psychology Today,* 5: 32–37, 1971.

Bandura, A.A. *Principles of Behavior Modification.* New York: Holt, Rinehart and Winston, 1969.

_____ ed. *Psychological Modeling.* New York: Lieber-Atherton, 1974.

Beck, H.L. *Don't Push Me, I'm No Computer: How Pressures to "Achieve" Harm Preschool Children.* New York: McGraw-Hill, 1973.

Becker, W.C. *et al. Teaching 1: Classroom Management.* Chicago: Science Research Associates, 1975a.

_____ *Teaching 2: Cognitive Learning and Instruction.* Chicago: Science Research Associates, 1975b.

Bellamy, G.T. "The Pygmalion Effect: What Teacher Behaviors Mediate It?" *Psychology in the Schools,* 12: 454–461, 1975.

Berlyne, D.E. "Curiosity in Education." In Glock, M.D., ed. *Guided Learning: Readings in Educational Psychology.* New York: John Wiley, 1971.

Bernard, H.W. *Mental Hygiene in the Classroom.* New York: McGraw-Hill, 1970.

Bernstein, D.A. "Anxiety Management." In Craighead, W.E., *et al.* Boston: Houghton Mifflin, 1976.

Bettelheim, B. "Psychoanalysis and Education." *School Review,* 77: 73–86, 1969.

Birney, R.C. and Teevan, R.C., eds. *Measuring Human Motivation.* New York: Van Nostrand, 1962.

Blackham, G. and Silberman, A. *Modification of Child and Adolescent Behavior.* 2d ed. Belmont, Cal.: Wadsworth, 1975.

Bledsoe, J.C. "Comparison of Interests of Urban Disadvantaged Boys and Girls." *Psychological Reports.* 36: 932–934, 1975.

Block, J.H. "Criterion-Referenced Measurements: Potential." In Clarizio, H.F. *et al.* eds. *Contemporary Issues in Educational Psychology.* 3d ed. Boston: Allyn and Bacon, 1977.

_____ *Mastery Learning in Classroom Instruction.* New York: Macmillan, 1975.

Boden, M.A. *Purposive Explanation in Psychology.* Cambridge, Mass.: Harvard University Press, 1972.

Bonney, M. "Self-Becoming as Self-Growth." *Theory Into Practice,* 13: 329–334, 1974.

Bridgeman, B. "Effects of Test Score Feedback on Immediately Subsequent Test Performance." *Journal of Educational Psychology,* 66: 62–66, 1974.

Brophy, J.E. and Good, T.L. "Teacher Expectations: Beyond the Pygmalion Controversy." In Gall, M.D., and Ward, B.A., eds. *Critical Issues in Educational Psychology.* Boston: Little, Brown, 1974.

Brown, C.C. "It Changed My Life." *Psychology Today,* Nov., 1976.

Brown, F.J. "Knowledge of Results as an Incentive in School Room Practice." *Journal of Educational Psychology*, 25: 532–552, 1932.

Bruner, J.S. "Child Development: Play Is Serious Business." *Psychology Today*, Jan., 1975.

——. *The Process of Education.* New York: Vintage Press, 1960.

——. *The Relevance of Education.* New York: Norton, 1973.

Bryan, J.F. and Locke, E.A. "Goal-Setting as a Means of Increasing Motivation." *Journal of Applied Psychology*, 51: 274–277, 1967.

Buhler, C. "Human Life Goals in the Humanistic Perspective." In Avila, D.L., et al. eds. *The Helping Relationship Sourcebook.* Boston: Allyn and Bacon, 1971.

Canfield, W. and Wells, H.C. *100 Ways to Enhance Self-Concept in the Classroom.* Englewood Cliffs, N.J.: Prentice-Hall, 1976.

Carpenter, F. *The Skinner Primer: Behind Freedom and Dignity.* New York: The Free Press, 1974.

Cartwright, C.A. and Cartwright, G.P. "Determining the Motivational Systems of Individual Children." *Teaching Exceptional Children*, 2: 143–149, 1970.

Cattell, R.B. and Child, D. *Motivation and Dynamic Structure.* New York: Halstead, 1975.

Chansky, N.M. "Reactions to Systems of Guided Learning." *American Educational Research Journal*, 1: 95–100, 1964.

Child, I.W. and Whiting, W.M. "Determinants of Level of Aspiration: Evidence from Everyday Life." *Journal of Abnormal and Social Psychology*, 44: 303–214, 1949.

Clarizio, H.F. "A Case against the Use of Corporal Punishment by Teachers and Some Myths about Its Use." In Hamacheck, D.E., ed. *Human Dynamics in Psychology and Education.* 3d ed. Boston: Allyn and Bacon, 1977.

Clarizio, H.F. *Toward Positive Classroom Discipline.* 2d ed. New York: John Wiley, 1976.

Clark, P.M. "Psychology, Education, and the Concept of Motivation." *Theory into Practice*, 9: 16–22, 1970.

Clarke, D.E. "Measures of Achievement and Affiliation Motivation." *Review of Educational Research*, 43: 41–51, 1973.

Clifford, M.M. "Competition as a Motivational Technique in the Classroom." *American Educational Research Journal*, 9: 123–137, 1972.

——. "How Learning and Liking Are Related—A Clue." *Journal of Educational Psychology*, 64: 183–186, 1973.

Cofer, C.N. *Motivation and Emotion.* Glenview, Ill.: Scott, Foresman, 1972.

Coffield, W.H. and Blommers, P. "Effects of Non-Promotion on Educational Achievement in the Elementary School." In Mouly, G.J., ed. *Readings in Educational Psychology.* New York: Holt, Rinehart and Winston, 1971.

Cohen, R.J. and Houston, D.R., "Fear of Failure and Rigidity in Problem Solving." *Perceptual and Motor Skills,* 40: 930, 1975.

Combs, A.W. and Snygg, D. *Individual Behavior.* Rev. ed. New York: Harper, 1959.

Combs, A.W. *et al. The Professional Education of Teachers.* 2d ed. Boston: Allyn and Bacon, 1974.

Coopersmith, S. *The Antecedents of Self-Esteem.* San Francisco: Freeman, 1967.

———— and Feldman, R. "Fostering a Positive Self-Concept and High Self-Esteem in the Classroom." In Coop, R.H. and White, K., eds. *Psychological Concepts in the Classroom.* New York: Harper and Row, 1974.

Covington, M.V. and Beery, R.G. *Self-Worth and School Learning.* New York: Holt, Rinehart and Winston, 1975.

Craighead, W.E. *et al. Behavior Modification.* Boston: Houghton Mifflin, 1976.

Cratty, B.J. *Active Learning: Games to Enhance Academic Abilities.* Englewood Cliffs, N.J.: Prentice-Hall, 1971.

Cullen, F.T., Jr. *et al.* "Effects of the Use of Grades as an Incentive." *Journal of Educational Research,* 68: 277–279, 1975.

Dalsimer, K. "Fear of Academic Success in Adolescent Girls." *Journal of the American Academy of Child Psychiatry,* 14: 719–730, 1975.

Day, H.I. and Berlyne, D.E. "Intrinsic Motivation." In Lesser, G.S. ed., *Psychology and Educational Practices.* Glenview, Ill.: Scott, Foresman, 1971.

DeCecco, J.P. and Richards, A.K. "Civil War in the High School." *Psychology Today,* Nov., 1975.

de Charms, R. "From Pawns to Origins: Toward Self-Motivation." In Lesser, G.S., ed. *Psychology and Educational Practice.* Glenview, Ill.: Scott, Foresman, 1971.

————. *Personal Causation.* New York: Academic Press, 1968.

Deci, E.L. *Intrinsic Motivation.* New York: Plenum Press, 1975.

Deutsch, M. "Cooperation and Trust: Some Theoretical Notes." In Jones, M.R., ed. *Nebraska Symposium on Motivation.* Lincoln, Neb.: University of Nebraska Press, 1962.

————. "The Effects of Cooperation and Competition upon Group Processes." In Cartwright, D. and Zander, A., eds. *Group Dynamics: Research and Theory.* New York: Harpers, 1960.

———— and Deutsch, C.P. "Intelligence, Heredity, and Environment: The Critical Appraisal of an Outmoded Controversy." In *Annual Editions: Readings in Education 76/77.* Guilford, Conn.: Dushkin, 1976.

Dewey, J. *Democracy and Education.* New York: Macmillan, 1924.

————. *How We Think.* Rev. ed. New York: D.C. Heath, 1933.

————. *Interest and Effort in Education.* Carbondale, Ill.: Southern Illinois University Press, 1975.

Dichter, E. *Motivating Human Behavior.* New York: McGraw-Hill, 1971.

Dinkmeyer, D., *et al.* "Increasing the Teacher's Understanding of Students' Self-Concepts." *Education, 96:* 180–183, 1975.

Dinkmeyer, D. and Dinkmeyer, D., Jr. "Logical Consequences: A Key to the Reduction of Disciplinary Problems." *Phi Delta Kappan, 57:* 664–666, 1976.

Dinkmeyer, D. and Dreikurs, R. *Encouraging Children to Learn.* Englewood Cliffs, N.J.: Prentice-Hall, 1963.

Dollar, B. *Humanizing Classroom Discipline.* New York: Harper and Row, 1972.

Doyal, G.T. and Friedman, R.J. "Anxiety in Children: Some Observations for the School Psychologist." *Psychology in the Schools, 11:* 161–164, 1974.

Dreikurs, R. *Psychology in the Classroom.* 2d ed. New York: Harper and Row, 1968a.

———— *et al. Maintaining Sanity in the Classroom.* New York: Harper and Row, 1971.

————and Cassel, P. *Discipline Without Tears.* Rev. ed. New York: Hawthorn, 1972.

———— and Grey, L. *Logical Consequences.* New York: Meredith, 1968b.

————. *A Parents's Guide to Child Discipline.* New York: Hawthorn, 1970.

Drew, W. *et al.* "Motivation Is a Matter of Trust and Dialogue." *Learning,* Jan., 1975.

Ebel, R.L. "A Case for the Use of Corporal Punishment by Teachers." In Hamacheck, D.E., ed. *Human Dynamics in Psychology and Education.* 3d ed. Boston: Allyn and Bacon, 1977a.

————. "Behavioral Objectives: A Close Look." In Clarizio, H.F. *et al.,* eds. *Contemporary Issues in Educational Psychology.* 3d ed. Boston: Allyn and Bacon, 1977b.

————. "Criterion-Referenced Measurements." In Clarizio, H.F *et al.*, eds. *Contemporary Issues in Educational Psychology.* 3d ed. Boston: Allyn and Bacon, 1977d.

————. "Shall We Get Rid of Grades?" In Clarizio, H.F. *et al.*, eds. *Contemporary Issues in Educational Psychology.* 3d ed. Boston: Allyn and Bacon, 1977c.

————. "What Are Schools For?" *Phi Delta Kappan,* 54: 3–7, 1972.

Elashoff, J.D. and Snow, R.E., eds. *Pygmalion Reconsidered.* Worthington, Ohio: Charles A. Jones, 1971.

Elkind, D. *et al.* "Motivation and Creativity: The Context Effect." *American Educational Research Journal,* 7: 351–357, 1970.

Elliot, A. "Student Tutoring Benefits Everyone." *Phi Delta Kappan,* 54: 53, 1973.

Enzer, N.B. "Parents as Partners in Behavior Modification." *Journal of Research and Development in Education,* 8: 24–33, 1975.

Ericksen, S. *Motivation for Learning.* Ann Arbor, Mich.: University of Michigan Press, 1974.

Erikson, E.H. *Childhood and Society.* New York: W.W. Norton, 1950.

————. *Identity: Youth and Crisis.* New York: W.W. Norton, 1968.

Ewell, J.L. and Grindley, G.C. "The Effect of Knowledge of Results on Learning and Performance." *British Journal of Psychology,* 29: 40–55, 1938.

Fancher, R.E. *Psychoanalytic Psychology: The Development of Freud's Thought.* New York: W.W. Norton, 1973.

Farson, R.E. "Praise as a Motivational Tool: Negative Aspects, Positive Functions, and Suggestions for Using It in Healthy Ways." In Hamacheck, D.E., ed. *Human Dynamics in Psychology and Education.* 3d ed. Boston: Allyn and Bacon, 1977.

Feldmesser, R.A. "The Positive Function of Grades." In Hamacheck, D.E., ed. *Human Dynamics in Psychology and Education.* 3d ed. Boston: Allyn and Bacon, 1977.

Finn, J.D. "Expectations and the Educational Environment." *Review of Educational Research,* 42: 387–410, 1972.

Fish, M.C. and Loehfelm, E.E. "Verbal Approval: A Neglected Educational Resource." *Teachers College Record,* 76: 493–498, 1975.

Flanagan, J.C. "Motivation and Achievement." In Ebel, R.L. and Noll, V.H., eds., *Encyclopedia of Educational Research,* 4th ed. New York: Macmillan, 1969.

Forlano, G. and Axelrod, H.C. "The Effects of Repeated Praise or Blame on the Performance of Introverts and Extroverts." *Journal of Educational Psychology,* 28: 92–100, 1937.

Frankl, V.E. *Man's Search for Meaning.* Boston: Beacon Press, 1962.

Freud, A. *The Ego and the Mechanisms of Defense.* Rev. ed. London: Hogarth Press, 1968.

————. *Psychoanalysis for Teachers and Parents.* New York: Emerson, 1935.

Freud, S. *The Complete Introductory Lectures on Psychoanalysis.* New York: W.W. Norton, 1966.

————. *The Ego and the Id.* New York: W.W. Norton, 1960a.

————. *A General Introduction to Psychoanalysis.* New York: Garden City Publishing Co., 1943.

————. *The Basic Writings of Sigmund Freud.* Edited and translated by A.A. Brill. New York: Modern Library, 1938.

————. *Beyond the Pleasure Principle.* New York: Bantam Books, 1959.

————. *Civilization and Its Discontents.* New York: W.W. Norton, 1961.

————. *The Interpretation of Dreams.* New York: Basic Books, 1955.

————. *Jokes and Their Relation to the Unconscious.* New York: W.W. Norton, 1960b.

————. *An Outline of Psychoanalysis.* rev. ed. New York: W.W. Norton, 1969.

————. *The Psychopathology of Everyday Life.* New York: W.W. Norton, 1965.

Frieder, B. "Motivator: Least Developed of Teacher Roles." *Educational Technology,* 10: 28–36, 1970.

Fromm, E. *The Art of Loving.* New York: Bantam Books, 1963.

Fuchs, E. "How Teachers Learn to Help Children Fail." In Hunt, J. McV., ed., *Human Intelligence.* New Brunswick, N.J.: Transaction Books, 1972.

Furth, H.G. *Piaget for Teachers.* Englewood Cliffs, N.J.: Prentice-Hall, 1970.

———— and Wachs, H. *Thinking Goes to School.* New York: Oxford University Press, 1975.

Gage, N.L. and Berliner, D.C. *Educational Psychology.* Chicago: Rand McNally, 1975.

Gagné, E.E. and Parshall, H. "The Effects of Locus of Control and Goal-Setting on Persistence at a Learning Task." *Child Study Journal,* 5: 193–199, 1975.

Gagné, R.M. "Behavioral Objectives Are Necessary for Good Instruction." In Hamacheck, D.E., ed. *Human Dynamics in Psychology and Education.* 3d ed. Boston: Allyn and Bacon, 1977.

Gibson, J.T. *Psychology for the Classroom.* Englewood Cliffs, N.J.: Prentice-Hall, 1976.

Gilman, R. "The Fem Lib Case Against Sigmund Freud." *New York Times Magazine,* Jan. 31, 1971.

Ginsburg, H. and Opper, S. *Piaget's Theory of Intellectual Development.* Englewood Cliffs, N.J.: Prentice-Hall, 1969.

Glasser, W. *Reality Therapy.* New York: Harper and Row, 1965.

_____. *Schools Without Failure.* New York: Harper and Row, 1969.

Glatthorn, A.A. *Alternatives in Education.* New York: Dodd Mead, 1975.

Gnagey, W.J. *Maintaining Discipline in Classroom Instruction.* New York: Macmillan, 1975.

Goldberg, C. "Some Effects of Fear of Failure in the Academic Setting." *Journal of Psychology,* 84: 323–331, 1971.

Goldstein, K.M. and Tilker, H.A. "Attitudes toward A–B–C–D–F and Honors-Pass-Fail Grading Systems." *Journal of Educational Resarch,* 65: 99–100, 1971.

Good, T.L. *et al. Teachers Make a Difference.* New York: Holt, Rinehart and Winston, 1975.

_____ and Brophy, J. "The Influence of Teachers' Attitude and Expectations on Classroom Behavior." In Coop, R.H. and White, K., eds. *Psychological Concepts in the Classroom.* New York: Harper and Row, 1974.

Gordon, T. *Parent Effectiveness Training.* New York: New American Library, 1975.

_____ . *Teacher Effectiveness Training.* New York: David McKay, 1976.

Graubard, P. and Rosenberg, H. *Classrooms That Work.* New York: E.P. Dutton, 1974.

Gray, S.W. and Klaus, R.A. "The Early Training Project: A Seventh-Year Report." *Child Development,* 41: 909–924, 1970.

Greene, D. and Lepper, M. "Intrinsic Motivation: How to Turn Play into Work." *Psychology Today,* Sept., 1974.

Gronlund, N.E. *Individualizing Classroom Instruction.* Riverside, N.J.: Macmillan, 1974.

Groobman, D.E., *et al.* "Attitudes, Self-Esteem, and Learning in Formal and Informal Schools." *Journal of Educational Psychology,* 68: 32–35, 1976.

Grossman, H. *Nine Rotten Lousy Kids.* New York: Holt, Rinehart and Winston, 1972.

Hackett, R. "In Praise of Praise." *American Education,* Mar., 1975.

Hales, L.W. *et al.* "The Pass-Fail Option." *Journal of Educational Research,* 66: 295–298, 1973.

Hall, C.S. *A Primer of Freudian Psychology.* New York: New American Library, 1954.

Hall, R.V., *et al.* "The Effective Use of Punishment to Modify Behavior in the Classroom." In Clarizio, H.F. *et al.,* eds. *Contemporary Issues in Educational Psychology.* 2d ed. Boston: Allyn and Bacon, 1974.

Hamacheck, D.E. *Behavior Dynamics in Teaching, Learning and Growth.* Boston: Allyn and Bacon, 1975.

———. "Removing the Stigma from Obedience Behavior." *Phi Delta Kappan,* 57: 443–447, 1976.

Hammil, D.D. and Bartel, N.R. *Teaching Children with Learning and Behavior Problems.* Boston: Allyn and Bacon, 1975.

Harris, M.B. and Trujillo, A.E. "Improving Study Habits of Junior-High School Students through Self-management versus Group Discussion." *Journal of Counselling Psychology,* 22: 513–517, 1975.

Hart, H.H., ed. *Summerhill: For and Against.* New York: Hart, 1970.

Hartman, C.L. "Describing Behavior: Search for an Alternative to Grading." *Educational Leadership,* Jan., 1975.

Havis, A.L. "Alternatives for Breaking the 'Discipline Barrier' in Our Schools." *Education,* 96: 124–128, 1975.

Heckhausen, H. *The Anatomy of Achievement Motivation.* New York: Academic Press, 1967.

Heider, F. *The Psychology of Interpersonal Relations.* New York: John Wiley, 1958.

Heller, M.S. and White, M.A. "Rates of Teacher Verbal Approval and Disapproval to Higher and Lower Ability Classes." *Journal of Educational Psychology,* 67: 796–800, 1975.

Herman, T.M. *Creating Learning Environments.* Boston: Allyn and Bacon, 1977.

Hill, J.C. *Teaching and the Unconscious Mind.* New York: International Universities Press, 1971.

Holt, J. *Freedom and Beyond.* New York: E.P. Dutton, 1972.

———. *How Children Fail.* New York: Pitman, 1964.

———. *How Children Learn.* New York: Pitman, 1967.

———. "Marking and Grading." In Gall, M.D. and Ward, B.A., eds. *Critical Issues in Educational Psychology.* Boston: Little, Brown, 1974.

Homme, L. *How to Use Contingency Contracting in the Classroom.* Champaign, Ill.: Research Press, 1970.

Horner, M.S. "A Psychological Barrier to Achievement in Women: the Motive to Avoid Success." In McClelland, D.C. and Steele, R.S., eds. *Human Motivation: A Book of Readings.* Morristown, N.J.: General Learning Press, 1973.

————— . "Toward an Understanding of Achievement-Related Conflicts in Women." *Journal of Social Issues,* 28: 157–175, 1972.

Hull, C.L. *Essentials of Behavior.* New Haven, Conn.: Yale University Press, 1951.

Hurlock, E.B. *Developmental Psychology.* 4th ed. New York: McGraw-Hill, 1975.

————— . "An Evaluation of Certain Incentives Used in School Work." *Journal of Educational Psychology,* 16: 145–149, 1925.

————— . "The Use of Group Rivalry as an Incentive." *Journal of Abnormal and Social Psychology,* 22: 278–290, 1927.

Johnson, C. and Cramer, J. "The O.K. Classroom." *Instructor,* May, 1973.

Johnson, D.W. and Ahlgren, A. "Relationship between Student Attitudes about Cooperation and Competition and Attitudes toward Schooling." *Journal of Educational Psychology,* 68: 92–102, 1976.

Johnson, D.W. and Johnson, R.T. "Instructional Goal Structure: Cooperative, Competitive, or Individualistic." *Review of Educational Research,* Spring, 1974.

————— . *Learning Together and Alone.* Englewood Cliffs, N.J.: Prentice-Hall, 1975.

Johnson, P.B. "Achievement Motivation and Self-Reported Grade Point Average." *Psychology in the Schools,* 12: 402–404, 1975.

Johnson, R.T. *et al.* "Cooperation and Competition in the Classroom." *Elementary School Journal,* 74: 172–181, 1973.

Johnston, J.M. "Punishment of Human Behavior." *American Psychologist,* 27: 1033–1054, 1972.

Jones, E. *Life and Work of Sigmund Freud,* edited and abridged edition. New York: Basic Books, 1961.

Julian, J.W. and Perry, F.H. "Cooperation Contrasted with Intra-Group and Inter-Group Competition." *Sociometry,* 5: 9–24, 1967.

Kal, E.F. "Survey of Contemporary Clinical Practice." *Journal of Individual Psychology,* 28: 261–266, 1972.

Kaplan, L. *Education and Mental Health.* New York: Harper and Row, 1971.

Keislar, E.R. "A Descriptive Approach to Motivation." *Journal of Teacher Education,* 11: 310–315, 1960.

Kelly, D.H. "Tracking and Its Impact upon Self-Esteem: A Neglected Dimension." *Education.* 96: 2–9, 1975.

Kelly, E.C. "The Fully Functioning Self." In Hamacheck, D.E., ed. *Human Dynamics in Psychology and Education*. 3d ed. Boston: Allyn and Bacon, 1977.

Kelly, G.A. "Man's Construction of His Alternatives." In Lindzey, G., ed. *The Assessment of Human Motives*. New York: Holt, Rinehart and Winston, 1958.

Kennedy, W.A. and Wilcutt, H.A. "Praise and Blame as Incentives." *Psychological Bulletin*, 62: 323–353, 1964.

Kersh, B.Y. "The Motivating Effect of Learning by Directed Discovery." *Journal of Educational Psychology*, 53: 65–71, 1962.

Kibler, R.J. *et al. Objectives for Instruction and Evaluation*. Boston: Allyn and Bacon, 1974.

Kipnis, D.M. "Inner Direction, Outer Direction and Achievement Motivation." *Human Development*, 17: 321–343, 1974.

Kippel, G.M. "Information Feedback, Need Achievement and Retention." *Journal of Educational Research*, 68: 256–261, 1975.

Kirkland, M.C. "The Effects of Tests on Students and Schools." *Review of Educational Research*, 41: 303–350, 1971.

Kirschenbaum, H., *et al. Wad-Ja-Get?* New York: Hart, 1971.

Klausmeier, H.J., *et al.* "Individually Guided Motivation." *Elementary School Journal*, 71: 339–350, 1971.

Kneller, G.F. "Behavioral Objectives Are Not Necessary for Good Instruction." In Hamacheck, D.E., ed. *Human Dynamics in Psychology and Education*. 3d ed. Boston: Allyn and Bacon, 1977.

Kohlberg, L. "The Cognitive-Developmental Approach to Moral Education." *Phi Delta Kappan*, June, 1975.

─────── . "The Quest for Justice in 200 Years of American History and in Contemporary American Education." *Contemporary Education*, 48: 5–16, 1976.

─────── and Turiel, E. "Moral Development and Moral Education." In Lesser, G.S., ed. *Psychology and Educational Practice*. Glenview, Ill.: Scott, Foresman, 1971.

Kolb, D.A. "Achievement Motivation Training Program for Underachieving High School Boys." *Journal of Personality and Social Psychology*, 2: 783–792, 1965.

Kolesnik, W.B. *Educational Psychology*. 2d ed. New York: McGraw-Hill, 1970.

─────── . *Humanism and/or Behaviorism in Education*. Boston: Allyn and Bacon, 1975.

_____. *Learning: Educational Applications.* Boston: Allyn and Bacon, 1976.

Komaki, J. "Neglected Reinforcers in the College Classroom." *Journal of Higher Education,* Jan./Feb., 1975.

Korman, A.K. *The Psychology of Motivation.* Englewood Cliffs, N.J.: Prentice-Hall, 1974.

Kounin, J.S. *Discipline and Group Management in Classrooms.* New York: Holt, Rinehart and Winston, 1970.

Kruglanski, A.W., *et al.* "Can Money Enhance Intrinsic Motivation? A Test of the Content-Consequence Hypothesis." *Journal of Personality and Social Psychology* 31: 744–750, 1975.

Krumboltz, J.D. and Krumboltz, H.B. *Changing Children's Behavior.* Englewood Cliffs, N.J.: Prentice-Hall, 1972.

Lepper, M.R. and Greene, D. "When Two Rewards Are Worse Than One: Effects of Extrinsic Rewards on Intrinsic Motivation." *Phi Delta Kappan,* 56: 565–566, 1975.

Lessinger, L. *Every Kid a Winner.* New York: Simon and Schuster, 1970.

Lewin, K. *Field Theory in Social Science.* New York: Harper, 1951.

_____. *Principles of Topological Psychology.* New York: McGraw-Hill, 1936.

_____. *A Dynamic Theory of Personality.* New York: McGraw-Hill, 1935.

Lindsey, B.L. and Cunningham, J.W. "Behavior Modification: Some Doubts and Dangers." *Phi Delta Kappan,* 54: 597–598, 1973.

Lytton, H. *Creativity and Education.* New York: Schocken Books, 1972.

Maccoby, E.E. and Jacklin, C.N. *The Psychology of Sex Differences.* Stanford, Cal.: Stanford University Press, 1974.

Maccoby, E.E. and Jacklin, C.N. "What We Know and Don't Know about Sex Differences." In Clarizio, H.F., *et al.,* eds. *Contemporary Issues in Educational Psychology.* 3d ed. Boston: Allyn and Bacon, 1977.

Maccoby, M. "A Psychoanalytical View of Learning." *Change,* 3: 32–38, 1972.

Macht, J. *Teacher/Teachim: The Toughest Game in Town.* New York: John Wiley, 1975.

MacMillan, D.L. *Behavior Modification in Education.* New York: Macmillan, 1973.

Madsen, C.H. and Madsen, C.K. *Teaching/Discipline: A Positive Approach for Educational Development.* 2d ed. Boston: Allyn and Bacon, 1974.

Madsen, K.B. *Modern Theories of Motivation.* Copenhagen, Denmark: Munksgaard, 1974.

Madsen, M.C. "Developmental and Cross-Cultural Differences in Cooperative and Competitive Behavior of Young People." *Journal of Cross-Cultural Psychology*, 2: 365–371, 1971.

Maehr, M.L. *Sociocultural Origins of Achievement*. Monterey, Cal.: Brooks/Cole, 1974.

———— and Sjogren, D.D. "Atkinson's Theory of Achievement Motivation: A First Step Toward a Theory of Academic Motivation." *Review of Educational Research*, 41: 143–161, 1971.

Maller, J.B. "Cooperation and Competition: An Experimental Study of Motivation." In Crofts, L.W., ed. *Recent Experiments in Psychology*. New York: McGraw-Hill, 1938.

Maslow, A.H. *Farther Reaches of Human Nature*. New York: Viking Press, 1971.

———— . *Motivation and Personality*. 2d ed. New York: Harper and Row, 1970.

————. "Some Educational Implications of the Humanistic Psychologies." *Harvard Educational Review*, 38: 685–696, 1968.

———— . "A Theory of Human Motivation." *Psychological Review*, 50: 370–396, 1943.

———— . *Toward a Psychology of Being*. 2d ed. Princeton, N.J.: Van Nostrand, 1968.

————. "Theory of Motivation." In Hamacheck, D.E., ed. *Human Dynamics in Psychology and Education*. 3d ed. Boston: Allyn and Bacon, 1977b.

———— . "Some Differences Between Intrinsic and Extrinsic Learning." In Hamacheck, D.E., ed. *Human Dynamics in Psychology and Education*. 3d ed. Boston: Allyn and Bacon, 1977a.

McCarthy, M.D. "Humanitarianism and Corporal Punishment." *Education*, 95: 212, 215, 1975.

McClelland, D.C., ed. *Studies in Motivation*. New York: Appleton-Century-Crofts, 1955.

———— . "Toward a Theory of Motive Acquisition." *American Psychologist*, 20: 321–333, 1965.

————. "What Is the Effect of Achievement Motivation Training in the Schools?" *Teachers College Record*, 74: 129–145, 1972.

———— et al. *The Achievement Motive*. New York: Appleton-Century-Crofts, 1953.

———— and Steele, R.S., eds. *Human Motivation: A Book of Readings*. Morristown, N.J.: General Learning Press, 1973.

McLaughlin, T.F. "The Applicability of Token Reinforcement Systems in Public School Systems." *Psychology in the Schools*, 12: 84–89, 1975.

Melby, E.O. "It's Time for Schools to Abolish the Marking System." In Clarizio, H.F. *et al*, eds. *Contemporary Issues in Educational Psychology*. 3d ed. Boston: Allyn and Bacon, 1977.

Miles, D.T. and Robinson, R.E. "Behavioral Objectives: An Even Closer Look." In Clarizio, H.F. *et al.*, eds. *Contemporary Issues in Educational Psychology*. 3d ed. Boston: Allyn and Bacon, 1977.

Miller, J., ed. *Freud: The Man, His World, His Influence*. Boston: Little, Brown, 1972.

Miller, N.E. and Dollard, J. *Social Learning and Imitation*. New Haven, Conn.: Yale University Press, 1941.

Morine, H. and Morine, G. *Discovery: A Challenge to Teachers*. Englewood Cliffs, N.J.: Prentice-Hall, 1975.

Mosak, H.H., ed. *Alfred Adler: His Influence on Psychology Today*. Park Ridge, N.J.: Noyes Press, 1973.

Moulds, H. "To Grade or Not to Grade: A Futile Question." *Intellect*, Summer, 1974.

Moulton, R.W. "Effects of Success and Failure on Level of Aspiration as Related to Achievement Motives." *Journal of Personality and Social Psychology*, 1: 399–406, 1965.

Murphy, J. "Teacher Expectations and Working-Class Underachievement." *British Journal of Sociology*, 25: 326–344, 1974.

Murphy-Berman, V. "Motive to Avoid Success: A Test of Basic Assumptions." *Representative Research in Social Psychology*, 6: 37–44, 1975.

Murray, H.A., *et al. Explorations in Personality*. New York: Oxford University Press, 1938.

Nagel, T.S. and Richman, P.T. *Competency-Based Instruction: A Strategy to Eliminate Failure*. Columbus, Ohio: Charles E. Merrill, 1972.

Nardine, F.E. "The Development of Competence." In Lesser, G.S., ed. *Psychology and Educational Practice*. Glenview, Ill.: Scott, Foresman, 1971.

Neill, A.S. *Summerhill: A Radical Approach to Child Rearing*. New York: Hart, 1970.

Noland, R.G. and Craft, L.H. "15 Approaches to Motivate the Reluctant Reader." *Journal of Reading*, 19: 387–391, 1976.

O'Leary, K.D. and Wilson, G.T. *Behavior Therapy: Application and Outcome*. Englewood Cliffs, N.J.: Prentice-Hall, 1975.

Orem, R.C. *Montessori: Her Method and the Movement*. New York: Putnam, 1974.

Page, E.B. "Teacher Comments and Student Performance: A Seventy-four Classroom Experiment in School Motivation." *Journal of Educational Psychology*, 49: 173–181, 1958.

Phares, E.J. "Expectancy Changes in Skill and Chance Situations." *Journal of Abnormal and Social Psychology*, 54: 339–342, 1957.

Piaget, J. *The Moral Judgement of the Child.* New York: Free Press, 1965.

———. *The Origins of Intelligence in Children.* New York: International Universities Press, 1952.

———. *To Understand Is to Invent.* New York: Grossman, 1973.

Podboy, J. and Organist, J. "A Discussion of Adlerianism and Behavioral Therapies: Their Similarities and Differences." *Journal of Applied Rehabilitation Counselling*, 6: 42–49, 1975.

Postman, N. and Weingartner, C. *The School Book.* New York: Delacorte, 1973.

Premack, D. "Toward Empirical Behavior Laws: I. Positive Reinforcement." *Psychological Review*, 66: 219–233, 1959.

Purkey, W.W. *Self-Concept and School Achievement.* Englewood Cliffs, N.J.: Prentice-Hall, 1970.

———. "Teacher Beliefs and Behaviors That Have a Positive Impact on Student Motivation and Self Concept." In Hamacheck, D.E., ed. *Human Dynamics in Psychology and Education.* 3d ed. Boston: Allyn and Bacon, 1977.

Read, D.A. and Simon, S.B., eds. *Humanistic Education Sourcebook.* Englewood Cliffs, N.J.: Prentice-Hall, 1975.

Redl, F. "Disruptive Behavior in the Classroom." *School Review*, 83: 569–594, 1975.

———. "Our Troubles with Defiant Youth." In Hamacheck, D.E., ed. *Human Dynamics in Psychology and Education.* 3d ed. Boston: Allyn and Bacon, 1977.

———. "The Concept of Punishment." In Clarizio, H.F. *et al.*, eds. *Contemporary Issues in Educational Psychology.* 3d ed. Boston: Allyn and Bacon, 1977.

Reiss, S. and Sushinsky, L.W. "Overjustification, Competing Responses, and the Acquisition of Intrinsic Interest." *Journal of Personality and Social Psychology*, 31: 1116–1125, 1975.

Richey, H.W. "Role Playing and Modification of Student Attitudes." *Education*, 96: 24–27, 1975.

Ringness, T.H. "Affective Differences Between Successful and Nonsuccessful Bright Ninth Grade Boys." *Personal and Guidance Journal*, 43: 600–606, 1965.

Roazen, P. *Freud and His Followers.* New York: A.A. Knopf, 1975.

Roberts, T.B., ed. *Four Psychologies Applied to Education.* New York: John Wiley, 1975.

Rogers, C.R. *Freedom to Learn.* Columbus, Ohio: Charles E. Merrill, 1969.

———. *On Becoming a Person.* Boston: Houghton Mifflin, 1961.

———. "Toward Becoming a Fully Functioning Person." In Combs, A.W., ed. *Perceiving, Behaving and Becoming.* Washington, D.C.: Association for Supervision and Curriculum Development, 1962.

———. "Learning to be Free." In Clarizio, H.F. *et al.* eds. *Contemporary Issues in Educational Psychology.* 3d ed. Boston: Allyn and Bacon, 1977a.

———. "To Be That Self Which One Truly Is." In Hamacheck, D.E., ed. *Human Dynamics in Psychology and Education.* 3d ed. Boston: Allyn and Bacon, 1977b.

——— and Skinner, B.F. "Some Issues Concerning the Control of Human Behavior: A Symposium." *Science,* 74: 1057–1066, 1956. (Reprinted in Glock, M.D., ed. *Guiding Learning.* New York: John Wiley, 1971).

Rosenham, D.L. "Effects of Social Class and Race on Responsiveness to Approval and Disapproval." *Journal of Personality and Social Psychology,* 4: 253–259, 1966.

Rosenthal, R. "When You Expect More, You Are Apt to Get More." In Hamacheck, D.E., ed. *Human Dynamics in Psychology and Education.* 3d ed. Boston: Allyn and Bacon, 1977.

——— and Jackson, L. *Pygmalion in the Classroom.* New York: Holt, Rinehart and Winston, 1968.

Rotter, J.B. "Generalized Expectancies for Internal versus External Control of Reinforcement." *Psychological Monographs,* 80: 1–28, 1966.

Russell, I. *Motivation.* Dubuque, Iowa: W.C. Brown, 1971.

Russell, W.A., ed. *Milestones in Motivation.* New York: Appleton-Century-Crofts, 1970.

Sahakian, W.S., ed. *Psychology of Personality: Readings in Theory.* 2d ed. Chicago: Rand McNally, 1974.

Schlosser, C.D., ed. *The Person in Education: A Humanistic Approach.* New York: Macmillan, 1976.

Schmidt, H.O. "The Effects of Praise and Blame as Incentives to Learning." *Psychological Monograph No. 53,* 1941.

Schmuck, R.A. and Schmuck, P.A. *Group Processes in the Classroom,* 2d ed. Dubuque, Iowa: W.C. Brown, 1975.

———. *A Humanistic Psychology of Education.* Palo Alto, Cal.: National Press, 1974.

Sears, P.S. "Levels of Aspiration in Academically Successful and Unsuccessful Children." *Journal of Abnormal and Social Psychology*, 35: 498–536, 1940.

Segal, R. *Got No Time to Fool Around*. Philadelphia: Westminister Press, 1972.

Selankovich, D. "An Experiment Attempting to Determine the Effectiveness of Frequent Testing as an Aid to Learning." *Journal of Educational Research*, 55: 178–180, 1962.

Shaw, M.E. "Some Motivational Factors in Cooperation and Competition." *Journal of Personality*, 26: 155–169, 1958.

Silbergeld, S. *et al.* "Classroom Psychosocial Environment." *Journal of Educational Research*, 69: 151–155, 1975.

Silberman, M.L. *et al.*, eds. *The Psychology of Open Teaching and Learning*. Boston: Little, Brown, 1972.

Simon, S.B. "Grades Must Go!" In Hamacheck, D.E., ed. *Human Dynamics in Psychology and Education*. 3d ed. Boston: Allyn and Bacon, 1977.

Sims, V.M. "The Relative Influence of Two Types of Motivation on Improvement." *Journal of Educational Psychology*, 19: 480–484, 1928.

Sizer, T.R. "Values Education in the Schools: A Practitioner's Perspective." *Religious Education*, 70: 138–149, 1975.

Skinner, B.F. *About Behaviorism*. New York: Random House, 1974.

——— . *Beyond Freedom and Dignity*. New York: A.A. Knopf, 1971.

——— . "The Ethics of Helping People." *The Humanist*, 36: 7–11, 1976.

——— . "The Science of Learning and the Art of Teaching." *Harvard Educational Review*, 24: 86–97, 1954.

——— . *The Technology of Teaching*. New York: Appleton-Century-Crofts, 1968.

——— . *Walden Two*. New York: Macmillan, 1962.

Solomon, D. and Kendall, A.J. "Teachers' Perceptions of and Reactions to Misbehavior in Traditional and Open Classrooms." *Journal of Educational Psychology*, 67: 528–530, 1975.

Solomon, D. and Oberlander, M.I. "Locus of Control in the Classroom." In Coop, R.H. and White, K., eds. *Psychological Concepts in the Classroom*. New York: Harper and Row, 1974.

Sperber, M. *Masks of Loneliness: Alfred Adler in Perspective*. New York: Macmillan, 1974.

Stacey, J., *et al.*, eds. *And Jill Came Tumbling After: Sexism in American Education*. New York: Dell, 1974.

Stainback, W.C., *et al.* *Establishing a Token Economy in the Classroom*. Columbus, Ohio: Charles E. Merrill, 1973.

Stanford, G. and Roark, A.E. *Human Interaction in Education.* Boston: Allyn and Bacon, 1974.

Steffenhagen, R.A. "Drug Abuse and Related Phenomena: An Adlerian Approach." *Journal of Individual Psychology,* 30: 238–250, 1974.

Stendler, C.B., *et al.* "Studies in Cooperation and Competition: 1. The Effects of Working for Group and Individual Rewards on the Social Climate of Children's Groups." *Journal of Genetic Psychology,* 79: 173–197, 1951.

Talmage, H., ed. *Systems of Individualized Instruction.* Berkeley, Cal.: McCutchan, 1975.

Taylor, R.G. "Personality Traits and Discrepant Achievement: A Review." *Journal of Counselling Psychology,* 11: 76–82, 1964.

Teevan, R.C. and Birney, R.C., eds. *Theories of Motivation in Personality and Social Psychology.* Princeton, N.J.: Van Nostrand, 1964.

Teevan, R.C. and Smith, B.D. "Relationship of Fear-of-Failure and Need Achievement Motivation to a Confirming-Interval Measure of Aspiration Levels." *Psychological Reports,* 36: 967–976, 1975.

Thompson, C.L. *et al.* "One More Time: How Do You Motivate Students?" *Elementary School Guidance and Counselling,* 9: 30–34, 1974.

Thompson, G.G. and Hunnicutt, C.W. "The Effect of Praise or Blame on the Work Achievement of 'Introverts' and 'Extroverts.'" *Journal of Educational Psychology,* 35: 257–266, 1944.

Thompson, M. *et al.* "Contingency Management in the Schools: How Often and How Well Does It Work?" *American Educational Research Journal,* 11: 19–28, 1974.

Thorndike, R.L. "Review of Pygmalion in the Classroom." *American Educational Research Journal,* 5: 708–711, 1968.

Tolman, E.C. *Purposive Behavior in Animals and Men.* New York: Appleton Century, 1932.

Torrance, E.P. "Motivation and Creativity." In Torrance, E.P. and White, W.F., eds. *Issues and Advances in Educational Psychology,* 2d ed. Itasca, Ill.: F.E. Peacock, 1975.

———. *Rewarding Creative Behavior.* Englewood Cliffs, N.J.: Prentice-Hall, 1965.

Tyler, L.L. "Curriculum Development from a Psychoanalytic Perspective." *Educational Forum,* 36: 173–179, 1972.

Vaughn, J. and Diserens, C.M. "The Experimental Psychology of Competition." *Journal of Experimental Education,* 7: 76–97, 1938.

Vernon, V.M. *Motivating Children: Behavior Modification in the Classroom.* New York: Holt, Rinehart and Winston, 1972.

Wadsworth, B.J. *Piaget's Theory of Cognitive Development.* New York: David McKay, 1971.

Wallen, C.J. "Teacher, Individual, and Group-Issued Incentives and Pupil Performance." *Journal of Educational Research,* 57: 413–416, 1964.

Waller, P. and Gaa, J. "Motivation in the Classroom." In Coop, R.H. and White, K., eds. *Psychological Concepts in the Classroom.* New York: Harper and Row, 1974.

Watson, J.B. "Psychology as the Behaviorist Views It." *Psychological Review,* 20: 158–177, 1913.

Wax, J. and Grenis, M. "Conflicting Views on Competition." *Phi Delta Kappan,* 57: 197–200, 1975.

Weiner, B. "Attribution Theory, Achievement Motivation and the Educational Process." *Review of Educational Research,* 42: 203–215, 1972.

———, ed. *Cognitive Views of Human Motivation.* New York: Academic Press, 1974.

———. "Motivation." In Ebel, R., ed. *Encyclopedia of Educational Research.* 4th ed. New York: Macmillan, 1969.

———. "Motivational Psychology and Educational Research." *Educational Psychologist,* 11: 96–101, 1974.

———. *Theories of Motivation: From Mechanism to Cognition.* Chicago: Rand McNally, 1972.

——— and Kukla, A. "An Attributional Analysis of Achievement Motivation." *Journal of Personality and Social Psychology,* 15: 1–20, 1970.

Welch, G.M. "Pressures on Children: Meeting of the Minds." *Theory into Practice,* 13: 358–361, 1974.

Wellington, C.B. and Wellington, J. *The Underachiever: Challenges and Guidelines.* Chicago: Rand McNally, 1965.

Wendel, R. "Inquiry Teaching: Dispelling the Myths." In Mueller, R.J., *et al. Readings in Classroom Learning and Perception.* New York: Praeger, 1974.

White, R.W. "Motivation Reconsidered: The Concept of Competence." *Psychological Review,* 66: 297–333, 1959.

White, W.F., "The Teacher's Personality Is the Primary Motive in the Classroom." In Torrance, E.P. and White, W.F., eds. *Issues and Advances in Educational Psychology.* 2d ed. Itasca, Ill.: F.E. Peacock, 1975.

Williams, R.L. and Anandam, K. *Cooperative Classroom Management.* Columbus, Ohio: Charles E. Merrill, 1973.

Winter, D.G. *The Power Motive.* New York: Free Press, 1973.

Wolman, B.B. *The Unconscious Mind: The Meaning of Freudian Psychology.* Englewood Cliffs, N.J.: Prentice-Hall, 1968.

Yura, M.T. and Gallassi, M.D. "Adlerian Usage of Children's Play." *Journal of Individual Psychology,* 30, 194–201, 1974.

Zanna, M.P., *et al.* "Pygmalion and Galatea: The Interactive Effect of Teacher and Expectancies." *Journal of Experimental Social Psychology,* 11: 279–287, 1975.

Name Index

Subject Index